REDISCOVERING GANDHI

VOLUME 7 : How Relevant is Gandhi Today? A Japanese View

Series Editor: ***Prof. R.P. Misra***

Vol. 1. Hind Swaraj: *Gandhi's Challenge to Modern Civilization*
—R.P. Misra

2. Ahimsa: *The Way to Peace*
—Jonathan K. Crane & Jordi Agusti-Panareda

3. Satyagraha: *Gandhian Approach to Conflict Resolution*
—Jainarain Sharma

4. Consensual Democracy: *Gandhi on State, Power, and Politics*
—Ashu Pasricha

5. Humanizing Science and Technology: *Some Case Studies*
—Vinnie Jauhari and Parul Wasan

6. Gandhi and Jesus : The End of Fundamentalism
—Wolfgang Sternstein

8. Gandhian Economics and Its Contemporary Relevance
—R.P. Misra and D.Gopal

9. Conflict Resolution and Peace Building: The Gandhian Way
—R.P. Misra and D.Gopal

10. Mahatma Gandhi: The Man, His Vision and Mission
—R.P. Misra

About the Author

H. Yamaguchi studied at the University of Tokyo, and got his B.A. and M.A. degrees in sociology. He worked at the IDE (Institute of Developing Economies, a semi-governmental research organization), then taught at Bunkyo University, both Tokyo-based. He was a Writer-in-Residence at the Mahatma Gandhi International Hindi University, Wardha, in 2005.

Yamaguchi's primary research interest may be termed the human factor in development, with his major regional moorings in India. His contact with India goes back to Jawaharlal Nehru's Prime Ministerial times. His secondary academic interest is modern Japan's relations with Asian nations.

Although his writings have been mostly in Japanese, he has co-edited *Tradition and Modernity: India and Japan towards the Twenty-first Century* (Munshiram Manoharlal, 1997), and written *Japan* (National Book Trust, India, 2006). He has participated in a number of academic conferences held in India, starting from "Nehru as Writer and Historian", sponsored by NMML, in 1989.

REDISCOVERING GANDHI

Series Editor
Prof. R.P. Misra

Volume 7

How Relevant is Gandhi Today?
A Japanese View

Yamaguchi Hiroichi

CONCEPT PUBLISHING COMPANY PVT. LTD.
NEW DELHI-110059

ISBN-13: 978-81-8069-374-8 (Set)
ISBN-13: 978-93-5125-168-2 (Vol. 7)

First Published 2015

Published and Printed by

Concept
Since 1974

Concept Publishing Company Pvt. Ltd.
A/15-16, Commercial Block, Mohan Garden
New Delhi-110059 (India)
T: 25351460, 25351794, *F*: 091-11-25357109
E: publishing@conceptpub.com, W: **www.conceptpub.com**
Editorial Office: H-13, Bali Nagar, New Delhi-110 015, India.

Cataloging in Publication Data--*Courtesy:* D.K. Agencies (P) Ltd. <docinfo@dkagencies.com>

Yamaguchi, Hiroichi, author.
How relevant is Gandhi today? : a Japanese view / Yamaguchi Hiroichi.
pages cm. -- (Rediscovering Gandhi ; volume 7)
Includes bibliographical references (pages) and index.
ISBN 9788180693748 (Set)
ISBN 9789351251682 (Vol. 7)

1. Gandhi, Mahatma, 1869-1948--Political and social views. 2. India--Politics and government--1919-1947. 3. India--Economic conditions--1918-1947. 4. Communalism--India--History. I. Title. II. Series: Rediscovering Gandhi ; volume 7.

DDC 954.035 23

Is Gandhi Out of Date?
Are Not Some of His Ideas Still Relevant Today?
Here I Have Given My Views.
But I Wish to Learn More.

Foreword

At a time when persons like Justice Markandey Katju, former Judge of the Supreme Court of India and many others of lesser importance are raising questions on the life, philosophy and contributions Mahatma Gandhi made to free India from British colonialism and thus to trigger freedom struggles in other parts of the world, H. Yamaguchi book "How Relevant is Gandhi Today: A Japanese View" being published as volume 7 of the series "Rediscovering Gandhi" is most welcome. To a great extent, this book answers many of the questions raised by the critics of Gandhi.

First, let us see what Justice Katju has to say about Gandhi.

1. *"... I submit that Gandhi was objectively a British agent who did great harm to India..."*

Justice Katju may right in branding Gandhi a British agent because Gandhi was the agent of humanity as a whole, the British included. He had no enemies; he did have adverseries though both in India and abroad who did not agree with his ideas, ideals and nonviolent method of solving problems that individuals, societies, countries and the world face from time to time. Gandhi wanted to win over his adverseries by love, which he translated in terms of Truth, *Ahimsa*, and *Satyagraha*. The British were the most formidable adversaries of India; Gandhi wanted to negotiate with them on equal footing and regain freedom for India peacefully. While in South Africa he did support the British in Boer War in the hope that the British attitude towards Indians in South Africa will soften. In India he supported the British during the World War II, because he considered

British better and more amenable to his ways of thinking than a dictator like Hitler. But these actions have to seen in the larger context of the world of which an independent India was to be a part. He was totally committed to India's freedom; he never deviated from his goal and the ideology of Truth and Non-violence to reach that goal. He carried forward his struggle against the British Raj without any break until India gained its freedom on August 15, 1947. Simply because Gandhi did not treat the British people as India's enemies, does not mean that he was a British agent. It was part of his philosophy, and this philosophy did succeed and show the war-torn world of the time that time-honoured Indian way of winning over the adversaries by soul force was relevant to modern times too.

2. *"Gandhi diverted the freedom struggle from this revolutionary direction to a harmless nonsensical channel called Satyagraha. This also served British interests."*

To depict *Satyagraha* as non-sensical and supportive of the British interests is to demonstrate one's ignorance of Indian values, which call for renunciation of all that is not good for humanity. While Gandhi was fighting the British non-violently, a good number of revolutionaries like Subhas Chandra Bose, Chandrasekhar Azad and many others were engaged in waging a war against the British using the same weapons which the British used to subjugate India. Gandhi's was the non-violent way while the revotionaries equally devoted to the motherland used the violent ways. Had Gandhi not been there, the freedom struggle would have led to the death of thousands of our countrymen and a rule over India, not necessarily based on democratic principles. One of the main aims the British rule over India was to make Indians British in thought and culture. Gandhi was not fighting just the British rule, he was also fighting the British values that were penetrating Indian culture and thought rather fast. Unfortunately, by the time India gained independence (August 15, 1947), Gandhi stood sidelined by the main current politicians led by J.L. Nehru. India, failed to do away with much of the British system of administration and British values.

3. *"By constantly injecting religion into politics continuously*

> *for several decades, Gandhi furthered the British policy of divide and rule."*

Gandhi, all through his life was in search of religion of religions. The fundamental principles of all religions being the same, for him God, Allah and Ishwar were different names of the same power. Gandhi tried to unite all religions. He called himself a Sanatani Hindu because being so did not contradict his mission to unite various religions. This apart, Gandhi learnt lessions from the majority of people of India, who followed Hinduism. Gandhi tried to unite Hindus and Muslims; this made the British thwart his efforts and launch the policy of divide and rule. In Gandhi's view one can be Hindu or Muslim, yet live in brotherly relationship. He got strength from Hinduism and followed fasting as a method of making the British concede the rights of the people. But he never brought Hindu sacraments in politics. Katju's comments in this regard are misplaced and not to be taken seriously.

4. *"Self-sufficient villages advocated by the Father of the Nation were casteist and in the grip of money lenders and landlords."*

According Mr. Katju, Gandhi's ideas about *Gram Swaraj* were reactionary because he wanted to perpetuate a village society which was marked by inequality – both social and economic. Here he was hinting at India's *varnas* and castes. On economic front, *Khadi* and *Charka* Gandhi propagated and encouraged would have not solved the problems of the village youth who sought employment in cities. The villages were dependent of money lenders and landlords. Each village was divided into upper caste and *Harijan* sectors. Gandhi's vision of self-reliant village republics was a dynamic one. His idea of self-reliant villages with *Charkha* as the symbol of rural industrialization did awaken the masses to the need for economic diversification in pre-independence India. All this, he was able to achieve at a time when no industrialist or businessman was prepared to invest in rural areas.

Gandhi's idea of *Gram Swaraj* was buried under the debries of city-centric development once the country became independent; but village India that houses 65 per cent of people of the country (estimate for 2015) still preserves the sweet memories of the days when Gandhi launched *khadi* and village industries movement. Today, our villages are being deserted by the youth on a mass scale. In the next two decades or so urban population of India would be equal to its rural population. If the village industries movement had continued, the living conditions in rural India in 2015 would have been far better. Had Gandhi been alive for a decade or so more, he would have advocated rural-urban integration through a network of large villages, small service towns, medium size towns, and large cities like Delhi and Mumbai. Yet, Katju denigrades the idea Gandhi put forward to add a new source of income to the rural masses, as sinister.

It is in this context that I consider the book "How Relevant is Gandhi Today: A Japanese View" by H. Yamaguchi a significant contribution to Gandhian thought and further elaboration of what Gandhi tried to accomplish in his life. The book has five chapters. 1. What Motivated Gandhi? 2. Gandhi's Democracy; 3. Gandhi's Socio-Economics; 4. Gandhi against Communalism and 5. Gandhi an Internationalist.

What Motivated Gandhi?

Yamaguchi rightly starts his book with the elaboration of the values that guided Gandhi. These values were summed up in the term manliness which measured the behaviour of individuals and people in general. The opposite of manliness, in Gandhi's view, was cowerdice. Manliness, in his scheme of things, did not mean muscle power and ever-readiness to retaliate, as it is commonly understood. For Gandhi, it meant adherence to the call of the soul force even in very adverse circumstances and violent attack. The soul force, to Gandhi was linked to pledges or vows one chose to adhere to. The idea had its roots in the upbringing of Gandhi from early childhood. Its first expression on a public platform was seen in 1906 when he was getting ready along with his fellow Indians in Transvaal, South Africa to fight against the 'Black Act' on the Asiatics' registration promulgated by the British. The idea of adherence to a pledge or vow one takes at any cost as a sign of manliness occurred to him. "Personally, I hold that a man, who deliberately and intelligently takes a pledge and then breaks it, forfeits his manhood...But everyone of us must think out for himself if he has the will and the ability to pledge himself...so long as there is even a handful of men true to their pledge, there can only be one end to the struggle, and that is victory". His conclusion was, "Everyone should fully realize his responsibility, then only pledge himself independently of others and understand that he himself must be true to his pledge even unto death, no matter what others do." Although the pledge or oath is individualistic, its adherence gives the pledger enough strength to face the mightiest in the world. He was even against the soldiers breaking their pledge even if it was in support of India's freedom.

"Personally, I hold that a man, who deliberately and intelligently takes a pledge and then breaks it, forfeits his manhood...But everyone of us must think out for himself if he has the will and the ability to pledge himself...so long as there is even a handful of men true to their pledge, there can only be one end to the struggle, and that is victory". The *Ekadashi* (eleven) Vows that he outlined touch every aspect of life and living, as they are inter-related and inter-dependent. To many Gandhi was not always true to his *Ekadashi* Vows. It was however, only partially ture if at all. Gandhi changed his views on various issues related to his nonviolent struggle against injustice. He did change his views through time and hence what Gandhi said or did last in his life, that only should treated as authentic.

What Gandhi has to say on each of these vows is given below in his own words.

Ekadashi (Eleven-fold) Vows

(Sanskrit)	*(English)*
1. *Ahimsa*	Non-violence
2. *Satya*	Truth
3. *Asteya*	Non-stealing
4. *Brahmacharya*	Self-discipline
5. *Aparigraha*	Non-possession
6. *Sharirshram*	Bread Labour
7. *Aswada*	Control of the Palate
8. *Bhayavarjana*	Fearlessness

9. *Sarva Dharma Samabhava*	Equality of all Religions
10. *Swadeshi*	Use Locally Made Goods
11. *Sparshabhavana*	Remove Untouchability

Ahimsa (Non-violence)

"*Ahimsa* is not merely a negative state of harmlessness, but it is positive state of love, of doing good even to the evil-doer". *Young India,* August 25, 1920.

"*Ahimsa* is a weapon of matchless potency. It is the *summum bonum* of life. It is an attribute of the brave, in fact, it is their all. It does not come within the reach of coward. It is no wooden or lifeless dogma, but a living and life giving force." *Young India,* September 6, 1926.

Two years later he wrote "*Ahimsa* is not the way of the timid or cowardly. It is the way of the brave ready to face death. He who perishes sword in hand is no doubt brave; but he who faces death without raising his little finger and without flinching, is braver". (*Young India*, October 11, 1928).

Satya (Truth)

"Truth should be Truth in thought, Truth in speech, and Truth in action. To the man who has realised this Truth in its fulness, nothing else remains to be known, because all knowledge is necessarily included in it. What is not included in it, is not truth and so not true knowledge" (*From Yeravda Mandir,* p. 2).

"Truth has no form. Therefore, everyone one will form such an idea or image of Truth as appeals to him, and there will be as many images of Truth as there are men. These will be true as long as they last. For they enable a man to obtain everything he wants" (*Diary of Mahadevbhai,* p. 120).

Asteya (Non-stealing)

"We are not always aware of our real needs, and most of us improperly multiply our wants and thus, unconsciously, make thieves of ourselves. One who follows the observance of Non-stealing will bring about a progressive reduction of his own wants. Much of the distressing poverty in this world has risen out of the breaches of the principle of Non-stealing" (*From Yeravda Mandir,* p. 20).

Brahmacharya (Self-discipline)

In *Bapu's Letters to Mira* (p. 257) Gandhi said "*Brahamchraya* means control of all the organs of sense. He who attempts to control only one organ, and allows all the others free play is bound to find his effort futile. ….To hear suggestive stories with the ears, to see suggestive sights with the eyes, to taste stimulating food with the tongue, to touch exciting things with the hands, and at the same time to expect to control the only remaining organ, is like putting one's hands in the fire and expecting to escape being hurt."

Aparigraha (Non-possession)

"Non-possession means that we should not hoard anything that we do not need today"(*Bapu-ke-Aashirvad,* November 25, 1944). "The less you possess, the less you want, the better you are. And better for what? Not for your enjoyment of this life but for enjoyment of personal service to your fellow beings; service to which you dedicate yourself, body, soul and mind" (*Mahatma,* Vol. 3, p. 155). "When you dispossess yourself of everything you have, you really possess all the treasures of the world. In other words, you really get all that is in reality necessary for you, everything. If the food is necessary, food will come to you" (*My Philosophy of Life,* p. 138).

Sharirshram (Bread Labour)

"Earn thy bread by the sweat of the brow"—says Bible. Bread labour means that everyone is expected to perform sufficient body-labour in order to entitle him to his living. It is not, therefore, necessary to earn one's living by bread labour, taking living' in its broader sense. But everyone must perform some useful body-labour" (*Young India,* November 5, 1925). The economics of Bread labour are the living way of life. It means that every man has to labour with his body for his food and clothing. If I can convince the people of the value and necessity of bread-labour, there never will be any want of bread and cloth" (*Harijan*, September 7, 1947). "The idea is that every healthy individual must labour enough for his food and his intellectual faculties must be exercised not in order to obtain a living or amass a fortune, but only in the service of mankind. If this principle is observed everywhere, all men would be equal, none would starve and world would be saved from a sin" (*Harijan,* August 3, 1935).

Aswad (Control of the Palate)

"Unless we are satisfied with foods that are necessary for the proper maintenance of our physical health and unless we are prepare to rid ourselves of stimulating heating and exciting condiments that we mixed with food. We will certainly not be able to control the over-abundant, unnecessary, and exciting stimulation that we may have. If we do not do that, the result naturally is that we abuse ourselves, and become less than animals and brutes" (*Speeches and Writings of Mahatma Gandhi,* p. 384). "The diet should be healthy and well-balanced. The body was never meant to be treated as a refuse-bin. Food is meant to sustain the body" (*My Philosophy of Life,* p. 111).

Sarvatra Bhayavarjana (Fearlessness)

"Fearlessness should connote absence of all kinds of fear - fear of death, fear of bodily injury, fear of hunger, fear of insults, fear of public disapprobation, fear of ghosts and evil spirits, fear of anyone's anger. Freedom from all these and other such fears constitutes fearlessness" (*Bapu Ke Ashirwad*, November 26, 194). "Fearlessness does not mean arrogance and aggressiveness. That in itself is a sign of fear. Fearlessness presupposes calmness and peace of mind. For that, it is necessary to have a living faith in God" (*Harijan,* November 3, 1946*)*.

Sarva Dharma Samabhava (All Religions are Equal)

"Religions have been interwoven. One sees a special quality in every one of them. But no one religion is higher than another. All are complimentary to one another. Since this is my belief, the speciality of any one religion cannot run counter to another, cannot be at variance with universally accepted principles" (*Harijanbandhu,* March 19,

1933). "For, I believe in the fundamental truth of all great religions of the world. I believe that they are all God-given, and I believe that they were necessary for the people to whom these religions were revealed. And I believe that, if only we could all of us read the scriptures of the different faiths from the standpoint of the followers of those faiths, we should find that they were at bottom all one and were all helpful to one another" (*Harijan,* February 16, 1934). "Just as men have different names and faces, these religions also are different. But just as men are all human in spite of their different names and forms, just as leaves of a tree though different as leaves are the same as the leaves of the same tree, all religions though different are the same. We must treat all religions as equals" (*Harijanbandhu,* July 22, 1934).

10. Swadeshi (Use Goods Made Locally and by People You Know)

"*Swadeshi* is that sprit in us which requires us to serve our immediate neighbours before others, and to use things produced in our neighbourhood in preference to those more remote. So doing, we cannot serve humanity to the best of our capacity, we cannot serve humanity by neglecting our neighbours" (*Young India,* April 20 1919). "It is sinful to buy and use articles made by sweated labour. It is sinful to eat American wheat and and let my neighbour, the grain dealer starve for want of customers. Similarly, it is sinful for to wear the latest finery of Regent Street when I know that if I had but worn the things woven by the neighbouring spinners and weavers, that would have clothed me, and fed and clothed them" (*Young India,* October 13, 1921).

"My definition of *Swadeshi* is well known. I must not serve my distant neighbour at the expense of the nearest. It is never vindictive or punitive. It is in no sense narrow, for I buy from every part of the world what is needed for my growth. I refuse to buy from anybody anything, however nice or beautiful, if it interferes with my growth or injures those whom Nature has made my first care" (*Young India,* March 12, 1925). "*Swadeshi* is that spirit in us which restricts us to the use and service of our immediate surroundings to the exclusion of the more remote and I should use only things that are produced by my immediate neighbours and serve those industries by making them efficient and complete where they might be found wanting. It is suggested that such *Swadeshi*, if reduced to practice, will lead to the millennium" (*Speeches and Writings of Mahatma Gandhi)*.

11. Sparshbhavna (Untouchability)

"Untouchability means pollution by the touch of certain persons in reason of their birth in a particular state or family. It is an excrescence. In the guise of religion, it is always in the way and corrupts religion" (*From Yeravda Mandir,* p. 31). "Removal of untouchability means love for, and service of, the whole world and thus merges into *Ahimsa*. Removal of untouchability spells the breaking down of barriers between man and man and between the various orders of being" (*From Yeravda Mandir,* p. 33). "I consider untouchability to be a heinous crime against humanity. It is not a sign of self-restraint but an arrogant assumption of superiority" (*Young India,* December 8, 1920)

To abolish untouchability, he asked the upper and middle class Hindus to open Hindu temples to them and observe penance for the cruelity inflicted on the *Harijans*. He called them *Harijans* (God's own) to differentiate them from the upper and middle-class Hindus. Yamaguchi points to two shortcomings in Gandhi's thinking at that early stage of life: 1. he did not consider men and women to be equal; and 2. he did not advocate inter-caste, interfaith and inter-regional marriages. In my view, Gandhi's views on women, as his other views evolved through time. He first had some tradition-based ideas, and then he tested those ideas to check their relevance and short-comings before he integrated them in his life and asked others to follow. One, therefore, finds contradictions in what he said earlier and what he said later on a given subject. He has himself said that he is not a static being; he is ever evolving and hence what he said later should be treated as authentic.

While in South Africa, Gandhi had not developed the concept of *Satyagraha*. The first, step in its evolution was Non-cooperation. It was easier for people to understand its meaning, i.e., not to cooperate with the government in implementing the unjust laws. The Civil Disobedience was the next stage wherein people were trained to disobey the laws without being violent. And finally, the term

Satyagraha was coined, which got global currency especially after his entry into India's freedom struggle in 1930s.

Yamaguch rightly commends Gandhi's adherence to Non-violence all through his life. He is right when he says that on certain occasions, he permitted mild violence to be used by the *satyagrahis*. In 1942, he asked the freedom fighters to do or die. In fact, he did not permit violence; he only meant that violence was better than cowardice. So, he asked people to face government's violence in the form of injustice to them non-violently but those who became violent in doing so were not to be disowned. This was especially so until 1931.

Manliness of Gandhi did not exclude the women. His *Ekadashi* Vows were applicable to men and women alike but he laid emphasis on men being in the fore front and the women helping the in men folks to observe the vows. To him men and women were equal as far as human rights were concerned but assigned a bit different duties to the two sexes at least in 1930s. Men and women were physiologically different. The latter were better fit to take responsibility of the household and upbringing of children. He did change his view in this respect too as many of his women followers entered active politics and various other pursuits.

Gandhi's Democracy

Gandhi was a democrat and he wanted the principles of democracy to reach the masses in rural areas. He wanted the Congress sessions to be held in rural areas and the elected leaders of the party including the ministers to be in direct touch with the masses. After independence in 1947, India became the largest democracy in the world which Gandhi had already said in 1930. Gandhi wanted democracy to penetrate down to the villages where nearly 80 per cent of the people in his time lived.

Gandhi wrote extensively on *gram swaraj* and village republics. He wanted Indian democracy not to be top down; he wanted the top-down democracy to be balanced and strengthened by bottom-up democracy. Gandhi talked of self-governing village republics. The idea was to keep the political leaders in constant touch with the people and thus to minimize the over-riding influence of beaurocracy on the government.

The state of Indian democracy today in 2015 is exactly what Gandhi had foreseen. India's villages are dying. In 2014, only 68 percent Indians lived in villages; the share was 72 per cent in 2002. In another 25 years, the share rural population is likely to come down to 50 per cent. Much of the rural migrant settle down in large cities. In 971, India had just 7 million plus cities; by 1991, the number went up 23; and in 2011 it more than doubled to 53. While the country is talking of developing 100 smart cities, villages are becoming dysfunctional and their economic base is getting eroded fast. India needs rural-urban integration and this possible unless along with smart cities India takes up the development of smart villages too, each having a population of at least 5000 people.

Gandhi's influence had had waned as he freedom struggle during the 1940s reached a point of no return and it became clear that the British were no longer in a position to keep India as a part of British Empire. The succeeded in dividing the people and prepared the ground for the partition of India into India and Pakistan. Later in 1971, Pakistan was also divided into two countries. West Pakistan became Pakistan and East Pakistan became Bangladesh. And Gandhi's villages turned into something worse than urban slums.

Gandhi's Socio-economics

In this chapter the author has covered, Gandhi's social and economic thoughts. In the early stages (1930s) of his movement in India, he was not thinking in terms of abolishing the *zamindari* system or doing away capitalists and 565 pricely states. This thinking emerged from the hope that people's power would subdue their superpower statuses and they will fall in line with areas under direct British control, and democracy wherein common man was freed from druggery of life, prevail all over the country. Later, his views changed, but his concern for the commonman continued to rule supreme, as he came close to launching the Quit India Movement in 1940s.

Gandhi introduced a few socio-economic innovations in his Constructive Programme for socio-economic development in villages and small towns. If accepted and introduced all over India, many of the problems that country faces today could have been avoided. These are: 1. Redistribution of land in rural areas to stop rural-urban migration; 2. Promotion of village industries with *khadi* (hand spinning and weaving) as the centre-piece; 3. Introduction of *Nayee Taleem* (Basic Education) with built-in training in other relevant economic and health promoting activities; 4. Abolition of untouchability and provision of better services to Harijans; and 5. Protection of cows to ensure adequate milk and milk products for all to keep themselves healthy, and of bullocks for agricultural operations. All these were integrated into his Constructive Programme.

To uplift the villages, his Constructive Programme included not only the above mentioned activities, but also health facilities and clean drinking water for all, conservation of forests and soil, irrigation facilities and use of organic fertilizers. Gandhi also called for redistribution of agricultural land. He himself practiced what he tried to teach the people through his Constructive Programme. For example, he drank only boiled water and urged his co-workers to follow his example.

As mentioned earlier, Gandhi considered men and women to be equal partners in the journey of life. But their roles were different in the freedom struggle and especially so in *Satyagraha*. He wanted the women to "Help the men in your families to honour their pledge. May God give you the wisdom to be loyal to that pledge." Gandhi considered women to be less suited for taking vows. "In the new order of my imagination all will work according to their capacity for an adequate return for their labour. Women in the new order will be part-time workers, their primary function being to look after the home' and help the husband be true to his vows" (*CWMG*, 71-324). Referring to his wife Kasturba, who was no more at the time, he said lovingly "It was that illiterate woman who helped me to observe all my vows with the utmost strictness and kept me ever vigilant" (*CWMG*, 88-105). Gandhi naturally was quite traditional in this respect unless he was referring to the women who lived in villages and were illiterate.

In my view, if Gandhi had lived longer, he would have advised India to opt for a rural development model similar to that of Israel's Kibutz and Moshavs and linked them physically as well as economically with India's large, medium and small cities (Growth Poles, Growth Centres, and Growth Points) and thus retained the republican status of Indian villages.

Gandhi against Communalism

Social Harmony

Gandhi was a spiritual man and wanted India to be a spiritual country. This he made clear in a Speech at Y.M.C.A., Madras, in April 1915, three months after his return from South Africa. He followed that G.K. Gokhale who wished to spiritualize the political life and institutions of India (*CWMG*, 13-66). In a Draft Resolution he wrote for the Congress Working Committee in mid-1940, he said "I have always derived my politics from ethics or religion and my strength is also derived by my deriving my politics from ethics…I came into the Congress with my religion" (*CWMG*, 72-243). "… For me, every, the tiniest activity is governed by what I consider to be my religion" (*CWMG*, 49-502).

The religion of Gandhi was not limited to observances of certain rituals in temples, mosque and churches. For him, it meant a general ethical or moral system, which he thought was more or less common to all the religions. As if he was in search of religion of religions, in *Hind Swaraj* he called it "that religion which underlies all religions" (*CWMG*, 10-24). His *Ekadasi* (eleven vows) in way provided the base to his religion. He declared himself to be a *Sanatani* (traditional Hindu), but he never visited a temple largely because Hinduism to begin with had no temples and also because *Harijans* were barred from entering Hindu temples. There was no Hindu temple in Gandhi's *ashrams*.

While asking Hindus to do away with untouchability and integrate the *Harijans* fully in Hindu society as equals, he advised the *Harijans* as early as 1932 to facilitate their own integration with the Hindu society by observing common cleanliness, refraining from eating the meat of dead animals and from drink, sending their children to schools, removing untouchability among themselves and carrying on other such reform from within which can bring all Hindus together. The Harijan Sevak Sangh was made a platform for upper caste Hindus for penance for the sins they committed in introducing untouchability.

Communal Harmony

Gandhi tried his level best all through his life bring Hindus and

Muslims on a common platform and to maintain communal harmony. But the very fact that India was divided into nations: India and Pakistan points to his utter failure in this respect. At the same time, we cannot ignore the fact that among his great followers were Khan Abdul Gaffar Khan (Frontier Gandhi) and his whole family, Maulana Abdul Kalam Azad, who became the first Education Minister of India and many others of equal or less prominence, points to the positive impact of Gandhi on the Muslims. Counter-posed to Gandhi's efforts at communal harmony was the British Policy of "Divide and Rule". The Muslim Leagues which spearheaded the movement for a separate homeland for Muslims found the British policy helpful in reaching its goals.

Gandhi's backing of the Khilafat Movement was, in my view a wrong decision. The issue of the recognition of the Caliph of Turkey was not even remotely related to India. Muslims of India and elsewhere in the world backed the Caliph simply because they were Muslims. To support this movement amounted to supporting pan-Islamic unity and a separate identity for Muslims. This thinking further strengthened the Muslim League in undivided India.

While in South Africa, Gandhi fought the Black Act and other discriminatory steps the British took to save the Eastern Civilization, not the Hindus or Muslims. His approach was similar in India. He was not prepared to concede the special privileges/rights, the Muslim League leaders demanded from time to time. True, Gandhi committed some strategic mistakes and India got divided into two nations, but his basic principles stood exonerated when Pakistan was divided into two nations, Pakistan and Bangladesh in 1971.

What the Muslim League started in India in 1940s has now taken a global form. Many countries like Sudan and Ethiopia in Africa stand divided on religious lines and even the predominantly Muslim countries like Syria and Iraq are engaged in religious wars involving different sects of Islam; Sunni and Shia. No Muslim country in the world is peaceful and the waves of its movement in the form of 'Islamic State of Iran and Syria' (ISIS) is now adversely affecting peace and harmony all over the world.

Concluding Remarks

After going through Mr. H. Yamaguchi's book "How Relevant is

Gandhi Today: A Japanese View" I conclude that the author has answered the questions raised on the Gandhi's contemporary relevance in a very scholarly and beautiful manner. While admitting that Gandhi was at fault on many occasions, he lived by his principles and changed his views as new situations, realities, and challenges he faced.

Yamaguchi goes into the depth of what motivated Gandhi to do what he did in his life? It was the manliness i.e. sticking to the pledges or vows one takes even at the cost of one's life. Then he dwells on Gandhi's Democracy and concludes that Gandhi advocated development from below and, therefore, empowering the Indian villages on a priority basis and involving the people in democratic governance. The new government of Independent India did not pay as much attention to this advice of Gandhi. The present pitiable state of Indian villages and mass scale rural-urban migration especially of the youth is the consequence of ignoring Gandhi's advice.

Gandhi stood for the removal of all those divisive forces from Indian society that weakened the social cohesion of Indian society. He took up communal harmony to bring the Hindus and Muslims together and to do away with untouchability in Hinduism. On both these fronts he was only partially successful but his intentions and efforts were honest. He also tried to lift the status of women though he believed that women must manage their home from well and help their male colleagues to perform their duties towards themselves, their families, society and the nation.

35-1, Stanley Road,
Allahabad-211001 (India)
27 April, 2015

Prof. R.P. Misra
Series Editor

Preface

Is there any need for having one more book on Gandhi when there are so many in our shelves already? The author would like to say 'yes'. There are two reasons for this. One is that, for the past some years by now, there has not been a full, integrated, and multi-angled study of him. Consequently, as the author sees, there has not been much debate about him, either. A passage of time makes it necessary, and also possible, to have some new perception. But why are such debates on Gandhi necessary? It will lead to the second, more important reason, that there has not been a new perspective on his contemporary relevance, whether in the affirmative or negative, to throw light on if Gandhi is a man of the past, or if he can talk to the present.

This book tries to be an attempt to fill the first gap while keeping the second fully in view. It aims to be Gandhi's full study, in the sense that the different aspects of his public life are analyzed and put together, so that his life and work would become understandable and meaningful as a whole. At the same time, it places him in the contemporary world, in 2016, to determine where his relevance lies today, what it is that we can extract from him today, and why he is being forgotten almost day by day, though imperceptibly. These two objectives are closely related. They are almost one and the same, although the title leans more on the second, reflecting the author's keener interest. This is not a biography. Rather, the above is not the task of a biography as such.

Is it true that he is being forgotten? There was a time when Gandhi was known even in the remote corners of the globe. A biographer of Kamaladevi Chattopadhyay (hereafter Kamaladevi) writes that when she visited Eritrea to see war graves, presumably of the Italian invasion of Ethiopia in 1935-36, she was captured by the bandits, but when she told them that she had come from India, the country of Gandhi, they released her and gave her a comb as a present.[1]

But we are in a different environment. When the first volume of D.G. Tendulkar's tremendous biography, *Mahatma: Life of Mohandas Karamchand Gandhi*, was published, Jawaharlal Nehru wrote in its Foreword that "A new generation grows up to whom he is almost a name, a great name to be revered, but nevertheless a name".[2] It was written on 30 June 1951, only three and a half years after his demise. Louis Fischer, an American journalist who interviewed Gandhi for one week during the Second World War, wrote on his birth centenary under the title "Where is Gandhiji" that "…Gandhiji is very much alive in America. But what of India?...young Indians…know far less than they should about Gandhiji's life and work."[3]

It must be much more so today. The author is not unaware that his name is mentioned, and is remembered anew, sometimes spontaneously, on many occasions. India's Kailash Satyarthi referred to his name, almost inevitably for one who has been active in social work for decades, in his acceptance speech for the Nobel Peace Prize on 10 December, 2014. But there is no denying the general tendency of knowing him less and less. Can't it be helped?

Many would say "no". But it is not possible for him to have a new lease of life until and unless we find in his work and writings messages appropriate to this age. Would that be possible? In a nutshell, that is the author's aim, and motivation, in writing this book, even though it means one more book to the huge existing literature. We will not find the whole answer in him to our problems, by which the author means not only India's, but our common problems. They are broadly two, peace and poverty alleviation. It is not humanly possible to expect answers to them from one person. But we may find in him the answers to them to a substantial degree, up to, say, 50 per cent. We may be compelled to discard some of his ideas. And we may also be compelled to find the other 50 per cent elsewhere, but that is beyond the scope of this book.

The author has depended most on the *Collected Works of Mahatma Gandhi,* published by the Publications Division, Government of India (hereafter *CWMG*).

Although this book is not Gandhi's anthology, the author has not hesitated to quote him often enough, so that he would dare to say that whatever is worth quoting from Gandhi has found its way into this book.

He has consulted a number of other books and articles which are mentioned in the Bibliography. He thanks the authors and publishers of those works, as this book is, on one hand, the result of the author's dialogue with those works, as well as the *CWMG*. The references from the *CWMG* are shown in the text itself, and those from other sources are shown in the Notes. The author regrets that there may still be quite a number of works which should have found their places in the footnotes and the Bibliography.

This is not a book to hero-worship, let alone deify, Gandhi. The author has not refrained from criticizing Gandhi. In its five chapters, and especially in the three key chapters, Gandhi's failure, miscalculation or even defeat will present themselves. In that sense this is a critical evaluation of Gandhi. At the same time the author does not conceal his respect for his remarkableness, even genius, as a public, and also a private person. It is his pleasure to find that after all Gandhi is a man worth writing about.

Yamaguchi Hiroichi
hyamaguchiblog@gmail.com

Notes

1. Shakuntala Narasimhan, *Kamaladevi Chattopadhyay: The Romantic Rebel*, p. 181.
2. D.G. Tendulkar, *Mahatma: Life of Mohandas Karamchand Gandhi*, Vol. 1, p. xi.
3. Louis Fischer, "Where is Gandhiji?", S. Radhakrishnan, ed., *Mahatma Gandhi 100 Years*, p. 84.

Acknowledgements

On the other hand, this book is also the result of a dialogue with a great number of people. We would like to present here with gratitude about sixty-five names of Indians whom the author has interviewed, sometimes more, or many more, than once, on Gandhi and related subjects. It has been the author's pleasure and privilege to talk to them. At the same time he regrets that he has not been able to meet many others whom he wanted to. Japanese names will be listed if and when the Japanese edition comes out. He, however, specifically thanks Tanaka Toshio, a Professor of Hindi literature in Japan, who has translated Gandhi's *An Autobiography*, *Hind Swaraj*, and *Satyagraha in South Africa* from the Gujarati original to Japanese. The author owes a great deal to those works for understanding Gandhi.

Om Prakash Aask, Arjun Asrani, Subrata Banerji, Sunderlal and Vimla Bahuguna, Gautam Bajaj, G. Balatchandirane, R.C. Bhargawa, Pratap Chandra Behera, Acharya Bhavananand, Himanshu Bourai, Suhashi Chakravarty, Sukhamoy Chakravarty, Bipan Chandra, Kamal Chenoy, Pran Chopra, M.S. Dadage, Narayan Desai, Kusum Deshpande, D.R. Dugar, Ashgar Ali Engineer, Partha Ghosh, S.D. Gokhale, Krishne Gowda, Anil Gupta, Pandurang Hegde, Narayan S. Jajoo and U.N. Jajoo (son and grandson of Krishnadas Jaju), P.C. Joshi and his wife, K.D. Kapoor, K.V. Kesavan, Jeevan Kumar and his wife, Lahiji, P.M. Lata, Annapurna Maharana and J. Maharana, Rashpal Malhotra, Dipak Malik, Naresh Mantri, Kuldeep Mathur and his wife, E.P. Menon, Anil Dutta Mishra, Pratibha J. Mishra, S.N. Mishra, Arun Mudhol, Aditya and Mridra Mukerji, Ram Dayal Munda, Sushila Narasimhan and her husband, Mansaram Nitnaware and his wife, Rajaram Panda, B.P. Pradhan, Acharya Ramamurthy, Shobhana Ranade, C.H. Hanumantha Rao, P.V. Rao, Subha Rao, Anil

Rawat, Ramaben Ruiya, T.N. Sareen and his wife, Anwar Ahmad Siddiqi, Y.C. Simhadri and his wife, Madhuri Santanam Sondhi, Kumar Sundaram, Brij Tanka, Manoj Kumar Teotia, Ramkrishna Tripathi, Vijay Upadhyay and his wife, P.C. Verma and his wife.

Anil Dutta Mishra has taken the trouble of introducing the author to the publisher, and the author is thankful to the Concept Publishing Company Pvt. Ltd., New Delhi for publishing the book. Nearly a dozen of the above-mentioned people are no more walking on this globe, and the author would like to wish their souls a peaceful rest. Needless to say, the author alone is responsible for whatever is written in the book.

Out of the several libraries where the author has worked, he likes to express his special thanks to the Library of the India International Centre, New Delhi.

Contents

Introduction

For the purpose of the book already stated, Gandhi's life and work which constituted an indivisible whole has been segmented into three more or less distinct areas of (1) his political thought and behaviour, (2) his socio-economic insight and practice, and (3) his struggle toward Hindu-Muslim unity. They have become the subject matter of Chapter Two, Three and Four, respectively. These three are the key chapters. His work and writings on the international sphere are dealt with in the last Chapter Five. The philosophical and religious basis of his activities is discussed in Chapter One.

Questions may be asked as to why a foreigner, a Japanese in this case, wants to write on Gandhi. Gandhi as a subject for research is open to anyone. If a foreigner writes on him, it may hopefully help generalize his work, his tasks and his problems, as the author has tried to do. But is there any advantage in being a Japanese in understanding Gandhi?

In the author's view, there are two merits, of not exactly being a Japanese national but, of being familiar with some aspects of modern Japanese history in writing on Gandhi. First is on the Russo-Japanese War of 1904-5 and its aftermath. Gandhi was closely following the War and wrote about it eleven times in his *Indian Opinion* in South Africa. But he was, partly under Tolstoy's influence, not favourable to the War itself and to Japan's victory. It is true that Japan's victory encouraged many Asian leaders, including Sun Yat-sen of China. Sun once said that Japan's victory over Russia was the first victory of the Asians over the Europeans. He established his Nationalist Party in Japan during the War where he was in exile. The movement in Vietnam to study in Japan was another example. It took those Asian leaders some years to get disillusioned with Japan's policies.

It was remarkable that Gandhi did not join their applause of Japan's industrial or military successes. This is clear from *Hind Swaraj,* written in 1909. The Reader says that if the British withdraws from India "we shall still keep their constitution and shall carry on the Government…we shall then hoist our own flag. As in Japan, so must India be. We must own our own navy, our army, and we must have our own splendour, and then will India's voice ring through the world".

This is the only place Japan is mentioned in *Hind Swaraj*. Since it is mentioned by the Reader, and since navy comes earlier than the army, presumably because the decisive battle in the Russo-Japanese War was a sea battle, we may suppose that Japan's victory is more or less known among the people of India. We may rather say that Japan is known by the victory in this War. But the Editor (Gandhi) refused to accept what the Reader said, and told him that "This is not the *Swaraj* that I want" (*CWMG*, 10-15). Here he drew a line between the two different ways before India, and by denying the one which may lead India to an industrial and military power, showed his determination to find India's future in the other direction, in whatever way it may be described. This is a crucial point in understanding Gandhi.

The second is on Gandhi's response during the Second World War when "Malaya, Singapore and Burma" had been conquered by the Japanese Army, and India, with her long Eastern coast undefended, and with Britain fighting the War in Europe almost single-handedly, was in danger of being invaded. Gandhi struggled hard to find a way of non-violent non-co-operation with the invading army. He did not take the side of the other Congress leaders who were anxious to share in the political power even during the war to fight the invaders not only in the non-violent way but in the violent way also. Ultimately the Quit-India Movement emerged out of Gandhi's groping. This was a significant landmark in the development of his thinking on non-violence.

India did not occupy a central place in Japan's imperial design. Still, a series of Japanese intellectuals came to visit Gandhi, mainly at Sevagram, to secure his tacit approval of such a design. It is outside the realm of this book to discuss this aspect of the war, but a reference will be made to a recent study of this point centring around two Japanese personalities, by a Japanese historian.[1]

Note

1. Naito Masao, "Japanese Approach Towards Gandhi during the Sino-Japanese War", Radhika Seshan, ed., *Convergence,* 109-129.

One
What Motivated Gandhi?

'...man is both matter and spirit, each acting on and affecting the other'. "Confusion about Ramanama".
—17 August 1946, *CWMG*, Vol. 85, p. 175.

1. Gandhi's Concept of Manliness

Taking an Oath

Gandhi was the first man, according to Vinoba Bhave (hereafter Vinoba), his life-long disciple and co-worker for thirty-two years since he met Gandhi at the Kocharab Ashram in 1916, to see that in the social service also *a vrat palan* (observance of an oath) is necessary to move toward the goal.[1] Vinoba says, incidentally, that 'The something that I am today is entirely the miracle of Bapu's blessings. He has made an uncivilized man like me into a social worker (*sevak*)'.[2]

Gandhi took a pledge together with his fellow Indians at the Empire Theatre, Johannesburg, to inaugurate the movement in the Transvaal against the 'Black Act' on the Asiatics' registration on 11 September 1906, and the movement came to be called *satyagraha*. At this meeting, attended by about 3,000 Indians, Abdul Gani, Chairman, British Indian Association, spoke first. He said toward the end that '...it is our duty firmly to resolve to defy the law and go to gaol. There is nothing to be ashamed of in going to gaol.' He concluded, '...we have to be humble and non-violent. We should not speak or listen to any bitter words.'(*CWMG*, 5-425) He was already speaking with the idea of civil disobedience and non-violence in mind. But he was not yet thinking of taking or proposing an oath at this time. Then Gandhi spoke. But he also, in his own words, 'had no intention of taking an oath or inviting others to do so…' (*CWMG*, 29-87).

When one of the other speakers, Sheth Haji Habib, spoke of supporting 'the Fourth Resolution', the main Resolution, 'with God as witness', or 'in the name of God' (*ibid.*), however, Gandhi immediately sensed its implications. So he stood up again and told the packed audience, 'We all believe in one and the same God, the differences of nomenclature in Hinduism and Islam notwithstanding. To pledge ourselves or to take an oath in the name of that God or with Him as witness is not something to be trifled with'. He was already speaking from the point of '*Ishwar Allah Tere Nam*' at this time and, moreover, could probably take it for granted that it was accepted by the audience. He continued, 'Personally I hold that a man, who deliberately and intelligently takes a pledge and then breaks it, forfeits his manhood…But everyone of us must think out for himself if he has the will and the ability to pledge himself…so long as there is even a handful of men true to their pledge, there can only be one end to the struggle, and that is victory'. His conclusion was, 'Every one should fully realize his responsibility, then only pledge himself independently of others and understand that he himself must be true to his pledge even unto death, no matter what others do'. (*CWMG*, 5-419~22, 29-88~90)

Here he is seen to respect the individuality of man, which is basic to his idea of building what may be called a civil society. It is another thing how his co-workers responded to it. At the same time his idea of 'manhood' can be seen here and there, in close connection with the observation of a pledge. One more noticeable thing is his belief that even a handful of men true to their pledge will be enough to achieve a goal whatever it is, even if it is such a large objective as the freedom of a country. It is his elitism. It emphasizes the importance attached to training. But it is not incompatible with his approach to the masses.

Back in India, it was at the time of the Kheda *satyagraha* that he first took such an oath. "The Pledge" he took together with some 200 villagers at Nadiad in Kheda District on 22 March 1918 reads, 'We the undersigned, therefore, (as the Government did not agree to the postponement of the collection of the land revenue in spite of a crop failure) solemnly declare that we shall not pay the assessment for the year whether it be wholly or in part; we shall leave it to the Government to take any legal steps they choose to enforce recovery of the same and we shall undergo all the sufferings that this may involve…But we shall not by voluntary payment allow ourselves to be regarded as liars and thus lose our self-respect'. (*CWMG*, 14-279) Nearly a month later, in his "Message to Satyagrahi Agriculturists", he reiterated the meaning of a pledge thus, 'A man owes it as a duty to refuse to do anything out of fear…This is a fight for asserting our manliness'.

As for the place of women in this fight, he called upon them in another speech on the same day, to 'Help the men in your families to honour their pledge. May God give you the wisdom to be loyal to that pledge'. So man and woman are to Gandhi not quite equal, and it is the man who should abide by his pledge, with the woman's help. Many years afterwards, Gandhi, in "Question Box" (subtitle, Women and Their Work), summed up the women's position by saying that 'In the new order of my imagination all will work according to their capacity for an adequate return for their labour. Women in the new order will be part-time workers, their primary function being to look after the home'. (*CWMG*, 71-324) Gandhi applied the same formula to his own family members. Some more years later he said in "Letter To Manilal Gandhi" about Sushila, Manilal's wife, that 'Her own desire is to help you and join in the struggle, but her duty is to do as you wish'. (*CWMG*, 85-132) Was this really 'the new order'? Even on Kasturba, his wife who was no more at the time, Gandhi said in "Talk to a Woman Relative", though with much respect, that 'It was that illiterate woman who helped me to observe all my vows with the utmost strictness and kept me ever vigilant'. (*CWMG*, 88-105)

Manliness vs. *Cowardice*

It was at the hilly station of Pietermaritzburg in South Africa in 1893 that he first hit upon this idea of manliness. It was shortly after he arrived at Durban, and he was on his way to Pretoria, without being familiar with the natural as well as social environment there. Consequently he was thrown out of his comfortable first-class compartment. Half-frozen, he wondered if he should go back or continue the journey. His *Satyagraha in South Africa* tells us that

'Late at night, I came to the conclusion that to run back to India would be cowardly'. (*CWMG*, 29-38) His *An Autobiography* or *The Story of My Experiments with Truth*, giving a more detailed account of the incident on the way, says on his determination in almost the same language that 'It would be cowardice to run back to India without fulfilling my obligation'. (*CWMG*, 39-94) Since then, cowardice became something even worse to him than violence, and manliness even more valuable than non-violence.

Thereafter he often examined his, or the co-workers', thought and action by using this manliness-cowardice yardstick. For example, he used 'manly' three times as an adjective in his "Speech on Reforms Resolution at Amritsar Congress" on 1 January 1920. It was in an amendment to the Resolution, tabled by C.R. Das, characterizing the Reforms Act (Montagu-Chelmsford Reforms) as, among other things, 'disappointing', and Gandhi demanded the deletion of the word. Gandhi's point was that, since the British have extended their hands like this, the Indians to be manly should not reject their advances. (*CWMG*, 16-363~67) Thus, we see that Gandhi was strongly motivated by the consciousness of if something he was about to do was manly or otherwise, in other words by the consciousness of personal honour. We will see that non-violence was extremely important to him, but the standard of manliness-cowardice seems to have even excelled it in importance. It is the same thing as observing an oath/pledge once it has been taken after careful thought.

Here is another example that Gandhi writes in *Autobiography* on his sense of humour. While he and his family were away from South Africa for the second time and settled down at Bombay, Manilal, the second son who was ten years old, became seriously ill. A Parsi doctor recommended eggs and chicken broth. Gandhi declined them, but was very anxious. He thought, 'What would people say of me? What would my elder brother think of me? My honour is in Thy keeping, oh Lord, in this hour of trial'. The boy recovered, but Gandhi says that 'For my part I was sure that God had saved my honour, and that belief remains unaltered to this day'. (*CWMG*, 39-199~201)

Eleven-fold Vow

It is the *Ekadas Vrata*, or the Eleven-fold vow, that expresses in a nutshell his idea of how the vow should be. It is a system of vows that the Ashramites have an obligation to observe. Vows are also called pledges, oaths, observances. It was explained in the "Constitution for the Ashram", the first such document for his *ashram*, which was decided in November 1915. The *ashram* was at Kocharab since 25 May 1915 till it moved to Sabarmati in 1917. The document mentions the following nine items as such vows and gives a brief comment on each of them. They are Truth, Non-Violence, Celibacy, Control of the Palate, Non-Stealing, Non-Possession, *Swadeshi*, Fearlessness, and Against Untouchability. Besides there are five items mentioned and commented upon, but it is not clear whether they are here as vows or not. (*CWMG*, 13-91~8) About three months later, Gandhi made a "Speech on 'Ashram Vows' at Y.M.C.A., Madras", in which he mentioned the above nine vows, but here also he mentioned three other items the place of which is not clear in the system of vows to be taken at the *ashram*. (*CWMG*, 13-225~35)

It was in the "Satyagraha Ashram", the next and probably the last version of the Ashram Constitution, published in June 1928, that the Eleven-fold vow was clearly mentioned. Besides the above nine, in some cases under slightly different titles, it also included Physical Labour, and Tolerance, making it eleven. (*CWMG*, 36-398~401) We will look at Gandhi's Constructive Programme in Chapter Three. One may be struck by the similarity between the above-mentioned items in the Eleven-fold and those in the Constructive Programme, though in the latter's case the number of items kept increasing with the passage of time. Gandhi himself later wrote in his "Letter to Jatindas M. Amin" in October 1945 that the 'constructive programme is included in the observance of the vows'. (*CWMG*, 81-405) It seems, however, that the weightage of the topmost three items in the Programme, communal unity, removal of untouchability and prohibition, is lower in the *Ekadas Vrata*.

Gandhi wrote on the distinction between what he called the primary observances (*mahavratas*) and other vows in his "History of the Satyagraha Ashram". According to him, Truth, *ahimsa* or Love, *Brahmacharya* or Chastity, Non-Stealing, and Non-Possession or Poverty belong to the first category. (*CWMG*, 50-213) We may add here one important change Gandhi introduced about this time in the way Truth is expressed in relation to God. In his "Speech at Meeting in Lausanne" on 8 December 1931, on his way home from the Round Table Conference (hereafter RTC) in London, Gandhi told the audience that 'for myself I have come to the conclusion that God is Truth. But two years ago I went a step further and said Truth is God. You will see the fine distinction between the two statements...'. (*CWMG*, 48-404) This God is Gandhi's general god we will talk about shortly. This change in placing God in relation to Truth has made God much more accessible and also understandable.

We will add one point each on Non-Stealing and Non-Possession. Living on alms is not always considered stealing. Very often it is necessary and inevitable. However, in the eye of Gandhi it was not a desirable thing to do. When an earthquake occurred in Bihar in 1934, Gandhi went there from the midst of his Harijan tour. In "Speech at Public Meeting, Patna", he told the audience 'But those who were able to work must earn the relief they sought by working for it. Let each suffering individual earn his relief by working for it'. (*CWMG*, 57-293) The idea of 'earn one's relief' and not 'live on relief' was always there in Gandhi's thinking, and he told so later to the refugees of the Partition, or the ex-INA soldiers as well.

In "Statement to the Press" at Delhi on 11 September 1947 he said that 'I understand...that it is well-nigh impossible to supply refugee camps with Bhangis for attending to the cleaning of the latrines and the general sanitation. Any infectious disease like cholera might break out. I have no doubt whatsoever that the refugees should look after the sanitation, including latrine cleaning in their own camps and should do some useful work ...All camps should be models of cleanliness, simplicity and industry'. (*CWMG*, 89-172) A month later he talked about the refugees in "Speech at Prayer Meeting" that 'The people who have been thrown on the streets must first realize that they belong to India, not to the Punjab...All those provinces are in India and the people from those parts also belong to India. They can become and remain Indians only on the condition that they are not a burden on others...They must be mutually helpful and cooperative and put in hard work. Then they can reform the province where they go and the people belonging to that province will say that they are willing to accommodate any number of such persons'. (89-329) Such an attitude may well be a part of the Non-Possession, but also of Physical Labour. Another point is inherent in what he said in "Speech

At Meeting of Gujaratis" in 1935, which was that 'You must bear in mind that you have the right to earn as much as you like, but not the right to spend as much as you like'. (*CWMG*, 60-465) He was here inducing the business people to spend for the sake of the community, or to be a trustee for their property. Some time ago, by the way, the author was told by a businessman in India that whereas formerly even a well-to-do did not eat a luxurious food, nowadays he would not mind it. This is an age of conspicuous consumption.

Narayan Desai, Gandhi's secretary Mahadev Desai's son (hereafter Narayanbhai), adds that apart from those five, two are auxiliary ones and the remaining four are of current nature. *Abhaya* (fearlessness) comes as one of the two auxiliary ones together with the control of the palate.[3] Hiren Mukerjee, a Communist Lok Sabha Member in independent India for five terms, in his compact *Gandhiji: A Study*, writes that 'This quality of fearlessness, rather than the more widely publicized notion of *ahimsa*, non-violence, was Gandhi's greatest contribution to Indian life—fearlessness of State repression and of social obloquy, fearlessness in respect not only of the coercive machinery of the State, but of landlords and moneylenders and vested interests, fearlessness even in the face of starvation and sorrow'.[4] Some of his other words are also worth noting, such as, 'India's debt to Gandhi is irredeemable. He, above all, taught our people as a whole to fear the conqueror no longer'.[5] Narayanbhai writes in the same tone that 'Among the many legacies of Gandhiji, *abhaya*—freedom from fear—can be considered the most significant'.[6]

One would wonder, however, why some of the human habits that Gandhi highly valued were not included here. For instance, he considered accounts of funds very important and said in "Speech at Convocation, Gujarat Vidyapith, Ahmedabad" in 1931 that 'let us be ready to account for every pie that we receive from the public'. (*CWMG*, 45-409) He also said in "Propaganda *vs.* Construction" in 1933 that 'Propaganda work should be self-supporting. Pamphlets ought not to be distributed free of charge…Pamphlets received free are thrown into the waste-paper basket'. (*CWMG*, 54-207) Another element missing here is to bc punctual. He said, 'Keep your appointments rigidly to the minute' in "Some Thoughts on U.P. Tour" in 1929. (*CWMG*, 42-221) Still another one is that he placed emphasis on arbitration by a third party. One example from the latter period of his life may be cited. While in Noakhali in 1946-7 he was urged by the local Muslim League to go to Bihar to look after the Muslim minority there. If the Government of Bihar had appointed a Commission to investigate into the alleged atrocities on the Muslims at the hand of the Hindus he would not have gone there. But as he wrote in "Letter to Vallabhbhai Patel", he thought that 'if a Commission is not appointed after all, I shall have no choice but to go to Bihar' (*CWMG*, 86-432), and he actually went there. For one reason or another Patel, Home Minister, was not looking kindly at the appointment (*CWMG*, 86-432, fn-1).

Manliness vs. *Non-Violence*

We will look at his behaviour at Noakhali a little in depth to comprehend his sense of manliness. Gandhi first mentioned the disturbances in Noakhali in "Speech at Prayer Meeting" at Delhi on 15 October 1946 when he said that 'what was far worse than the news from Assam (of floods) was the fact that there was rioting in Noakhali in Eastern Bengal…Ever since he had heard the news of Noakhali, indeed ever since the blood bath of Calcutta (the 'Direct Action' of the Muslim League on 16 August of that year) he had been wondering where his duty lay'. (*CWMG*, 85-464) He then made up his mind, got on board a train for Calcutta on 26 October. This was the start of the last fifteen months of his life, characterized by placing himself in the midst of riots, disturbances, and danger to himself. During this time what sustained him was his notion of manliness. He said, 'Do or die' a number of times there, which he had made famous at the time of the 'Quit-India' Movement, but which actually he first used in describing the attitude of the Japanese people during the Russo-Japanese War of 1904~5. Also in Bihar where he moved from Noakhali, he said, 'I have come here determined to emerge successful from this ordeal' in "Letter to G.D. Birla"(*CWMG*, 86-162), or 'if this thing is pulled through, it will be the crowning act of my life' in "Discussion with Amiya Chakravarty"(*CWMG*, 86-193), and 'I don't want to die a failure but as a successful man. But it may be that I may die a failure' in "Discussion with Hindu Mahasabha

Leaders" (*CWMG*, 86-200), or 'I don't want to return from Bengal defeated' in "Remark to a Friend" (*CWMG*, 86-224).

Was not there any contradiction between his manliness on one hand and non-violence on the other? Here is a historic example of such a conflict. On 24 April 1930, when the nationwide Salt Satyagraha was at its peak, two platoons of 18th Royal Garhwal Rifles, a Hindu regiment, were ordered to shoot at the huge Muslim crowd, unarmed and peaceful, at Peshawar, but refused to do so. If they had done so, there would have been a countless number of casualties among the Muslims, the second Amritsar Massacre would have been created, and a deep and irreparable injury in the Hindu-Muslim relations would have resulted. One might have expected Gandhi to praise such a behaviour of non-violence on the part of the Hindu soldiers, as it was non-violence in action, by the armed and, therefore, the strong, practiced at a great risk. Moreover the Muslims were led by Khan Abdul Ghaffar Khan, Gandhi's disciple and co-worker in the Frontier Province, who was known as the "Frontier Gandhi". Kamaladevi quoted him. 'Yes, our Khudaikhidmatgars remained so completely non-violent and non-provocative, that the hearts of the hill-jawans, could not but melt'.[7] Narayanbhai writes that they were court-marshalled, and four officers were sentenced to life imprisonment and fifty-three others received light sentences.[8]

But, 'strangely enough'—to use Hiren Mukerjee's words[9]—this was precisely what hurt Gandhi. He admitted that the terms were sometimes too long, but once the soldiers took an oath they could not break it and complain about the punishment. In his "Speech at Meeting" at Geneva on 10 December 1931, he said, 'I would consider it unmanly for a soldier who has taken an oath to deny himself the consequences when he defies the order by shooting in the air…he should lay down arms and pay the penalty of insubordination'. (*CWMG*, 48-417) Therefore, it is as if there is a great difference between shooting in the air and laying down arms. Did he not go too far in upholding his idea of manliness when apparently scores of human lives were at stake? Where did the principle of Non-violence go? But he also said in "A Letter" of April 1932 that, in the context of having to defend a helpless person in the absence of any other means, 'cowardice is worse than violence' even though violence in such a case does not cease to be violence. (*CWMG*, 49-321) Rajmohan

Gandhi writes in his *Ghaffar Khan* on this point that '...soldiers of the Raj's Garhwal Rifles refused to obey their officer's order to fire at a crowd of unarmed Pathans...the Raj's demise had been scripted by *their* non-violent revolt in Peshawar's Kissa Khwani Bazaar'. He, however, does not seem to be discussing Gandhi's response to this non-violence.[10]

2. Gandhi's Religion

An All-pervading Religion

If Gandhi was so strongly motivated by his sense of honour, where does his religion stand? He said in a "Speech at Y.M.C.A., Madras", in April 1915, three months after his return from South Africa, that 'The message (of G.K. Gokhale, by which he wished to be guided in his life) is to spiritualize the political life and the political institutions of the country'. (*CWMG*, 13-66). In mid-1940, exactly a quarter of a century afterwards, he wrote in his "Draft Resolution for the Working Committee" that 'I have always derived my politics from ethics or religion and my strength is also derived by my deriving my politics from ethics...I came into the Congress with my religion'. (*CWMG*, 72-243) Therefore, at least in letters, and probably in thinking also, his and Gokhale's ideals must have been the same. This he could say in "A Letter" of 1932 that 'I do not conceive religion as one of the many activities of mankind. The same activity may be either governed by the spirit of religion or irreligion. There is no such thing for me, therefore, as leaving politics for religion. For me, every, the tiniest, activity is governed by what I consider to be my religion'. (*CWMG*, 49-502) Vinoba wrote on this point that 'It seemed to me that this was a kind of man who wanted to achieve both the political independence and spiritual development of the country at the same time.[11]

The religion Gandhi was talking of in the above speeches and writings was not particularly Hinduism, but a general ethical or moral system, which he thought was more or less common to all the religions. In *Hind Swaraj* he called it 'that religion which underlies all religions'. (*CWMG*, 10-24) We will call it his general religion. We may recall his *Ekadasi* and put it on a par with this general religion. Like the former, the latter was omnipresent in all his activities. It is not possible to consider it as just one sector of his life. It must have been about this general God that he said to Vinoba that 'My life exists to search for God and to see Him'.[12] Gandhi told him also that 'I have not seen His shape but have heard His voice'.[13]

Still he had no hesitation in calling himself a devout Hindu. He did not usually practice it. Judith Brown, a British historian, writes, 'He used the stories of Hindu mythology as he spoke on religious matters, but he showed little of the veneration of particular Hindu deities common among Hindus who expressed their beliefs in temple-going or in cults of devotion to specific gods. He engaged in none of these popular practices…'[14] Narayanbhai says that there was no Hindu temple in Gandhi's *ashrams*. Even after his demise he was not enshrined, if you exclude naming the streets after him. In this sense he was no longer a Mahatma, but just MG in MG Marg. It was good for him not to be worshipped as a god, and he would have liked it as he could thus be nearer the people.

'A Devout Hindu'

If he did not practice Hinduism, or did not bring Hinduism with him to the Congress, where do we find his Hinduism in action or in practice? In the author's view it was in his policy toward the untouchables more than anywhere else. We will discuss it later in more detail at the end of Chapter Three, but we may ascertain here what his basic stance was concerning the untouchables. In his perception, as he wrote in "Warning To Me" in April 1933, 'The *sanatanists* (orthodox Hindus) assert that the *Antyajas* have been a distinct class from time immemorial and say that they will sacrifice their lives to keep them so'. In contrast to this his policy toward them was essentially one of upper Hindu caste reformers aiming 'to secure their assimilation into the Hindu fold and end their separation'. (*CWMG*, 55-4)

Gandhi often told the Harijans what to do to be integrated with the Hindu socicty. In "Interview to P.N. Rajbhoj" in November 1932, for instance, he said, 'They should observe common cleanliness, should refrain from eating the meat of dead animals and from drink, send their children to schools, remove untouchability among themselves and generally carry on such reform from within as is possible' (*CWMG*, 51-406) Gandhi clearly said that The Harijan Sevak Sangh, which was one of his brainchildren to debate the policy toward them, consisted entirely of the men and women from non-Harijan castes, at least after the initial period. The "Draft Constitution of the Harijan Sevak Sangh" of March 1933 stated that B.R. Ambedkar and some others from this group were among the members of the Central Board, and also that 'Every Board or committee shall have as many Harijan members as it is possible to secure consistency with its maximum...' (*CWMG*, 54-17~21) The constitution was finalized early in 1935.

It was probably at this time that changes were introduced which Ambedkar and the like-minded people in the Central Board could not swallow. They resigned from the Board. Ambedkar wrote in "An Anti-Untouchability Agenda" that while he had to be away to attend the third RTC in London, which Gandhi did not, he wrote a long letter to A.V. Thakkar, Secretary, on 14 November 1932, shortly after the Poona Pact, suggesting what the Board should do.[15] But, he says, 'To my great surprise, I found that no attention was paid to my proposals. Indeed, my letter was not even acknowledged! I felt that there was no use in my remaining in the Sangh...I found that in my absence the aims and objectives had undergone a complete change'. And 'Since the first batch of the Untouchables (Ambedkar and two others) left the Sangh no attempt was made by Mr. Gandhi to appoint other Untouchables in their places'.[16] Thus the only opportunity of Gandhi and Ambedkar hugging each other, so to speak, was lost. At least this was the Ambedkar version. Against this there is hardly anything in the *CWMG*, especially on the circumstances concerning the reconstitution of the Central Board. It would not be an exaggeration to say that Gandhi to the end treated the untouchables as the monopoly of the Hindu society to the exclusion of other communities like the Muslims, though their problem was more or less a problem of the Indian society as a whole.

Valerian Rodriguez writes in the "Introduction" in *The Essential Writings* that 'He (Ambedkar) felt that Gandhi was too soft on orthodoxy and its proponents. As the 1930s advanced, Ambedkar increasingly turned against Gandhi and also against what he called Brahminism'.[17] In Ambedkar's words in his "Reply to the Mahatma",

'He (Gandhi) is the most influential apologist of it (this archaic social structure of the Hindus) and, therefore, the worst enemy of the Hindus'.[18] On the other hand Ambedkar had a high regard for Ranade. He wrote, for example, in "Ranade, Gandhi, Jinnah" that 'Ranade argued that there were no rights in the Hindu society...There were...privileges for a few and disabilities for a vast majority. Ranade struggled to create rights'.[19] Gandhi was of the view that the Indian society was more duty or obligation-oriented. But, as a quote from D.P. Mukerji would show later, he had a different perspective on the duty and the right.

On the appointment of Harijans, however, Gandhi was not, as he wrote in "Letter To H.J. Khandekar" in 1938, after the Congress Ministries were set up in different Provinces, against having a Harijan in a cabinet, if 'among the members of the C.P. Assembly there is a competent Harijan prepared to accept the Congress discipline, enjoying the confidence of the Harijan members and able to shoulder Ministerial responsibility'. (*CWMG*, 67-228) This was regarding a trouble in the C.P. (Central Provinces) Congress Committee. A little later Gandhi wrote about the matter in a more general way in "Message To Harijan Satyagrahis" and said that 'it is the duty of every Congress Ministry to include a Harijan in the Cabinet if a capable Harijan is forthcoming'. (*CWMG*, 67-292) But no such appointment was made during 1937-39 period. S.S. Gill, for instance, writes in his *Gandhi A Sublime Failure* that in the 1937 Provincial Elections 78 untouchables were elected from the Congress, but 'not even one of them was made a minister'.[20]

The appointment of Ambedkar later as Chairman of the Drafting Committee of the Constituent Assembly, and then the Law Minister of Nehru's first cabinet was, according to Narayanbhai, suggested by Gandhi himself.[21] But the all caste-Hindu composition of the Harijan Sevaks naturally brought difficulties. Gandhi wrote in *Harijan Sevak Sangh* of May 1942 that 'Many workers, while they do not observe untouchability themselves, are unable even to convert their own families'. (76-81) Gandhi himself said in "Talk with Members of Harijan Sevak Sangh" in 1946 that 'He could not convert his own sister'. (*CWMG*, 85-28) We may recall here how his own wife Kasturba was opposed to a Harijan family coming to stay at the Kocharab Ashram, almost as soon as Gandhi's family themselves moved there as their first ashram in India. In "Interview To K.R. Narayanan" in 1945, one of the questions was 'The Harijan Sevak Sangh after years of work had not yet produced even a dozen leaders from among the Harijans themselves'. Unfortunately Gandhi's answers were in writing and, therefore, short. He wrote only that 'That charge is only partly true'. (*CWMG*, 79-363)

In "Speech At Central Board, Harijan Sevak Sangh", in August 1945, he was reported to have said that 'only caste Hindus and no Harijan should be taken on the Executive of the Sangh, as it was the caste Hindus who had to atone for their sin of prolonging untouchability'. (*CWMG*, 81-126) Did not the Harijans themselves protest against this? Gandhi published a letter from a Harijan in "What Has the Congress Done?" in 1946 which was questioning the Congress policy toward the Harijans in general. It said, 'What is the place of Congress Harijans in the Congress? Why are not Harijan candidate made to stand for election to the various committees of the Congress? When they do stand, why are caste Hindus allowed to oppose them?... Why has it (the Congress) not yet succeeded in educating them sufficiently and making them capable?'. (*CWMG*, 84-334) Gandhi's reply to this was a little vague. He said, 'It is true that the Congress has not done all it should. Much remains. Equally true is the fact that none has done as much as the Congress. Therefore, the Harijans must be patient. There is no doubt that there is a limit to one's patience. But the limit has not been reached'. (*CWMG*, 84-335)

'Harijan'

Another aspect of this question was the way he gave them the name of Harijan. In "Use Another Name" in the middle of 1931, he wrote that an *Antyaja* man had written to him to say that this term was humiliating, and requested Gandhi to coin some new word in its place. Gandhi went on, 'Formerly the name *antyaja* was not felt as expressing contempt. The names Dhed and Bhangi were disliked. I think the term '*dalit*' was first used by the late Swami Shradhanand. Now it seems that name is also not liked.' He concluded that 'if a better word than *Antyaja* or *Dalit* occurs to anyone he may send it to me'. (*CWMG*, 46-342~343) This was published in the Gujarati monthly *Navajivan*. In "My Notes" after a little less than two months in the same journal, he wrote that 'I asked serious readers of *Navajivan* to suggest to me a substitute for the word '*Antyaja*'. One of the three or four suggestions received has appealed to me'. That was the Harijana (men of God). He gave reasons why it had appealed to him. (*CWMG*, 47-244~245) In 'Speech at Ahmedabad' at about the same time he said 'I am delighted to adopt that word...' to substitute for *Antyaja* (the last born). (*CWMG*, 47-248) He was speaking with the best of intentions. However, did he try to have the view of the people themselves, who were going to be called by this name? Did it ever occur to him to do so?

His "How They Should Act", in 1934, would throw light on this matter as well as the matter of Harijan Sevak Sangh. He begins with 'The reader is aware that I have dissuaded Harijans from pressing for representation on Harijan boards, for the very simple and complete reason that these boards are meant to be composed of *savarna* Hindus who regard untouchability as a sin and who would do reparation to Harijans for past wrongs done to them...I have, therefore, suggested the formation of advisory committees of Harijans to assist Harijan Sevak Sangh boards'. But that was not a 'complete reason', as he also said, 'But the question of asserting themselves does not arise just yet, because the vast mass of Harijans have been rendered so completely helpless that they have no power of resisting injustice, even if they wanted to'. (*CWMG*, 57-416~417) He thus, at least by implication, wanted the Harijans to be guided by the awakened caste Hindus.

'A Personal Affair'

Gandhi was at first strictly against inter-caste and inter-religious marriage and dining. Would it not be possible to call it also an upper caste Hindu attitude? When his second son, Manilal, sent a letter from South Africa, where he was in charge of the works left behind by Gandhi like editing the *Indian Opinion*, to express his wish to marry a Muslim girl, an angry Gandhi, even without showing the letter to Kasturba, turned it down in his "Letter to Manilal Gandhi" of 3 April 1926. As his reason he wrote, 'If you stick to Hinduism and Fatima (the Muslim girl) follows Islam it will be like putting two swords in one sheath...'. He condemned his son saying that 'In proposing this marriage you have thought only of momentary pleasure'. (*CWMG*, 30-229) Manilal may, but may not have, done so. After several weeks Gandhi also wrote a "Letter to Harilal", his eldest son, criticizing inter-marriages in a more general way.

Gandhi's attitude to the inter-marriage and inter-dining, however, became increasingly tolerant with the passage of time. When Manilal got married, Gandhi welcomed it and wrote in "Letter to Manilal and Sushila Gandhi" in 1929 that 'if the proposal for Sushila (Manilal's wife) had not been received, I had nearly decided to betroth you to a Bengali girl…it has been my considered opinion that inter-provincial marriages are a very good thing'. (*CWMG*, 41-370) Gandhi's fourth son, Devdas, had an inter-caste and inter-provincial marriage. A good example of Gandhi's growing tolerance would be "A Letter" of May 1932 where he said, 'I would say that marriage between persons following different faiths was a risky experiment…but I do not regard it as irreligious…But I do not advocate marriages between persons of different faiths as I advocate inter-caste marriages because I desire the disappearance of sub-castes…'. (*CWMG*, 49-478)

If Gandhi had given his OK to Manilal, it would have given a subtle, but on the whole favourable, influence on the Hindu-Muslim relations in India. Even Mohammad Ali Jinnah's speech at the time of the Lahore Resolution of 1940 would have been different, as Jinnah then said that 'They (Hindus and Muslims) neither intermarry…', thus stressing the difference between the two communities, as we will see in Chapter Four. Gandhi's attitude slowly but steadily changed in favour of both inter-caste and inter-religious dining and marriages. As Vinoba said he was a developing (*Vikashil*) person, although the change came rather late.

A different aspect of this was that from the second half of 1930s Gandhi began to say that a religion was a purely personal thing. He probably made it clear for the first time when he wrote in "Notes" in 1936 that 'Religion is essentially an individual matter which each one has to decide for himself'. (*CWMG*, 63-294) Then he wrote in "Unseemly If True", his last writing before the arrest early next morning, 9 August 1942, that 'Religion is a personal matter which should have no place in politics. It is in the unnatural condition of foreign domination that we have unnatural divisions according to religion'. (*CWMG*, 76-402) True, co-religionists do not automatically have common interests whether they are Hindus or Muslims or any other. Left alone, they have the same socio-economic cleavages as others. The author, however, is of the view that, although Gandhi was perfectly correct on this point, this realization also came too late at a time when the individual matter could no longer be looked at as such.

Notes

1. Vinoba, "Gandhi: Jaisa Dekha-Samjya", Gautam Bajaj, ed., *Vinoba Sahitya*, Vol. 17, 391. The references to Vinoba in this book are from here (translation by the author).
2. *Ibid.*, 378.
3. Narayanbhai, *My Life Is My Message*, II, 387.
4. Hiren Mukerjee, *Gandhiji:A Study*, 20.
5. *Ibid.*, 93.
6. Narayanbhai, *ibid.*, II, 265.
7. Kamaladevi, *Memoirs*, 200~1.
8. Narayanbhai, *ibid.*, II, 637.
9. Hiren Mukerjee, *ibid.*, 94.
10. Rajmohan Gandhi, *Ghaffar Khan*, 86.
11. Vinoba, *ibid.*, 376.
12. *Ibid.*, 360.
13. *Ibid.*, 446.
14. Judith Brown, *Gandhi*, 81.
15. *Essential Writings of B.R. Ambedkar*, 360~5.
16. *Ibid.*, 365~7.
17. Valerian Rodriguez, Introduction, *Essential Writings of Ambedkar*, 11.
18. *Essential Writings of Ambedkar*, 318.
19. *Ibid.*, 123.
20. S.S. Gill, *Gandhi*, 108.
21. Narayanbhai, III, 178.

Two
Gandhi's Democracy

'Deshabhakta Venkatappayya is older than I am. But he shows the same intellect and energy as before. May he live long and die in harness'. "Letter to G. Sitarama Sastry".
—26 January 1945, *CWMG*, Vol. 79, p. 66.

1. Gandhi in the National Tradition

Gandhi in the Main Stream

We will then discuss Gandhi's politics, particularly as it relates to the masses of India, in other words his concept of democracy. Historian Bipan Chandra writes that 'the founding fathers' of India's nationalism 'had worked out an understanding of the three modes of colonial exploitation' in the last quarter of nineteenth century. These were '(a) (direct exploitation) taxation, plunder and large-scale employment of Englishmen; (b) unequal exchange; and (c) investment of British-owned capital'. Therefore 'the nationalist leaders...opposed all the three forms of surplus appropriation by the metropolis'.[1]

Seen in this light, we will easily notice that Gandhi was strongly opposed to all these three forms of exploitation, although expressing it in his own words. We may look at his criticism of the salt tax, which already appeared twice in his *Hind Swaraj* of 1909, anticipating some action against it on his part, of the high salaries of the civil service men, of the alteration of the exchange rate without consulting the Indians, or of the investment in the railways and communications. Thus Gandhi may safely be placed in the mainstream of Indian nationalism side by side with the 'founding fathers'.

This applies to his political idea also, which is clear from the tribute he has paid in *Hind Swaraj* to the role of the Indian National Congress. He says, 'The Congress brought together Indians from different parts of India, and enthused us with the idea of nationality. The Government used to look upon it with disfavour.'(*CWMG*, 10-11) More than twenty years later, while leading the Salt March and relying on more political experience of his own, he wrote in "Untouchability" that 'without *swaraj* there will be neither communal unity nor removal of untouchability'. (*CWMG*, 43-264) Clearly he had come to know the value of independence.

About a year and a half later, on the eve of his departure for the RTC, Gandhi said on the relation of his social work and political work in "Speech at Ahmedabad" that 'The fact is, that when I saw that to a certain extent my social work would be impossible without the help of political work, I took to the latter and only to the extent that it helped the former'. (*CWMG*, 47-246) Similarly in "Further Clearance" of about the same time, he wrote that his emphasis was 'on political power as a weapon for enabling the reformer to achieve his reforms in the quickest manner possible'. (*CWMG*, 47-252) One more example can be drawn from "Letter to C.F. Andrews" in June 1933, which says 'Full and final removal of untouchability I can show you to your satisfaction, is utterly impossible without *swaraj*'. (*CWMG*, 55-199) It was with such understanding of the political work and the social work that he came to place himself at the forefront of the national movement.

We may add, however, that there was one exception to all this. Almost all the 'founding fathers' were keen advocates of industrialization. Indulal Yajnik wrote that when Gandhi arrived in the political scene of India in 1915, 'The way was...clear for a new leader to stir the still waters of political life in India. And Mr. Gandhi really stepped in at a psychological moment'.[2] But take Tilak, for example, who, as Yajnik saw in comparison with Gandhi, 'was a thorough-bred modernist in his industrial outlook, and never believed in the vagaries of the Charkha cult'.[3] In Gandhi's own time also, as we will see, there were intellectuals like M. Visveswaraya who were strong supporters of industrialization. We must say in this sense that Gandhi, and perhaps he alone among the first-rank political leaders, stood outside the mainstream of Indian nationalism.

2. Gandhi's Satyagraha

Satyagraha as Peaceful Rebellion

In his fight with the British, and even before that with the South African government, Gandhi used a weapon he named *satyagraha*, which was indeed unique to him. There is no doubt that *satyagraha* is the word that best represents Gandhi. According to Narayanbhai, who has published an almost definitive four-volume biography of Gandhi, 'Gandhiji had presented three gifts to the people of India…*satyagraha, ekadas vrata* and constructive programmes'.[4] These are the three major elements of his activities. The *ekadas vrata* has been discussed in Chapter One. The Constructive Programme will be taken up in Chapter Three. Here we will examine his *satyagraha*.

We take it that there were broadly three major stages of its evolution, in accordance with the three great national movements Gandhi led or planned to. They were NC (Non-Co-operation) of 1920~2, CD (Civil Disobedience) of 1930~4, and the Quit India Movement of 1942.

It is difficult to define *satyagraha*, as Gandhi himself said something different in a different context on *satyagraha*. But as long as we are able to appreciate its importance in accordance to its different aspects, it would not be necessary to try to give its precise definition. We will make a round-about way and first examine what Gandhi said on "Why was India lost?", the title of Chapter 7 of *Hind Swaraj,* in order to find out Gandhi's idea of the relations between the ruler and the ruled in India then. His answer to this question was 'The English have not taken India; we have given it to them. They are not in India because of their strength, but because we keep them'. (*CWMG*, 10-22) But before giving his answer in more detail, he begins to give 'my views as to the poverty of India', and says that 'Railways, lawyers and doctors have impoverished the country so much…'. (*CWMG*, 10-26) Therefore, we may take it that these two questions of why India is kept under the British rule and why India has become poor are closely intertwined.

Gandhi also brings in the religious conflict in this connection, and says that 'With the English advent quarrels (between the Hindus and the Muslims) recommenced...These thoughts (of the difference between the two) are put into our minds by selfish and false religious teachers. The English put the finishing touch'. (*CWMG*, 10-29, 31) On each of the above three causes of poverty, namely railways, lawyers and doctors, Gandhi makes a devastating remark. On the lawyer, for instance, he says, 'My firm opinion is that the lawyers have enslaved India, have accentuated Hindu-Mahomedan dissensions and have confirmed English authority'. (*CWMG*, 10-32) Gandhi also brings in the role of education, particularly that of English education, and writes, 'It is we, the English-knowing Indians, that have enslaved India'. (*CWMG*, 10-56)

From all this indictment of the British rule in India, and perhaps even more of the subservience on the part of the Indians, it is natural and logical for Gandhi, given that while comparing India with Italy he has already committed himself to Non-violence, to proceed to the discussion of peaceful rebellion against such a rule, which is *satyagraha*. Vinoba says that 'The idea of *satyagraha* was precisely Gandhi's. I have done nothing for its enhancement, change or purification. I have only spread it'.[5]

Subservience and Rebellion

The discussion of *satyagraha* in *Hind Swaraj* is mostly that of CD (Civil Disobedience). As of October 2014 this term is being heard from Hong Kong and Burkina Faso. In chapter 17, "Passive Resistance", which is the core of this booklet, Gandhi says, 'If man will only realize that it is unmanly to obey laws that are unjust, no man's tyranny will enslave him. This is the key to self-rule or home rule'. (*CWMG*, 10-49) And indeed the key to this booklet. The emphasis on CD suggests that it is a wider concept and NC (Non-co-operation) is actually a part of it. Gandhi continues this with a brief discussion of the four 'observances' or 'attributes' of perfect chastity, poverty, truth, and fearlessness which are required from a *satyagrahi*, or a passive resister, as he is called here. (*CWMG*, 10-52~53)

One is impressed by the presence of the concept of manliness which is considered to be the motivating factor behind *satyagraha*. Indeed the word appears in *Hind Swaraj* countless times. One is also led to believe that the above four 'observances' are a proto-type of the eleven vows already discussed. Gandhi later gave a more precise definition to CD by writing in "Constructive Programme: Its Meaning and Place", 1941, that 'Civil disobedience can never be directed for a general cause such as for independence. The issue must be definite and capable of being clearly understood and within the power of the opponent to yield'. (*CWMG*, 75-165) Therefore, *satyagraha* presupposes negotiation or compromise. The Salt March, for instance, was a CD in this sense as it was aimed at achieving Gandhi's Eleven Points, and not independence at one stroke. Yajnik was right when he wrote that 'His (Gandhi's) political career...in India has really proved to be a series of campaigns for the redress of separate and special grievances...', but, as he saw, Tilak was different and "dominated like a giant the whole scene with his single slogan of 'Home Rule' and 'Self-government' as a panacea for all evils..."[6]

It is this logical connection between man's subservience to the existing power and his consequent rebellion, though peaceful, which constitutes the core of Gandhi's *satyagraha*. He may not like it to be called rebellion, preferring it to be called 'conversion' or 'change of heart'. On the eve of his first national Movement, NC, he concluded his discussion in "The Mohammedan Decision" by saying 'No Government can possibly withstand the bloodless opposition of a whole nation'. (*CWMG*, 17-485) Let us also quote his explanation in "My Notes" written in late November 1929. He could not yet have hit upon the idea of the Salt March. 'At the root of a peaceful struggle lie the hope and the effort to bring about a change of heart in the adversary. It is my confirmed belief that if India adheres to the path of peace till the very end, the hearts of the most callous of British officers is bound to undergo a change. Hence, if an honourable settlement is possible, I am always ready to accept it'. (*CWMG*, 42-209) It was the idea of 'an honourable settlement' that has invited criticism more than once that he has diverted the national struggle in favour of some other issues.

Yet it is still a rebellion, and that is the way people have looked at it. This formula had been extracted from the past experience, especially of the struggle in South Africa since 1906 by himself and his co-workers. It has also guided his struggles afterwards. That is why he continued to express his unchanged allegiance to this booklet,

Hind Swaraj, not only to the above formula but almost in its entirety. The last time he did so was probably when he wrote in his "Letter to Jawaharlal Nehru", 5 October 1945, that 'I fully stand by the kind of governance which I have described in *Hind Swaraj*...My experience has confirmed the truth of what I wrote in 1909'. (*CWMG*, 81-319)

Clarification by Gene Sharp and Narayanbhai

Among the scholars who have studied Gandhi, it is Gene Sharp who has made an outstanding success in clarifying the meaning of *satyagraha*, especially its Non-violent aspect together with its revolutionary character, through his analysis of the old numbers of the *Indian Opinion*. In his *Gandhi as a Political Strategist with Essays on Ethics and Politics*, 1979, especially in its chapter 2 entitled "Origins of Gandhi's Use of Non-violent Struggle; A Review-Essay on Erik Erikson's Gandhi's Truth", Sharp discusses 'Gandhi's acquaintance with various cases of non-violent action' like the boycott in China and Bengal, the Russian Revolution of 1905 which was overwhelmingly non-violent and of which Gandhi wrote that 'The present unrest in Russia has a great lesson for us' and 'We, too, can resort to the Russian remedy against tyranny'. The case of Bengal was of 'no mean significance'. Gandhi also discussed Ireland and Britain. Therefore, Gandhi and his associates must have known them by 11 September 1906, the Day One of their struggle against the 'Black Act' in the Transvaal. Thus, the Non-violent action did not originate from Gandhi, and he himself was aware of it. Sharp also discusses 'his first contact with the theory of power upon which it (non-violent action) is based', and writes, 'The view of the power of rulers as being dependent on the ruled continued throughout his life to be the fundamental political insight upon which Gandhi's struggle rested'.[7] This was Sharp's great discovery.

In this connection Narayanbhai's biography is also worth noting as it contains statements here and there which are similar to Sharp's. Some of the typical ones are as follows. 'An oppressor's efforts will be in vain if we refuse to submit to his tyranny...Slavery consists in submitting to an unjust order...' (from Gandhi's "Preface to Leo Tolstoy's "Letter to a Hindoo"", 18 November 1909, *CWMG*, 10-1), 'Gandhiji realized that untruth, injustice, oppression and tyranny last only so long as their victims accept them. The moment one learns to say NO to untruth and injustice, their edifice collapses immediately', 'Non-cooperation was the only dignified and constitutional form of such direct action, for it is the right recognized from time immemorial of the subject to refuse to assist a ruler who misrules' (from Gandhi's "Letter to Viceroy", 22 June 1920, *CWMG*, 17-504), 'The Government's power is maintained ...because of our deluded love for it. This love has taken three forms: Love for the councils...love for the courts and love for education. I say nothing about titles and similar honours, for very few have them. But we are very much in the grip of the three above-mentioned infatuations...To my mind, it is a sin to enter councils and attend courts and an altogether heinous sin to attend schools' (a sentence added from Gandhi's "Speech to Students and Teachers, Surat", 6 October 1920, *CWMG*, 18-330), 'Among the many legacies of Gandhiji, *abhaya* (freedom from fear) can be considered the most significant. It is true that Gandhiji considered *ahimsa* to be the supreme value. But, this country did not accept the principle of *ahimsa* to the same extent as it did *abhaya*', 'Authority will not yield without a tremendous effort even to non-violent pressure' (from Gandhi's "The Inevitable", *CWMG*, 38-29), 'Injustice and oppression continue because of expressed or implicit co-operation with the oppressor', and 'In the final analysis every regime is based on co-operation of the people with the rulers. A regime, however, powerful and oppressive, cannot last without co-operation of the people'.[8]

Thus both Sharp and Narayanbhai have made a great contribution to the theory of political power and of democratization by non-violent non-co-operation, defiance and disobedience. In other words they have gone deep into the logical connection, or the formula, inherent in *Hind Swaraj* mentioned above.

We will not call Sharp's more recent work, *From Dictatorship to Democracy: A Conceptual Framework for Liberation*, 1993, simply a study of Gandhism. It has underlined the rebellious character of *satyagraha*, and by doing so has encouraged the democratization movement in a number of countries. Written originally as a 'generic analysis' of 'how a dictatorship can be disintegrated', by the request of the Committee for the Restoration of Democracy in Burma in exile in Thailand, it stands on the same theoretical basis as Sharp's previous work. It talks of 'non-violent defiance' and says that 'Contrary to popular opinion, even totalitarian dictatorships are dependent on the population and the societies they rule'.[9] Sharp, therefore, may be said to have put forth Gandhi's views in more universal terms than Gandhi himself, and in so doing have shown Gandhi's contemporary validity before the world.

The BBC broadcast on 21 February 2011 conveyed a scene from Cairo showing that a number of Egyptian youths were absorbed in reading *From Dictatorship to Democracy* in its Arabic translation by the side of the tanks deployed in the Tahrir Square by the light of the torch during the night, and discussing how to put into practice what is written there. By this time many of Sharp's readers had been detained. Sharp also appeared on the BBC's Hardtalk programme on 31 January 2012 and, while pointing out to the danger of negotiation in the process of democratization, said in connection with Egypt that it was a mistake to negotiate with President Mubarak as 'Dictators do not negotiate themselves out of power', and there was no precedence to it. Did he imply that it also applies to Gandhi's numerous negotiations? Probably yes, although Gandhi hardly wanted to negotiate the Viceroys out of power. But *From Dictatorship to Democracy*, and the readers of its many translations, have shown that *Hind Swaraj* can be reformulated today into a message for a more democratic world. Has Gene Sharp gone beyond Gandhi in presenting non-violent *satyagraha* as an idea of peaceful revolution, as Vinoba has done so in the field of property redistribution, as will be shown in Chapter Three? Not quite, but it may be said that he has put Gandhi in a more clear-cut and contemporary shape as far as the idea of *satyagraha* is concerned.

A word of caution here may be called for. Very often Gandhi's other aspects, particularly his indifference to the property redistribution, though coupled with sympathies with the poor, are ignored while discussing his role in democratic movement. A prominent exception was Martin Luther King, Jr., in that he came to notice the necessity of the 'Poor People's Campaign' in his last years, 1967-8, over and above the various civil rights movements in which he had been involved. The 'Poor People's Campaign' actually started when King was no more. It is recorded that 'Just four weeks after the April 4 murder of Martin Luther King, Jr., SCLC (Southern Christian Leadership Conference)'s new head, Ralph Abernathy, set out from

Memphis to lead the first group of marchers to Washington, D.C., opening the Poor People's Campaign'.[10]

Back to *Hind Swaraj*, we may note that Gandhi had to face some new problems which he had not, quite naturally, foreseen at the time of writing. In the author's view there were five such major issues, which were not clearly present and were at best latent in *Hind Swaraj*. They were, broadly, the questions of (1) poverty alleviation, (2) control of the armed forces after independence, (3) mass education, (4) decentralizing of administration, and (5) position of women. Gandhi did not consider them in *Hind Swaraj* either because, in the cases of (1), (3) and (5), he was not familiar with the conditions of India then, and in the cases of (2) and (4), India was still far away from the achievement of independence. We will discuss these issues also under appropriate headings, and see how he tried to cope with them after he returned to India, and in so doing if his ideas had changed. Yajnik said that 'Mr. Gandhi...as is well known, is a man of fixed ideas'. Was he right? The author has given a preliminary sketch of the first four issues of the above and Gandhi's attitude to them in his recent article.[11]

NC and CD

The difficulty with *satyagraha* is for one thing about the respective places of non-co-operation (NC) and civil disobedience (CD) within it. But Gandhi himself gives a very precise description of the two. In "Speech to Congressmen, Poona" in the middle of 1944, he said, 'We have the mighty weapon of *ahimsa*. In action, it takes the form of civil disobedience and non-violent non-co-operation. Civil disobedience is a very potent weapon. But everyone cannot wield it. For that, one needs training and inner strength. It requires occasions for its use. But non-violent non-co-operation can be practiced by everybody'. (*CWMG*,.77-341~342)

Narayanbhai also extends us a helping hand from a different angle in understanding the difference between the two by pointing out that 'The non-cooperation movement was a movement of titleholders, legislators, lawyers, teachers and professors' as in NC the so-called triple boycott of the legislature, the courts and the government schools would play a dominant role, while 'The civil disobedience movement had a much larger appeal as it touched all social sections. The non-cooperation movement was carried out by middle-aged men, while thousands of women and adolescents participated in the civil disobedience struggle'.[12]

We see from *Hind Swaraj*, and the research by Gene Sharp, that Gandhi was not the sole inventor of *satyagraha*, though the term is definitely his. He may well have taken the idea from the movement against the Partition of Bengal of 1905. He says, as the Editor, 'what you call the real awakening took place after the Partition of Bengal...The *Swadeshi* movement was inaugurated. People, young and old, used to run away at the sight of an English face; it now no longer awes them. They do not fear even a row, or being imprisoned'. (*CWMG*, 10-12~13)

In order to understand the meaning of *Satyagraha* as a weapon, we will do well to go by how none other than Winston Churchill saw it. Arthur Herman in his *Gandhi and Churchill* quotes Wilfred Blunt's *My Diaries,* which says that Churchill told him in as early as 1909 that if the Indians 'could agree to have nothing at all to do with us, the whole thing would collapse'.[13] Churchill correctly foresaw the shape of things to come in India sooner or later. In a similar vein, D.A. Low, a British political historian, writes, as B.R. Nanda quotes, that the period of 1920-21, when the NC Movement was at its peak, was 'probably the worst moment for Britain's imperial rulers...between the Mutiny and 1942'.[14]

It was, however, mainly not NC but CD, as we have seen, that Gandhi was keen on propagating in *Hind Swaraj*. This was probably the reason why, as Vinoba wrote, 'He always used to say that *ahimsa* should be for the brave'.[15] In fact it was the most important part of the booklet, where the Editor tries to impress upon the Reader, to the latter's great surprise, the significance and moral justice of disobeying the unjust law. That is what is called *satyagraha* in the book. Therefore we notice two types of *satyagraha*, NC and CD. The mass movement started at the Empire Theatre in Jonannesburg in 1906 was CD. *Hind Swaraj* may be said to have theorized the experience of this movement. It may also be called a provisional report of this struggle.

The mass movements led by Gandhi in India procceded from the NC in 1920-22 to CD of 1930-34. In the case of the former also, Gandhi had decided to launch a CD on a small scale at Bardoli Taluka of Surat District. Although this was called off, it implies that the CD is a politically more advanced form of *satyagraha*, involving more preparation, above all more training of people.

This does not mean that NC was discontinued for good at a certain time. These two could be mixed, or be shifted to one another. There is one interesting passage in Gandhi's "Mr. Montagu on the Khilafat Agitation" at the end of July 1920 which was on the eve of the starting of NC. As will be discussed in Chapter Four, his NC originated in the Khilafat Movement. It said 'Non-co-operation in itself is more harmless than civil disobedience, but in its effect it is far more dangerous for the Government than civil disobedience. Non-co-operation is intended so far to paralyze the Government, as to compel justice from it. If it is carried to the extreme point, it can bring the Government to a standstill'. (*CWMG*, 18-88) This is exactly what Churchill was apprehensive of. At the same time Gandhi also said in his "Duty of Disloyalty", which must have been written while marching in March 1930, that 'civil disobedience is a necessary part of non-co-operation'. (*CWMG*, 43-133)

Means more than the Ends

What is implicit in *satyagraha* is non-violence. In India's nationalist movement, the person who is considered to be the immediate forerunner of Gandhi was Bal Gangadhar Tilak, the Lokamanya. According to Vinoba, the difference between the two was that in Tilak's view non-violence should have a place in the private life, but not in the public life, but Gandhi denied it and thought that the public life itself was the proper place for non-violence.[16] This means that while Gandhi emphasized means more than the end, by saying, for example, that the means would take care of the ends, Tilak was not able to present any means of struggle unique to him.

G.P. Pradhan, in his biography *Lokamanya Tilak*, writes that 'He came forth with a four-point programme of *swadeshi*, boycott, national education and *swarajya*'. In the author's view all these four found their way into Gandhi's thinking. In that sense Tilak was Gandhi's forerunner. Putting it in a different way Pradhan writes that 'Both of them had enormous faith in the strength that lay in the common man's sacrifice, and in this regard Gandhi carried aloft the torch handed over to him by Tilak'.[17]

On their differences, Tilak himself wrote to Gandhi early in 1920 that 'Politics is a game of worldly people and not of *sadhus* and instead of the maxim 'Anger should be won over with love', as preached by Buddha, I prefer to rely on the maxim of Shri Krishna who said, 'I treat humans equally when they seek refuge in me'.[18] Did he look at Gandhi as a *sadhu*? Another difference, in Pradhan's view, was that 'Lokmanya was of the opinion that a nation striving for freedom had the moral right to use all means and methods in its struggle'.[19] This would support Vinoba's view on their differences shown in the above. At the same time when he said, 'When law is divorced from morality, we should abide by morality, break the law if necessary and bravely accept the punishment for breaking the law',[20] he seems to be very close to *Hind Swaraj*. Tilak died before Gandhi's method was really tested nation-wide.

When the author interviewed Pradhan in the freedom fighters' quarters in a hospital in Pune early in November 2007, he said that if alive Tilak would have co-operated with Gandhi. The author was impressed, after taking leave, by seeing him, in his mid-eighties, going for an evening walk with a stick.

NC of 1920~2 and CD of 1930

Gandhi in launching the NC, his first nationwide Movement in India, had 'a rude shock' three times when violence occurred in the process. First, he sent a "Telegram to G.A. Natesan" writing 'Decided Suspend Civil Disobedience Temporarily Owing Critical Situation That Has Developed...' on 18 April 1919 when riots had erupted in some places. (*CWMG*, 15-243) This was a few days after the Massacre at Jallianwala Bagh. Second, six policemen were killed in Bombay in November 1921 and he went into a fast. (*CWMG*, 21-461~467) Third, when twenty-one policemen were killed at Chauri Chaura, Gorakhpur District, UP, on 4 February 1922, he wrote a "Letter to Members of Working Committee" on 8 February from Bardoli, where he was preparing the CD planned from 12 of that month, calling a meeting of the Committee to consider 'first whether mass civil disobedience should not be suspended for the time being'. (*CWMG*, 22-350-351) The letter was his announcement of the stoppage of the entire NC, much to the annoyance of many of his co-workers.

After this stoppage, how was his CD, or his second Movement, brought about in 1930? After Gandhi presided over the Congress Session at Belgaum at the end of 1924, and brought the NC formally to an end, he had confined his activities almost entirely to the Constructive Programme for about three years, 1925 to 27, keeping himself away from the political events of the country like the completion of the *Nehru Report* in 1928. His health was also not very good during this time. It was, however, the arrival of the Simon Commission, an all-white body, to look into the question of revising the existing constitution of India, namely the 1919 Government of India Act, and its successful boycott by the Indians, that not only made the political atmosphere in India heated again, but also created an opportunity for Gandhi's 'return to politics'. Soon after the *hartal* in Bombay of 3 February 1928 opposing their visit, he wrote "After *Hartal*?", where he said that 'I tender my congratulations to the organizers for the very great success they achieved on the *hartal* day', and 'there is (after the *hartal*) nothing before the nation other than boycott of foreign cloth' although for himself 'I have no desire even now to interfere with the present evolution of the national movement except through occasional writings'. (*CWMG*, 36-14~15)

Then there occurred a struggle at the two Taluks of Bardoli and Valod in Surat District later in 1928, which was closely associated with the name of its leader Sardar Patel, but also required Gandhi's consistent 'interference' since it was in his Gujarat and Patel was one of his close associates. It was a movement by the peasants against the sharp upward revision of land revenue by the Government in spite of the continuing bad harvest. An enquiry by three independent persons was conducted in its midst. Finally the Government agreed to entrust an enquiry to two officers in August 1928 (*CWMG*, 37-424~26), and they recommended that the initial 22 per cent increase should be lowered to 5.7 per cent in the midst of 1929. Gandhi gave his help to the peasants by, for instance, his scathing attack on the Collector of Surat District's arrogance and lack of a sense of honour in his "At the Hour of Doom". (*CWMG*, 36-458~461) When the recommendation was made, he called it 'the Bardoli triumph' in his "Bardoli Enquiry Report". (*CWMG*, 41-39~41)

Regarding the role of the Sabarmati Ashram in this victory, he wrote in "Letter to Motilal Nehru" in August that, 'I do not know whether you are aware that Bardoli was possible because the *ashram* was in existence. The majority of the workers in Bardoli owe their preparation to the *ashram* directly or to its indirect influence'. Then significantly he continued, 'If I could but make of the *ashram* what I want, I should be ready to give battle on an extensive scale'. (*CWMG*, 37-194) Incidentally during the struggle Gandhi wrote in "Non-co-operation or Civil Resistance" that he would prefer to use the term 'civil resistance' in a movement like this 'with the redress of a specific grievance as its object'. (*CWMG*, 37-73~74) It seems doubtful, however, if he was consistent in the use of this term.

Anyway he felt, as he wrote in "Letter to C.F. Andrews" in August after an enquiry had been entrusted, that 'It (Bardoli victory) has almost restored the shattered faith in non-violence on the political field'. (*CWMG*, 37-200) In referring to 'the shattered faith in non-violence' Gandhi probably had in mind the Hindu-Muslim riots which were on the increase after the Khilafat struggle on one hand and the equally increasing terrorist activities culminating in those by Bhagat Singh and his associates on the other.

Valod Taluka is now a part of the Tapi District which has separated from Surat. It is where Jugatram Dave was running an ashram at a place called Vedchhi for the benefit of the tribal population for many years. At present Narayanbhai is in charge of the ashram where he gave the author an interview for four days in October 2012.

Around this time Gandhi seemed to have been in two minds as to his own political future. He wrote in "Letter to Dr. B.C. Roy" in May 1928 that 'I am keeping fairly fit. I am bidding my time and you will find me leading the country in the field of politics when the country is ready...But my time is not yet and may never come to me in this life'. (*CWMG*, 36-287) This was before Bardoli. In "Letter to C.F. Andrews" in November he wrote, 'I have not the courage yet to bury myself there (Sabarmati Ashram). Somehow or other I feel that I must go out for a while...'. (*CWMG*, 38-122) Then he moved a resolution in his "Speech on Resolution on Nehru Report, Calcutta Congress-2" at the end of 1928, at the Congress Session of the Congress which he attended at the request of Motilal Nehru, the President. It was a memorable resolution which moved, "This Congress, having considered the constitution (the *Nehru Report*) recommended by the All-Parties Committee Report, welcomes it…and…approves of the constitution drawn up by the Committee as a great step in political advance…this Congress will adopt the Constitution, if it is accepted in its entirety by the British Parliament on or before December 31, 1929, but in the event of its non-acceptance by that date or its earlier rejection, the Congress will organize a campaign of non-violent non-co-operation …'. (*CWMG*, 38-287) Unlike the Khilafat Movement the proposed action here was thus first approved by the Congress.

The *Nehru Report* proposed that India would be a Dominion. Some radical elements in the Congress opposed this and proposed complete independence instead. Jawaharlal Nehru moved a proposal for complete national independence already in the year before, in 1927, at the Madras Session of the Congress. It was several years since such a resolution came up at a Congress Session. But Gandhi in explanation of the above resolution said that 'I warned you against drawing any distinction between Dominion Status and Independence'. Why then not Independence but Dominion Status? The *Report* also stipulated a strong centralized government. This point will be discussed later in this chapter.

The proposal of 'a campaign of non-violent non-co-operation' itself must have strongly suggested that if such a campaign was forthcoming it could not but be placed under Gandhi's leadership. Gandhi himself said in the same speech that after the Session 'my back is turned upon Calcutta and I retire to Sabarmati'. He did return there, but within a month or so he openly wrote in "My Apologies", published in *Young India* of 31 January 1929, that 'I must prepare myself for the next year's struggle, whatever shape it may take'. (*CWMG*, 38-416) This was apparently in conformity with the above resolution, and the 'next year' was 1930.

Gandhi's "Letter to Chhaganlal Joshi", the Secretary of the Sabarmati Ashram, on 6 October 1929 was perhaps the first indication that 'something can certainly be done through them (ashram inmates)'. (*CWMG*, 41-519) Gandhi then wrote a "Letter to Jawaharlal Nehru" on 10 January that 'I have not seen my way clear as yet. But I have come so far that, in the present state of the Congress, no civil disobedience can be or should be offered in its name and that it should be offered by me alone or jointly with a few companions…' (*CWMG*, 42-382) In "Letter to Mathuradas Trikumji" a week later he says,

'The plan of the struggle that is taking shape in my mind is of a fight of such magnitude that no one can say how it will end'. (*CWMG*, 42-414)

On 30 January he wrote "Clearing the Issue" in the *Young India* where he put eleven demands and said that 'let the Viceroy satisfy these very simple but vital needs of India. He will then hear no talk of civil disobedience…'(*CWMG*, 42-434~435) Item 4 was 'Abolition of the salt tax'. He himself wrote in "Some Implications" that 'I venture to claim that in formulating the eleven points, I have somewhat and to the extent of my ability given a concrete shape to their (masses') feeling'. (*CWMG*, 42-451) It was an ultimatum to the Viceroy. But he in fact informed the British the specific conditions for suspending the movement even before it started.

3. Violence and Non-violence in Satyagraha

Ashram in 1930

In "Speech at Prayer Meeting, Sabarmati Ashram" of 15 February 1930, it was said that 'Gandhiji addressing the inmates referred to the names he had received (for participation in the coming struggle) and said that it was not necessary that one and all should give their names'. (*CWMG*, 42-477) This shows that the recruiting of his fellow travellers (literally!) had started already, and was being done not by the Congress organization but by the ashram itself.

This is also shown in the CWC resolution of the same day, quoted in Gandhi's "'Never Faileth'", which says that 'the Working Committee welcomes the proposal of Mahatma Gandhi and authorizes him and those working with him who believe in non-violence as an article of faith…to start civil disobedience as and when they desire and in the manner and to the extent they decide'. Explaining the resolution Gandhi wrote that 'I saw that I could not work out *ahimsa* through an organization holding a variety of mentalities'. (*CWMG*, 42-480) Soon afterwards he wrote in "Some Questions" that 'I propose at present to confine myself only to those who are amenable to the *ashram* discipline and have actually undergone it for some time'. (*CWMG*, 42-482)

One will find here that the observance of the *Ekadasi*, namely, the ashram vows, is crucially important in his enrolling. Shortly before the departure on the March he wrote in "Letter to Jaisukhlal Gandhi" that '(he would be) accompanied by most of the men in the *ashram*'. (*CWMG*, 43-21) As of the mid-1928 the number of 'the men in the *ashram*' was one hundred and thirty-three. (*CWMG*, 36-410) Narayanbhai writes on the departure of the Salt March that 'It was not a gloomy and melancholic leave taking. The mood was one of festivity'.[21] Thomas Weber writes in his *Gandhi, Gandhism and Gandhians* that two marchers came late and the total amounted to eighty-one, the eightieth being a Nepali.[22] The first chapter of his book is entitled from his name as "Kharag Bahadur Singh: The Eightieth Marcher".

Coming to know the plan of salt-making, the Anglo-Indian press wrote that 'It is difficult not to laugh...'. [23] They were also in the mood of festivity in their own way. We may recall that the idea of breaking the salt law was not new to Gandhi. It was his familiar ground. In *Hind Swaraj* he said twice, either straight away or by implication, that the Salt Law should be abolished. During the 'National Week' in April 1919 he proposed before the *Satyagraha Sabha* that the Salt Law should be broken and some prohibited literature should be published, but the former was not accepted by the *Sabha*.[24]

At the same time, Gandhi was deeply conscious of the growing violence in the country, and wrote in "Letter to C.F. Andrews" early in February that 'I see as clearly as never before that the spirit of violence must be dealt with by non-violent *action* if the situation is to be at all saved'. He was talking of 'double violence', by the government on one side and its reaction on the educated in India on the other. (*CWMG*, 42-444) In the latter's connection he wrote some time later in "Foul Play" that 'The Bhagat Singh worship has done and is doing incalculable harm to the country'. (*CWMG*, 47-232) Judith Brown writes that at the Lahore Session of the Congress at the end of 1929 'Eventually the main resolution was passed almost unanimously with shouts of triumph for Gandhi; but the very narrow majority for the resolution deploring a recent bomb attack on the Viceroy's train showed how near to supporting violence were many in Congress as well as outside it'.[25] There was also communal violence, and he said in "Some Questions" later in February that 'Indeed this campaign should take the attention of the nation off the communal problem and to rivet it on the things that are common to all Indians....'(*CWMG*, 42-484)

Gandhi wrote in "The Final Test" that it was Sardar Patel who recommended Jalalpur Taluk of Surat District as the destination of the March where he and his party would pick up salt from the sea. (*CWMG*, 43-31) His "Letter to Lord Irwin", the Viceroy, on 2 March says that 'I shall proceed with such co-workers of the *ashram* as I can take, to disregard the provisions of the salt laws'. (*CWMG*, 43-7) Notice the word 'disregard'. He said somewhat later in "Speech to Congress leaders, Allahabad" that 'Who would describe the breaking of the salt law as civil disobedience? Breaking of a law would be civil disobedience only if we intended to obey it after peace was concluded'. (*CWMG*, 45-133) This is a little difficult to understand, as a law to be disobeyed must be a bad law anyway and it must be, therefore, difficult to take its continuance after the peace, and more so after the independence, for granted.

The March started, with Gandhi and an all-male group of seventy-eight. According to N.K. Bose, anthropologist and Gandhian social worker, 'Forest laws were also defied, and in numerous localities taxes were also refused'.[26] The list of 'Persons Who Accompanied Gandhiji on the Dandi March' shows that thirty-seven of them, besides Gandhi, were from Gujarat and Cutch, including Manilal Gandhi. (*CWMG*, 43-454~455) Kamaladevi, at this time, took a bus from Surat to a village near Jambusar, met Gandhi and requested him to let women participate in the March, but Gandhi said that he preferred to assign some other works to them.[27]

The immediate object of the March was achieved and a green signal was given to 'an all-India start' when Gandhi picked up a lump of salt from the Beech of Dandi and thus broke the Salt Law in the morning of 6 April 1930, the anniversary of the anti-Rowlatt national *hartal* in 1919. Ten years after the March, Gandhi said, in "Discussion with B.G. Kher and Others" that 'The Dandi March was entirely my conception. Pandit Motilalji first laughed at it, he thought it to be a quixotic adventure...Later when he saw me in Jambusar, he was completely converted for he saw with his own eyes the awakening that had come over the masses. And it was an almost magical awakening'. (*CWMG*, 72-390) Jawaharlal Nehru wrote in the Foreword to Tendulkar's book mentioned above that 'Many pictures rise in my mind of this man…But the picture that is dominant and most significant is as I saw him marching, stuff in hand, to Dandi on the Salt March in 1930'.[28]

Violence in Non-violence at Dharana Depot

In the Salt March, there was not such a large-scale violence occurring from within the Movement to disturb Gandhi. Rather, violence was used by the rulers in repressing the Movement. In fact the Movement was conceived of to counter the 'double violence'. The most spectacular example of both the Non-violent action and of the violent repression during the Salt Movement was at the Salt Depot called Dharana. It started with the march of the volunteers on the Depot on 15 May 1930. Gandhi had been arrested early in May.

During the twenty-four days of Non-violent march on the Depot, which was called off by Chhaganlal Joshi on 6 June, because of the arrival of the monsoon, four volunteers were killed and 1,329 were injured by the police beating.[29] It was Gandhi who first mentioned the attempted Raid at his "Speech At Chharwada" on 26 April, without specifically mentioning when it would take place. After completing the March he was left alone by the authorities, who might have feared violent nation-wide protest by his arrest. In the above speech he said 'I have made it clear to you that only if you wear *khadi* and give up liquor will I let you join me in the raid on the Dharasana salt-beds. If you do not fulfil the condition and still insist on coming, I will offer *satyagraha* against you. (*CWMG*, 43-333) Was he planning to lead this March also, and to bear the consequences? The example of Lala Lajpat Rai, a foremost Congress leader from the Punjab, who was badly beaten by the police at Lahore and died because of the injury in 1928, was there. The above speech seemed to make it clear that it was so.

For four weeks from 6 April to 5 May, when he was arrested, it seems Gandhi did not take any initiative. Yajnik said that 'he might have at least picked up the threads of the no tax movement from where he left it in 1922'.[30] He also said that Gandhi 'exhorted the village folk to lop off the vast forests of the most precious Toddy trees…'[31] If he had been out of jail, in view of his concept of manliness alone, he would probably have marched at the head of the columns.

He probably knew roughly when the assault would begin, and he could have known how brutal it would turn out to be. He also wrote in "Letter to Narandas Gandhi" on 26 April, the same day he announced the raid, that 'I think I shall be arrested in about eight or ten days'. (*CWMG*, 43-325) Would it have been within his power to postpone the raid till he was not on the scene? Yajnik's book ends with Gandhi's announcement of the proposed Raid. No one can tell what was in Gandhi's mind in the early hours of 5 May when he was being escorted to prison by the police.

Anyway, the Raid would make one wonder if the violence used by the rulers on this scale would make it impossible for the struggle to be called non-violent. The repression was too cruel. Also, what would happen if the rulers were not the British who were at least officially committed to the rule of law, though this is an oft-debated question. Of course we have seen that, even under the British, an order was given to shoot an unarmed crowd at Amritsar in 1919, and in Peshawar about the same time as the Dharana Raid.

In "Letter To President, Mysore State Congress" in 1938, though cancelled afterwards, Gandhi wrote that 'I am well aware that such meticulous observance of non-violence and truth is not to be expected from the rank and file. But then *satyagraha* cannot be launched by the rank and file. It has to be launched by responsible persons who are versed in the law of *satyagraha*'. (*CWMG*, 67-45) This was a letter to the people of an Indian State where the experience of *satyagraha* had not been much shared by then. But even for the general masses Gandhi said, in "Not Guilty" written in the middle of 1939, that 'I regret to have to say that in most cases the peasants are not being educated for non-violent action'. (*CWMG*, 70-10) It may be an irony of history that this letter on non-violence was written at a place called Abbottabad, now known as a place where Osama-bin-Ladin was murdered in 2011.

Bringing the Struggle to the End

In the above we saw how Gandhi started a struggle. Also interesting is how he tried to bring it to an end. In the NC, his first, he made the best use of his third 'rude shock' mentioned above to suspend it. But it was so sudden, so unexpected, that Yajnik wrote that, when the

AICC (All India Congress Committee) discussed the plan for suspension on 24~25 February, already passed by the CWC on 11~12, 'The discussion was naturally centred on the meaning and content of non-violence…Mr. Gandhi thus sacrificed the political campaign on the altar of an impossible fetish of non-violence'.[32] Gandhi himself wrote after the AICC in "The All-India Congress Committee" that 'I confess I was totally unprepared for the hurricane of opposition' (*CWMG*, 22-501).

Even before the third 'rude shock' occurred, Gandhi wrote a "Letter to Viceroy" on 1 February 1922, in which he said that 'India's resolve regarding the *Khilafat*, the Punjab and *swaraj*' was certainly the issue at the time, but under the ongoing repression 'The immediate task before the country…is to rescue from paralysis freedom of speech, freedom of association and freedom of the Press', and 'If you can see your way to make the necessary declaration within the seven days of the date of publication of this manifesto, I shall be prepared to advise postponement of civil disobedience…'(*CWMG*, 22-302~5) This was also an ultimatum to the Viceroy. One would suspect, however, that Gandhi had an eye on throwing out his plan of the final battle in exchange for the three freedoms which were in themselves important but not among the original demands of the Congress. It may have been still short of surrender, but it would almost amount to that if the crucial battle was postponed not as the result of a trial of force but before that. In this sense it was similar to "Clearing the Issue" he wrote on 30 January 1930 which we have seen already. The "Government of India "Communique" on Gandhiji's Letter to Viceroy" dated 6 February was not at all sympathetic to Gandhi's proposals. (*CWMG*, 22-512~5) An angry Gandhi immediately dictated a "Rejoinder to Government of India" on 7, but then Chauri Chaura happened.

Therefore what actually happened was something close to surrender, and thus caused the 'hurricane opposition' at the AICC. This was the *de facto*, if not the formal, end of the NC by Gandhi, who had almost single-handedly defeated the opposition to his NC plan at the Special Congress Session at Calcutta in 1919. Yajnik wrote on this Session that, first in the Subjects Committee, '…the speech that Mr. Gandhi delivered in reply to the entire debate', by C.R. Das, Bipan Chandra Pal, Malaviya, Jinnah, Mrs. Beasant, Lala Rajpat Rai and a host of others, which means a really formidable combination, 'practically demolished the entire edifice of this able opposition...It remains in my memory as the ablest and the most convincing masterpiece of Mr. Gandhi's oratory...'. And in the open Congress also, 'Mr. Gandhi again rose to the height of the occasion in replying to the entire debate...'.[33] Gandhi's NC had already started on 1 August of the same year but it became a Congress policy by the Calcutta Session. It collapsed after a year and a half later. Does Chauri Chaura give a sufficient explanation for the collapse?

But in the CD, his second, what happened was not something very different from the first. After Gandhi succeeded in manufacturing salt at the beach, he wrote his second ultimatum, or the third if we also count the 30 January article, in "Letter To Viceroy" on 4 May, the same day of his arrest, following "Letter to Lord Irwin" of 2 March forewarning the Viceroy of the coming March. In the second one, he wrote that 'I would...ask you to remove the (salt) tax...If, therefore, you cannot see your way to remove the salt tax, and remove the prohibition on private salt-making, I must reluctantly commence the march adumbrated in the opening paragraph of this letter (where Dharasana is mentioned)'. (*CWMG*, 43-392~3) If the salt tax had been withdrawn, the Dharasana, the most important battle-ground, and by implication many others, and probably all the rest of the Eleven Points, also would have been withdrawn. But the British have chosen a different way, by retaining Gandhi in jail, greatly damaging the volunteers at Dharasana and elsewhere, concluding the Pact with Gandhi with hardly any concessions, and ensuring the attendance of the Congress at the RTC for making a constitution which was far from the Dominion Constitution in substance. Yajnik's comment that 'a policy of personal negotiations ending in the temporary pacts and settlements was an integral part of Mr. Gandhi's technique of a non-violent war. It escaped us then though it has now been thoroughly understood in India, and should also have been clear to us from the history of his South African movement'[34] is very much to the point.

In his third major nation-wide movement, the abortive Quit-India, as we will see in the next Section, the question of organizing non-violent struggle against possible Japancse invasion of India was foremost in Gandhi's mind. By this time his *satyagraha* had been almost exclusively aimed at the dominating political power at the time, whether in South Africa or in India. But at the time of the Quit-India he had to consider the question of how to cope with the armed foreign aggressors with the same means. Actually, he had to face one more trial after the Second World War, namely coping with the communal violence. While proceeding to Srirampur, Noakhali, he wrote in "Letter to Vallabhbhai Patel" on 14 November 1946 that 'My non-violence is being tested here in a way it has never been tested before'. (*CWMG*, 86-119) But he did not plan to organize a nation-wide movement to face this test.

Gandhi's Finest and Darkest Hours

What was the period, if any, when Gandhi was most high-spirited, and when was his lowest moment ?

As to the former, the period we were discussing right now, leading to his planning of the Salt March in detail, handpicking the fellow travellers and the March itself, was his brightest moment. But even before this period he had never lost his sense of humour. He wrote for instance "Letter to Hakim Ajmal Khan" on 10 April 1926 to say that 'We must attend also the ceremony of establishing *swaraj*'. (*CWMG*, 30-263) It was not written simply as a joke. In his Preface to *Satyagraha in South Africa*, Gandhi wrote that 'From my reminiscences of that history (of *satyagraha* in South Africa) I see that there is nothing in our present position which I had not encountered in South Africa on a smaller scale'. He also said, 'The final phase of India's battle is yet to arrive. I expect the repetition here of the experience I had of the final phase in South Africa'. (*CWMG*, 29-6) This was written in 1925. From his success in South Africa Gandhi had already had a conviction that India would achieve her independence, and also some idea, however vague, of how and in what form it would be achieved. This was his great advantage over the other leaders.

Another example of his high state of mind at this time, before the Salt March, was a passage in his "Honest Differences", an indirect but a startling reply to J.B. Pennington, a Britisher, in November 1929. Gandhi said, 'I do remember his question about the first president of the future Indian republic. If I must for the time being give up my modesty, I must tell Mr. Pennington in confidence that if there was an Indian republic in my lifetime and the burden was imposed upon me by the simple people of the country, I dare to say that it would not break me. At any rate I should make a fair effort to shoulder it'. (*CWMG*, 42-193)

An Australian mentioned to the author about a dozen years ago a name, a famous aborigine lady athlete, as a probable candidate for the first President of his country. May be it was a current joke Down Under at that time. But here Gandhi was openly admitting that he was ready to be the first President of the independent India. Was he not a believer in India's Dominion Status rather than her becoming a republic? But it was clearly a republic that he was talking about here. He continues to write that 'What however I am striving for is not a life of isolation for India but a life of association with the British on absolutely equal terms…it (the Indian republic) would not need to drive the English out…'. This was written only four months before the Salt March.

Another question would be what kind of a President he meant, the American type of a strong President or more or less a figurehead type? We may be reminded that, in spite of aiming at a Republican polity under the name of *Poorna Swaraj*, India did not have any prototype of the future Presidency. It is, therefore, not likely that Gandhi had any clear idea of what kind of the Presidency he would assume.

Still, after all is said, it is difficult to imagine that Gandhi was really keen on such a government post, even the highest in a republic. It would be truer to imagine that he was not interested in a public post all his life. A question in "Interview to *The New York Times*" in 1940 was 'Supposing India does become free in your lifetime, what will you devote the rest of your years to?', and his reply was 'If India becomes free in my lifetime and I have still energy left in me, of course I would take my due share, though outside the official world, in building up the nation on a strictly non-violent basis'. (*CWMG*, 72-12) The idea of assuming the Presidency must have gone by now.

Gandhi goes on in the above letter of 1929, 'If such a consummation comes to pass, it would be something of which India will have every reason to be proud and for which the world will be the richer. It may be a dream never to be fulfilled but it is enough for me that it makes me happy'. (*CWMG*, 42-193~194) The dream, probably including that of himself as the first President in this case, makes him happy, he says, and that itself shows he must have been in a physically and mentally good condition. As a part of the dream he is talking of a possibility of India making the world richer. It cannot be a one-way traffic, and if India makes the world richer the world also will make India richer. Such must have really been his happier moment.

Sucheta Kripalani writes that Gandhi while at the Birla House a few days before his death said, 'he would like to see a Harijan woman as the first President of India'.[35] This was when India was already independent, but her Republican constitution had not yet been in place. These words would show that the idea of himself becoming the President was not with him any more. They would also show that, by talking of a Harijan woman, probably the weakest person in the society, Gandhi's mind was with the underprivileged people.

As to his lowest moment, we cannot help remembering that Gandhi said in his "Speech at Prayer Meeting" on 19 January 1948, one of his last, that, 'Delhi is poorer for the disappearance of the exquisite workmanship of the Muslims'. (*CWMG*, 90-462) Things were going in an opposite direction from the one of India enriching the world that Gandhi dreamt of nearly two decades ago.

His "Letter to Hariprasad Desai" written before 25 July 1947 is another such example. There he said, 'For me Sabarmati is far off, Noakhali is near'. (*CWMG*, 88-418) He was in Delhi at this time and needless to say Ahmedabad is much nearer to Delhi than Noakhali. Gandhi was approached on the possibility of returning to Sabarmati now that India's independence had become certain. He had said on the eve of the Salt March that, in "Message to Andhra", 'This is a battle to the finish' (*CWMG*, 43-38), in "Interview to H.D. Rajah", that 'I hope to return to *ashram* triumphant in our struggle for India achieving her independence' (*CWMG*, 43-38), and in "Speech at Prayer Meeting, Sabarmati Ashram" that 'Only with complete victory can we return to this place' (*CWMG*, 43-45). Even after the March he said 'I have all along been saying that this is a do-or-die struggle…'. (*CWMG*, 45-285) So Gandhi was bound by something like a vow prohibiting his return to Sabarmati. For Noakhali, on the other hand, his work stood unfinished, and he heard a strong call to go back there from inside himself, but he had to be at other places, and also wanted to visit Punjab. Those were the darkest moments in his life. At the same time it was in these last fifteen months of his life, from his arrival in Noakhali till his last day, when Gandhi's greatness was most clearly shown.

On the question of returning to Ahmedabad, Tridip Suhrud says in his *Reading Gandhi in Two Tongues and Other Essays* that his last visit to Ahmedabad was in November 1936, and that to Gujarat was in January 1942. He writes, 'If we understand something of this obvious turning away from Gujarat on the part of Gandhi, we might be able to capture something of the relationship that present-day Gujarat has with him'.[36] A very attractive subject, but Suhrud himself, at least in the above-mentioned work, does not seem to be tackling it.

The Noakhali episode itself is best described in N.K. Bose's *My Days with Gandhi,*[37] and Pyarelal's *The Last Phase*.[38] Sushila Nayar, Pyarelal's younger sister who was among Gandhi's entourage in Noakhali together with these two, writes that when dispatching them to different villages Gandhi interviewed everyone of them, presumably to ascertain his or her will and capacity.[39] An equally impressive and moving chapter is in Narayanbhai's biography. It is that of "The Miracle of Calcutta" in Volume IV, a part of the Noakhali episode.

Here is a brief chronological table of the last 15 months of Gandhi's life.

1946

26 October—Got on board a train from Delhi to Calcutta.
6 November—Arrived from Calcutta in Chandpur, Tippera District.
20 November—Arrived in Shrirampur, Noakhali District (43 nights).

1947

2 January—Arrived from Shrirampur in Chandpur.
7 January—Set out on a pilgrimage to 40 villages in Noakhali and 7 in Tippera (54 nights).
2 March—Got on board a ship from Chandpur to Calcutta.
5 March—Arrived from Calcutta in Patna (25 nights).

31 March—Arrived from Patna in Delhi (12 nights).
13 April—Arrived from Delhi in Patna (17 nights).
1 May—Arrived from Patna in Delhi (6 nights).
9 May—Arrived from Delhi in Calcutta (5 nights).
15 May—Arrived from Calcutta in Patna (9 nights).
25 May—Arrived from Patna in Delhi (67 nights).
8 August—Arrived from Delhi *via* Kashmir in Patna (1 night).
9 August—Arrived from Patna in Calcutta (29 nights).
9 September—Arrived from Calcutta in Delhi (143 nights till the end).

Judith Brown, however, writes that 'His work in the next few weeks (leading up to the Gandhi-Irwin Pact) probably represented the highest point of his political career'.[40] In this connection Narayanbhai quotes William Shirer's book *Gandhi: A Memoir* as it relates his mood immediately after the signing of the Pact. 'In none of the talks I had in those days in Delhi with the Viceroy and his principal aides did I discern a feeling that time and the course of history might be running against them. Gandhi was sure of it. He hammered into me again and again that, though the British did not sense it, *time* was with him and his nationalist movement. *Time and the course of history*. He understood what few Indians and fewer Englishmen realized, even in 1931...*I shall see India free before I die!*'[41]

Satyagraha after Freedom

What happens to *satyagraha* after independence? Gandhi himself has given some thought to this already. He said in *Satyagraha in South Africa* that 'Probably there would not have been any scope for *satyagraha* if they (Indians) had the franchise'. (*CWMG*, 29-94)

In late 1944, he also said, in "Interview To N.G. Ranga", a socialist peasant leader, that, 'Civil disobedience and non-co-operation are designed for use when people, i.e., the tillers of the soil, have no political power. But immediately they have political power, naturally their grievances, whatever their character, will be ameliorated through legislative channels...If the legislature proves itself to be incapable of safeguarding *kisans*' interests they will of course always have the sovereign remedy of civil disobedience and non-co-operation'. (*CWMG*, 78-247) A little more than a year afterwards while the Cabinet Mission Plan was debated, Gandhi told the AICC meeting that 'this is no occasion for a fast or civil disobedience. I regard the Constituent Assembly as the substitute of *satyagraha*. It is constructive *satyagraha*. The alternative is constructive work which you have never done justice to'. (*CWMG*, 84-421)

In post-independence India, there have been moments when action on the principles of *satyagraha* seemed to be well justified. The Chipko Movement which we will see later was certainly one of these examples. In *Goodbye to Gandhi*, Bernard Imhasly quotes an Indian, who said on the present conditions of the NGOs in India that 'There are 1.2 million NGOs here, engaging and employing seven million people...The NGO sector lacks professionalism. They have Gandhi's idealism, but they don't have Gandhi's pragmatism. And they work in isolation.'[42] Still they must be representing the emerging initiative of the civil society in India, and if there is going to be *satyagraha* they must be in the leading position.

The most difficult to judge among such movements in independent India was the JP Movement, which became gradually one of CD. It will be discussed later together with the Bhoodan Movement. Recently India saw the Anna Hazare Movement in the midst of Delhi in 2011, which was a fast against corruption, and as such was NC rather than CD.

Vivek Pinto in his *Gandhi's Vision and Values* discusses Hazare as one of the 'three contemporary Indian alternatives I explore and explain principally draw upon Gandhi's philosophy and emulate his agricultural experiments', besides The Self-Employed Women's Association (SEWA) of Ahmedabad and 'the self-imposed land-use plan in the village of Seed' in Rajasthan.[43] It is an example 'of the little known story of Baburao Hazare of Ralegan Siddhi in drought-prone Ahmednagar district, Maharashtra'. Here Hazare, 'a retired army jeep driver', involved the villagers from 1978 to fight alcoholism and achieve prohibition, worked to maintain soil and water in various ways using also local wisdom, procured '*shramdan*' (voluntary donation of labour), and succeeded in getting two crops a year. The land under irrigation increased nine times over a dozen years or so.

Moreover, electrification, schools, health service, afforestation and stall-feeding of cattle were also introduced.[44]

The author had an opportunity of watching on TV what was going on at the Ramlila Maidan, Delhi, on 17 August 2011, in the midst of the movement, around the person of the then 74 year-old Anna Hazare who had gone on fast on the stage at the centre in the full view of the camera and thousands of people. This was the fourth day of the fast. Among the things that hit his eyes were, great many Indian flags in people's hands including Anna's, Gandhi caps not usually seen in the city, Gandhi's photographs shown on the stage, some people shouting that this is India's second freedom movement, politicians were said to have been barred from coming up the stage, Anna's blood pressure frequently measured but not in his health bulletin, 'From Kashmir to Kanyakumari', 'Anna is India's voice', 'Hold referendum on Lokpal' but is there any ways and means for a referendum in the Constitution?, 65 per cent were of the view that they were winning the war against corruption but 35 per cent were not, Some said the Indians have got a vote but the counter-opinion was that Democracy is not a five-year poll, thousands of people telling their story of bureaucratic corruption, some social workers joined the movement with other problems like education, public health and so on, completely peaceful, not even a stick in hand, no sign of people mobilized by trucks as usual, people apparently unknown to each other but broadly of middle-class origin and well-clad walking hand in hand for miles around the stage, something of a non-violent revolution!

4. INA and Gandhi's Non-violence on Trial

Non-violence and Decentralization in 1942

Let us ask how Gandhi was thorough in his non-violence. The possible Japanese invasion and the trial of the three Indian National Army (INA) officers who had fought the British and the Indian Armies under Subhash Bose provide two excellent examples of examining it.

We will not discuss here the relative importance of the roles played by Gandhi and Bose in the achievement of India's independence. Samar Guha in his *The Mahatma and the Netaji* discussed, among others, that according to the secret survey by the British of the 8,000 Indian officers, who had swelled from the pre-war level of 400, 95 per cent were of the opinion that the INA defendants were patriots and were, therefore, to be released,[45] and concluded that these two were the 'two co-architects'[46] of the independence of India. Gandhi would not have agreed as in his view Bose had been misled and took to violence.

We will begin by seeing how Gandhi tried to find the way to resist the possible Japanese invasion. When its threat increased, Gandhi sent Mirabehn to the Orissa coast to see the things there. This was in May 1942. Mira's report did not please him, as it said that the local people were so anti-British that they would welcome whoever was opposed to them. Narayanbhai writes that 'She (Mira) realized that the British had no plans of engaging the advancing Japanese army in the coastal regions…'.[47] It put Gandhi to serious thinking on how to fight the Japanese by Non-violence. He had already published "Foreign Soldiers in India", and had sent his draft resolution to the AICC. These became the origin of the 'Quit-India' Movement and will be discussed later. He said afterwards that he had wanted to try his idea of such resistance to the invaders. Moreover he had repeatedly said by this time, and would do so likewise afterwards, as he did in "History of South African *Satyagraha*" in 1928, that '*Satyagraha* is not conceived as a weapon merely of the weak. It is the strongest force that one can possibly imagine or wish for…'. (*CWMG*, 36-330)

But he was arrested much too soon to try his method against the external aggressors, and was in prison till the tide of the war had been decisively turned, his second longest imprisonment. Unlike in the NC or CD before, therefore, it is difficult to tell if the Quit-India was planned as an NC or a CD. Maybe it was intended to combine both as it would have taken much more than NC to resist an invading army. It must have been in Gandhi's plan to think it out in the interval which he hoped he would find after the AICC passing the resolution on 8 August. It was not even possible to issue an ultimatum this time unlike on the previous occasions. Therefore, in none of these three nation-wide Movements, an all-out national offensive could be made against the *Raj*, although each of the three Movements had its own glory to remember.

It is common to take up these three Movements as representing Gandhi's political action in India, and to make a comparative study of them. For the study of *satyagraha* itself, a different selection could be possible. For example, Joan V. Bondurant's *Conquest of Violence* is an early attempt to place *satyagraha* in the spectrum of the Western political thought. In a section "An Analysis of Five *Satyagraha* Campaigns", the Vykom temple road *satyagraha* in the then Travancore State in 1924-5, the Bardoli campaign of peasants against the Government of Bombay in 1928, the Ahmedabad labour *satyagraha* in 1918, nationwide *satyagraha* against the Rowlatt Bills, and the Salt *satyagraha* are studied.[48]

In June 1942, while Gandhi was still preparing for the movement, he gave one hour everyday for a week to an American journalist which culminated in his *A Week with Gandhi*. About twenty-five pages of its excerpts were reproduced in the *CWMG* under the title "Interview with Louis Fischer". There in reply to a question what shape the coming movement would take, Gandhi said, 'In the villages, the peasants will stop paying taxes. They will make salt despite official prohibition…Their next step will be to seize the land'. Probably taken aback, Fischer asked, 'With violence?', and the reply was 'There may be violence…'. (*CWMG*, 76-445~446) When asked if it went violent would he call it off as before, Gandhi said, 'In my present mood it would be incorrect to say that no circumstances might arise in which I would call off the movement. In the past, however, I have been too cautious. That was necessary for my own training and for the training of my collaborators. But I would not behave as I have in the past'. (*CWMG*, 76-448~449)

When Fischer asked about the cities Gandhi said, 'Workingmen in the cities would leave their factories. The railroads would stop running.' Fischer thereupon said 'General strike'. Gandhi's response to this in terms of yes or no is not recorded. (*CWMG*, 446) But, as the quotation below from Yajnik would show, it was so rare that Gandhi should talk about the factory or transport labour in such a way.

Gandhi was of course not blind to the possibility of violence. But probably he was aware of the possibility of a far greater violence arising from the external threat and the resulting possible land battle inside India itself. Compared to it any smaller violence would be paled. The above quotation therefore is important in understanding

Gandhi's perception of violence. He saw things in relative terms. Gandhi also said in connection with China that 'My heart goes out to China...Even for China's sake alone I must do this'. (*CWMG*, 76-450)

In *Hind Swaraj* Gandhi referred to the Italians who were armed by Garibaldi in the process of their national integration, and said 'But the fact is that the Indian nation will not adopt arms, and it is well that it does not'. (*CWMG*, 10-42) Italy had achieved her integration not very long ago, and its process had attracted some Indian leaders like Surendranath Banerjea, who made clear his interest in the Italian integration in his autobiography *A Nation in Making,* 1925. Gandhi went against such a stream of thinking. Gandhi also did not join the feeling of sympathy to Japan, then and now. In "To Every Japanese", dated 18 July 1942, he warned them not to make a mistake and think that the Indians would heartily welcome them.

Shriman Narayan Agarwal published *Gandhian Constitution for Free India* in 1946, with Gandhi's "Foreward". Faithful to the title, Narayan wrote in the way as if Gandhi himself would have done. Gandhi said in the Foreward that 'the merit of his attempt consists in the fact that he has done what for want of time I have failed to do'(*CWMG*, 88-393~4). It seems it was with the possibility of the Japanese invasion of India in mind that Narayan wrote in the book that 'Decentralisation and ruralisation are imperative for successful defence against foreign aggression; they alone can defy modern warfare'.[49] Gandhi wrote "Question Box" (subtitle, Village Swaraj), which begins with 'My idea of village *swaraj* is that it is a complete republic.', and gives a sketch of the self-supporting and self-governing village. It is significant that this article and "To Every Japanese" mentioned above were written on the same day, 18 July, and published in the same issue of the *Harijan* of 26 July 1942, only two weeks before the AICC passed the Quit-India Resolution. (*CWMG*, 76-308~9, 309~312) It is easy to see, therefore, that, in his idea of defending India in a non-violent manner, he gave his 'village republics' a central place.

In the state machinery envisaged in the book, the village is considered to be the 'Basic Unit', and then the Taluka and District Panchayats, the Provincial Governments, and finally the Central Government, in that order, are organized upward on this basis, 'with the largest measure of local autonomy for the federating unit'.[50] Thus 'the whole system will be turned upside down'.[51] This is in tune with what Gandhi told Louis Fischer in the interview mentioned above, where Gandhi said that after each villager voted in his village 'Each village...would have one vote. The villages would elect their district administrations, and the district administrations would elect the provincial administrations, and these in turn would elect a president who would be the national chief executive'. (*CWMG*, 76-438)

INA Trials and Gandhi

Shortly after the end of the war, the trial of the first batch of three INA officers began in Delhi. It was a military tribunal, and the defendants were accused, first, as they had fought the King of England, and second, as they had committed atrocities in the name of punishing deserters and so on. The Congress formed the INA Defence Committee led by Bhulabhai Desai. By a strange turn of fate, he happened to be one of the Congress Working Committee members who ousted Bose from the Congress Presidency in 1939.

As the trial was coming to an end, Desai read his concluding *Defence Address* on 18 December 1945. It said, among others, that, when the INA began fighting HMG's troops, the Provisional Government of Free India had already been constituted, had been recognized by several governments like Japan, and had some territories (Andaman and Nicobar islands) ceded to it. Such a government had every right to declare war as belligerent rights, and it actually did so. Once they became belligerents, the second charge would not arise. Moreover, when the British surrendered to the Japanese at Singapore, the Indian soldiers were handed over to Japan as prisoners of war by a British officer on 17 February 1942. Therefore, the question of allegiance was no longer left with those Indians.

What was crucial from the point of view of non-violence was that, although the *Address* said the INA's fighting should be recognized as a war, from which immunity followed, it did not discuss war, and violence in that form, as such. It simply said that war was 'a necessary evil in this infirm world'[52], and did not put forward any critical comment either on this war, or war in general, or violence, or the INA. By implication this is a clear approval of war in general and the war the INA had fought. True, it was necessary here to defend Bose and the INA for political reasons. The wave of opposition against the military tribunal greatly enhanced the nationalistic feeling among the Indians and the desire for independence. But the justification employed here of a war, quoted in the above, is capable of being used for any other war. Therefore the *Address* did not contribute to any advancement of the theory of non-violence either in the Indian or the international context, either in legal or political terms. In that sense it was different from the Nuremberg Trial or Tokyo Tribunal, though both of them were yet in preparation at this time. It is difficult to believe that this was all that was said by the Congress Defence Committee. In spite of this, it, and its author, were highly praised all over the country.

Alone for Gandhi, this was not the end. Neither could it be. He was probably the only person who did not join the praise. He was consistent in calling Bose and the INA misled. What was in his mind was known by the message he conveyed to the ex-INA men who came into contact with him after the war. To Shah Nawaz, for example, who had declared that now he was back he would work with the spirit of non-violence, Gandhi expressed a feeling of welcome (*CWMG*, 83-135). To a question by an ex-officer what Gandhi would have done if the INA had come marching victorious, his answer was he would have requested them to pile up the weapons in front of him (*CWMG*, 84-189). Something like this actually happened in Calcutta when the rioters surrendered their weapons before him early in September 1947.

The INA was thus not simply an episode. Gandhi would not probably have reflected over his non-violence so intensely if there had been no war. His conclusion was consistent with what he had written in *Hind Swaraj* on Garibaldi. Thus he was exceptional among the Congress leaders, not only on industrialization, but also on the war-time violence. This will easily lead to the issue of armament to be discussed in the next Section. Before that we will recall what Vinoba said on the relation between Gandhi and Subhash. He seems to be summing up a broad view held among the people, like Samar Guha mentioned earlier, rather than giving his own. 'People think that for Gandhi and for Subhash there are two different ways, but both are needed for the country, and the two will make one…'.[53]

5. Non-violence and Non-armament

Gandhi on Armed Forces

When and how, then, did Gandhi's Non-violence reflect itself on the question of whether India should have armed forces after independence? In *Hind Swaraj*, as we saw, the Editor criticized the Reader who wanted to have an army and a navy after independence. But Gandhi's thinking was not consistent at this time. Not only at the time of the South African War and the 'Zulu Rebellion', but also during the First World War after he returned to India, he tried to help the government's recruiting activities. On the latter occasion, unlike in the first two, it was not simply the nursing personnel but the fighting soldiers. He justified this by saying that 'We are not entitled to demand *swaraj* till we come forward to enlist in the army' (*CWMG*, 15-1). He was nearing 50, and was not likely to 'come forward' himself to be enlisted. But the logic itself was the same as in South Africa when he said that the Indians should participate in the war effort to demand a respectable position in the society. But the question of India's own fighting soldiers did not arise there.

It was after the *Purna Swaraj* Resolution, the Salt March, Gandhi-Irwin parley on an equal footing, the Karachi Congress, and the attendance at the Second RTC that Gandhi came to embrace a more or less systematic idea on the question of India's future armament. Probably the Karachi Congress of 1931 was the first step in this process. Before Karachi, there had been little in what he said that lead us to believe that some idea was evolving in his mind on the armed forces of the future India. For instance, in his Eleven Point demands to Irwin under the title "Clearing the Issue", the fifth item was 'Reduction of the military expenditure to at least 50 per cent', and the eleventh was 'Issue of licences to use firearms for self-defence subject to popular control'. (*CWMG*, 42-434) These two were incorporated in the Karachi Resolution, but they were only remotely related to the subject here. As to the last item, which coming from a man of non-violence is very controversial, Gandhi also talked about it in his "Letter to Lord Irwin" on 2 March 1930 that 'by the policy of cruel disarmament, it (the British rule) has degraded us spiritually. Lacking the inward strength, we have been reduced, by all but universal disarmament, to a state bordering on cowardly helplessness'. (*CWMG*, 43-3) We find words like 'cowardly' which are already familiar to us. A German scholar Dietmar Rothermund has given a remarkable interpretation on this in his handy *Mahatma Gandhi: An Essay in Political Biography*. He said that the item was meant to make non-violence 'a deliberate option of the strong'[54].

But what was new at Karachi was that Gandhi also said in 'Interview to *The Statesman* 'that 'I myself do not believe that any Army, Indian or British, is necessary at all, but there the Working Committee disagrees with me'. This was the beginning of a series of his comments on the army in independent India. His view did fluctuate, and he talked vaguely, for example, about the possibility of India having 'the smallest army imaginable' (*CWMG*, 47-388~9).

Evolution in his Views

The epoch-making remarks were made during his stay in Britain and first in a speech on 12 October 1931. There he said, '...people who have been able to gain liberty through these means (non-co-operation and *satyagraha*) are able to retain it through these means...' (*CWMG*, 48-144). On 15 October, he said, 'if per chance India wins her deliverance through non-violence, we may perhaps show to the world that it is not necessary to have an army State...' (*CWMG*, 48-158). In still another on 20 October, he said once again that 'If we really succeed in demonstrating that we have won our freedom through non-violent means, the people of India will not require much argument to convince them that non-violence will also enable them to retain their freedom' (48-200).

By these remarks Gandhi opened up a new road to politics and political thinking which had been virtually unknown in history. Why did he entertain the idea at this time? Partly because he saw that, even though the RTC had produced nothing constructive and, if anything, had emphasized the split among the various Indian political forces by giving unnecessarily loud voices particularly to the Princes and their representatives, still the arrival of freedom to India was no longer infinitely far away, just as he was sure in Delhi at the time of the Pact and told so to William Shirer. This must have stimulated him to give more serious thinking to the problem of the future armed forces, in other words, of the self-defence of India in the age of imperialism. It was an applied science of Non-violence.

He may also have remembered that the Congress itself had demanded that the military expenditure of India should be halved. It was also because he took notice of what he may or may not have expected to see in Europe. He made it clear in his speech at Lausanne, Switzerland, which he visited on his way to see Romain Rolland, that in his view 'You seem to be tired of the military burden under which Europe was groning...'.[55]

The Lausanne speech was remarkable in other ways also. Gandhi talked of a hypothetical situation of the neutral Switzerland invaded by a foreign army, and said, '(in that case) I would have invited every citizen to refuse all supplies to invading armies...and build a living wall of women and children and invite the invading armies to walk over their bodies.... Non-violence is not and has never been the weapon of the weak'.[56] Seldom has Gandhi talked about the power of his Non-violence in such strong words, before or after. He seems confident here that the armed forces are absolutely unnecessary. We may also be reasonably sure, from what we saw in the previous Section on the INA, that he would have uttered those same words if he were to face the invading army during the Second World War. On the same occasion at Lausanne he also said, 'She (India) could not enter into war if she had gained her freedom through non-violent means'.[57] The remarks at Lausanne have been quoted from Narayanbhai, originally taken from *Entertaining Gandhi*, 1932, the memoir of Muriel Lester, Gandhi's host in London, who accompanied him through Switzerland until he got on board a ship at Brindisi, Italy. Those remarks are not in the *CWMG*, but the Chronology in there says that he 'Addressed three meetings at Lausanne' on 8 December (*CWMG*, 48-512).

Gandhi and Japan's Article 9

Once thus determined, Gandhi did not look back. For instance, he said in his "Statement to the Press", on 6 February 1940, that 'so far as Defence is concerned unarmed peaceful India would rely upon the goodwill of the whole world. But I know that that is only a dream at the present moment'. (*CWMG*, 71-187) As a Japanese, the author is attracted by the first sentence, as the words are similar to a passage in the Preamble to the Japanese Constitution of 1946. It says that 'we have determined to preserve our security and existence, trusting in the justice and faith of the peace-loving peoples of the world'.

This passage is embodied in Article 9 of the Constitution in more concrete terms. It states, 'Aspiring sincerely to an international peace based on justice and order, the Japanese people forever renounce war as a sovereign right of the nation and the threat or use of force as means of settling international disputes. In order to accomplish the aim of the preceding paragraph, land, sea, and air forces, as well as other war potential, will never be maintained. The right of belligerency of the state will not be recognized'. It is this Article which has had a great appeal to 'the peace-loving peoples of the world'. It would have surely appealed to Gandhi, who would have found his own thought in the second paragraph. But it is also this Article that is under attack by the Conservative and rightist elements in Japan, backed by the Neo-Conservatives abroad. As to the former, they should study the history of how and why modern Japan fought one war after another continuously for half a century from 1894 to 1945, and learn the lessons. With regard to the latter, they would, to their benefit, learn whom they are calling their allies, and where they are together heading for. We will not make it 'only a dream'.

One more point may be taken up in connection with Gandhi and the Article 9. The latter uses the term renunciation of war. The term originally comes from the Kellogg (the then US Secretary of State) Treaty, or Treaty of Paris, also known as the Treaty for the Renunciation of War, signed in August 1928. When Gandhi came to know about it, he strongly criticized it in his article "The Kellogg Pact" on 4 July 1929, saying that while it 'has great possibilities', 'The parties to the Pact are mostly partners in the exploitation of the peoples of Asia and Africa...The Peace Pact, therefore, in substance means a desire to carry on the joint exploitation peacefully'. (*CWMG*, 41-153~4)

The Treaty was a step forward towards world peace, and that was why Article 9 borrowed those words from it. But Gandhi was very shrewd in his analysis. The joint imperial design he talked about was to break up not long afterwards by the action of the Axis Powers, all signatories of the Treaty, and by the national and revolutionary movements of the oppressed peoples.

Vinoba said candidly that the independence of India did not solve the problem of *himsa* (violence) versus *ahimsa* (non-violence), implying that the independence was not achieved solely by non-violence and, therefore, India is perturbed by a lot of *himsa* even now.[58] This was why Gandhi's dream did not come true, as it was based on the assumption that the freedom of India would be achieved by non-violence only.

But Gandhi's view on the armed forces did not change afterwards. He said at a "Speech at Prayer Meeting" in April 1946 referring to this that 'The Congress has declared that she would carry on the struggle for India's independence through the method of non-violence. But she has not yet decided whether she would adhere to that method for the protection of that freedom against possible foreign aggression'. (*CWMG*, 83-378) The Congress has never fulfilled Gandhi's wish on this point. For one more example of Gandhi's thinking, he said at another "Speech at Prayer Meeting" in July 1947, in less than a month before the Partition, that 'Keeping an army, whatever its nature or size, can have no support from me…If I am asked I will still say that I am not for maintaining an army'. (*CWMG*, 88-399)

Shriman Narayan writes in the chapter on National Defence in his *Gandhian Constitution* mentioned above that 'He (Gandhi) would like Free India not to maintain any armed defence against foreign aggression'.[59] So this was surely Gandhi's thinking. Interestingly Narayan goes a bit further than Gandhi, and writes that 'if India…is able to attain political independence through non-violence, she will surely release tremendous forces of amity and good-will among the warring nations of the world'.[60]

"What if Gandhi had lived on?"

But how should we perceive the external threats India has faced after independence? Rajmohan Gandhi wrote on "What if Gandhi had lived on?".[61] Since Gandhi did not die a natural death, and as Rajmohan says, 'was in 1948 mentally and even physically more vigorous than many of the Congress leaders', it would be valid to ask this question. According to Rajmohan, as the result of a series of coming and going by some emissaries early in 1948, 'On January 27(1948), it was agreed that Gandhi would arrive in Pakistan on February 8 or 9'. We find the same narrative in his *Mohandas*.[62] This arrangement is not found in *CWMG*, where Gandhi is only talking of visiting Sevagram for twelve days on 2 February. Pyarelal wrote on the state of mind of Gandhi at this time that 'Gandhiji, too, felt that having done his bit for the minority community in the Indian Union (by his last fast in January) he must now do the same for the minority community in Pakistan for which the way had now been set clear for him'.[63]

If done, it would have been a glorious fulfilment of his long entertained wish to visit the riot-torn Pakistan. If done, it would no doubt have eased the tension between the two newly born countries, and lessened the need on both sides to face each other with mighty arms ready. It would also have made it possible to divert resources to more urgent need of the time. Why was the thread not picked up by someone else on the Indian side when Gandhi was suddenly removed from the scene? Was any sounding made, but unsuccessful?

If India and Pakistan have been able to have better relations, it was bound to have a significant impact on the Indo-Chinese relations among others. It is not easy to make meaningful comments on such an assumption. Let us, however, dare to point to three factors which could have avoided the War between India and China in 1962. First, China should have conveyed its views on the Indo-Chinese border to India at least two or three years earlier, so that the two could have had inter-governmental negotiations in a much calmer atmosphere. Second, the Opposition parties in India should have restrained their demands on Prime Minister Nehru on the border issue. Third, the political asylum to Dalai Lama should not have been given so easily. Dalai Lama himself, if he wanted to claim to be a Gandhian, should not have sought asylum, remembering that Gandhi always advised the refugees to go back to their native land. These three may be said only with hindsight. But they have been presented to explore if the war could have been avoided at all on the basis of India not being a military power, and, by so doing, to see if Gandhi's 'dream' of 'unarmed peaceful India' could have been valid at all.

Rajmohan, by the way, concludes the above "What If" article by saying that 'If he had remained alive, the Indian state might have become less a master and more a servant of the Indian people, empowering them might have become a mainstream rather than a marginal exercise, and the hierarchies that continue to mark India's society and polity might have become less steep'. Here, however, on the basis of what is discussed mainly in Chapter Three, the author is not prepared to go all the way with him.

There is one more point to be discussed in connection with Gandhi's idea of disarmament. It is the theory of deterrence, particularly of nuclear deterrence. When India exploded her nuclear devices on 11 May 1998, Vinod Mehta, Editor-in-Chief, *Outlook*, wrote a full two-page article in his journal's next issue of 25 May sharply criticizing the tests. It concluded by saying that 'India was already a great nation before May 11. It would become an even greater nation if 44 per cent of its population did not live in absolute poverty'. In spite of such criticism, India, and also Pakistan, has been keen on expanding their nuclear arsenal in the name of deterrence. Not only these two, but all the five Permanent Members of the UN Security Council are nuclear powers, and legitimately so in terms of the Nuclear Non-proliferation Treaty (NPT), believe in the nuclear deterrence, and as such all violating 'the threat or use of force' clause of the Article 2(4) of the UN Charter. Deterrence here is really an excuse for diverting the resources from 'work and wages' in which, in Gandhi's words, God reveals Himself to the 'hungry and unemployed'.

The use of the concept of 'deterrence', however, may not be limited to the nuclear weapons issue alone. On arriving at Patna from Noakhali, Gandhi gave "Speech at Prayer Meeting" on 5 March 1947, his first one in Bihar this time, in which he said, 'Dr. Rajendra Prasad told me today that some people believed that the Bihar riots had arrested the crimes in Noakhali, otherwise Hindus everywhere would have suffered a similar fate…Those who are under the illusion that Bihar has saved other people by committing these barbarities are talking nonsense'. (*CWMG*, 87-45) What Gandhi was criticizing here was exactly a kind of deterrence theory. It was to justify the atrocities Biharis committed on the Muslims in the name of preventing further atrocities.

Incidentally, Rothermund writes that it was on 1 July 1946, nearly a year after the dropping of the Atomic Bombs on Japan, that Gandhi wrote about it for the first time in "Atom Bomb and *Ahimsa*". (*CWMG*, 84-393~4) According to his analysis, Gandhi at this time had a deep suspicion of the 'Big Three'—Britain, USSR and the USA—, particularly the last-mentioned, so that he thought it wise not to criticize the dropping explicitly.[64] It took him that much of time to regain confidence. This was Gandhi's diplomacy. He also wrote that '...it (the bomb) resulted for the time being in destroying the soul of Japan. What has happened to the soul of the destroying nation is yet too early to see'. Gandhi here was really far-sighted. Several decades on, and we hear more of the high incidence of suicide and PTSD among the survivors who have seen the battle in Afghanistan and Iraq.

6. The Constitution of Free India demanded in the Quit-India Resolution

Unitary vs. *Federal*

The AICC's famous Resolution of 8 August 1942, which decided launching the Quit-India Movement 'under the leadership of Gandhiji', also in part refers to the future constitution of India. It says that a free India will have a constituent assembly to prepare a constitution, and 'This constitution, according to the Congress view, should be a federal one, with the largest measure of autonomy for the federating units, and with the residuary powers vesting in these units'. (*CWMG*, 76-459) Beginning in May 1942, the Congress adopted three resolutions in all on 'Quit-India', and this was the final and the decisive one. The earlier two will be discussed later.

The significance of these constitutional proposals was that for one thing they were meant for the Muslims, and possibly other minorities. Muslims, at least some of their groups including the Muslim League, were persistent in demanding these as we will see in Chapter Four. But the Congress, Motilal Nehru's Committee who had drafted the *Nehru Report* in 1928, and Gandhi himself, were not known to have responded to these demands quickly and sympathetically. Yajnik writes on Gandhi that 'He is not reported to have attended any of the All Party Conferences or conventions that were held so frequently during the year of 1928'.[65] The Congress by and large stuck to the idea of independent India as a unitary and centralized state, more or less on the pattern of the *Nehru Report*. In its Recommendations, the *Report* says on the future 'Commonwealth of India' that 'Parliament shall...have power to make laws (a) for the peace, order and good government of the Commonwealth in relation to all matters not coming in the classes of subjects by this Act assigned to the legislatures of provinces', thus keeping the residuary powers with the Centre.[66]

But these demands in the August Resolution were not there basically for the sake of appealing to the Muslims. The idea of decentralization was not foreign to Gandhi from the beginning. His view as was enunciated in "Spinning-Wheels *vs*. Mills" at the end of 1939 was that 'I suggest that, if India is to evolve along non-violent lines, it will have to decentralize many things. Centralization cannot be sustained and defended without adequate force'. (*CWMG*, 71-56) His thinking was thus very unique. It was in tune with his idea of disarmament, or rather non-armament, as discussed above. Also it fits in well with what he told Fischer, or what Shriman Narayan wrote on his behalf. Already in *Hind Swaraj,* when the Reader spoke of 'our own splendour', which was strongly militarily-oriented, the Editor refused to subscribe to it. In his view, 'when you look at it in its nakedness', what the British had established in India was 'nothing but a highly organized efficient military control'. (*CWMG*, 67-226)

When the CD in 1930s petered out, and it became apparent to everybody that the mass energy would take some time for recovery, the Swarajya Party, the legislature wing of the Congress, as in 1924, came to be born again in 1934, ten years later. The difference was that while earlier the Congress split into the Pro-Changers who wanted to go into the legislature and the No-Changers who were more interested in Constructive Programme, and as such were seen as the Gandhites, thus shaping two more or less clear-cut camps within the Congress, this time the Congress as a whole gave the legislative activities its approval. Yajnik once characterized the Swarajist Pro-Changers in this way, 'I designated the whole Swarajist movement as the revolt of the political intelligentsia of the country against the cast-iron doctrine of non-co-operation'.[67] But now it was an old story. This was with the new 1935 Government of India Act coming into the background, and with it the greater opportunity of Congressmen becoming MLAs with a much greater power and privilege.

Gandhi foresaw this, and in "Letter to K.M. Munshi" in the middle of April 1934 said that 'Council-entry will remain a permanent feature of the Congress like civil disobedience and constructive work'. (*CWMG*, 57-397) He continued that he himself was qualified for the other two but not for the Council-entry. In the same letter he wrote 'My hopes are pinned on you and Bhulabhai. I do not know who else might go...Rajagopalachari, Rajendrababu, Jairamdas, etc., will probably stay out...Possibly Jawaharlal also may be tempted...'. Thus in Gandhi's eyes there had been a considerable transformation within the Congress.

But we wonder if he was still minimizing the aspiration within the Congress to go into the Legislature in the changing circumstances. He was also minimizing the necessity of practicing the Congress policies within the framework of Parliamentary democracy. He still thought the other two activities were more important than the council-entry. He, however, himself moved a "Resolution on Council-Entry" before the AICC at Patna in mid-May 1934 to create the Congress Parliamentary Board with M.A. Ansari as President. (*CWMG*, 58-8) The venue and timing of the AICC at this time were so fixed to coincide with Gandhi's Harijan tour going on since November 1933 and the earthquake that struck Bihar in January of this year. The Congress Socialist Party (CSP) was also formed then. With all this in the background, "Manifesto of Congress Parliamentary Board", at the end of July 1934, said to have been drafted by Gandhi, said that 'The Working Committee *has.....suggested an infallible alternative-a constituent* assembly to be elected on the basis of adult suffrage or as near as it may be'. (*CWMG*, 58-256)

This was the first time the Congress proposed a Constituent Assembly as a means of making India's constitution with the Indians' hands, and not by the British Parliament. It is also noteworthy that they stressed the universal suffrage at this time. After the first elections to the Provincial Assemblies under the new Act, and the Congress's decision to form its Ministries in those Provinces where they had won, Gandhi in "Statement to the Press" called it 'the largest and fullest democracy known to the world' even under a still very limited, though expanded, suffrage under the Act. (*CWMG*, 65-38) It is now common to call India the largest democracy in the world, but Gandhi, in spite of his skepticism of the legislature since *Hind Swaraj*, knew that India's achieving independence would mean exactly this, and worked for it.

As for the working of the new Act, the Election Manifesto of the Congress, decided by the AICC on 22 August 1936, demanded India's independence and a Constituent Assembly, made it clear that the

Congress would take part in the Provincial Elections, declared that 'The new Legislatures...are totally incapable of solving the vital problems of poverty and unemployment', reiterated the resolution at Karachi in 1931 for its economic programme, and said that since 'the Congress stands for the rejection of the new Act...every endeavour will be made to prevent the introduction and functioning of the federal part of the scheme'. ("Extracts from the Congress Election Manifesto", *CWMG*, 65-459-462)

The Election Manifesto also said that 'The A.I.C.C. is of opinion that it will be desirable for this decision (on forming Ministries) to be taken after the elections'. (*CWMG*, 65-461) It must have been written by Jawaharlal Nehru as Congress President as the text has been taken from the *Selected Works of Jawaharlal Nehru*. As such the Manifesto was couched in strong words such as 'to combat it (the Act) and seek to end it'. When the Congress decided to form the Ministries after the victory, it was Gandhi himself who wrote in "Extract from A.I.C.C. Resolution" of 16 March 1937 that 'the A.I.C.C. authorizes and permits the acceptance of the Ministerial offices in Provinces where the Congress commands majority in the Legislatures'. (*CWMG*, 65-4) Hereafter Gandhi became a guide on the working of the Ministries, and, as he himself said in "Letter to C. Rajagopalachari", '*Harijan* is becoming a weekly letter to the Congress Ministries'. (*CWMG*, 66-4) He also saw to it that the Congress Ministries resigned once the War started in 1939.

As we have seen the Congress demanded a Constituent Assembly for the first time in 1934. The "Working Committee's Manifesto" issued immediately after the breaking out of the Second World War demanded, among other things, that 'the Indian people must have the right of self-determination by framing their own constitution through a Constituent Assembly without external interference...'. (*CWMG*, 70-411) Gandhi supported it by saying in "The Only Way" that 'The only way out (of communal trouble) is a Constituent Assembly'. (*CWMG*, 70-364).

Gandhi further wrote in "Question Box" (subtitle, Use of Force Against Muslims) six months later that 'My hope in desiring a Constituent Assembly is that...the representatives (of Muslims) when they are face to face with the reality will not think of cutting up India according to religions but will regard India as an indivisible whole and discover a national, i.e., Indian solution of even specially Muslim questions'. (*CWMG*, 71-345) This was written on 17 March and appeared in the *Harijan* of 23 March 1940. This was the time when the Congress was meeting at Ramgarh and the Muslim League at Lahore. Few other remarks by Gandhi would surpass this quotation in showing him a true nationalist. But Jinnah, as was quoted in Gandhi's "My Answer to Quaid-e-Azam", said in his Presidential address of the League on 22 March that 'May I point out to Mr. Gandhi and the Congress that they are fighting for a Constituent Assembly which we cannot accept?' (*CWMG*, 71-371) Jinnah did not make any counter proposal. He did not need to, for the reasons explained in Chapter Four. So Gandhi's idea of the Constituent Assembly collapsed. The August Resolution shows what he would have wanted to be put into the Constitution to be made by it.

The Constitution of independent India, which took effect in 1950, in stating the Legislative Relations between the Union and the States, says that 'Parliament has exclusive power to make any law with respect to any matter not enumerated in the Concurrent List or State List' (Article 248), thus keeping the residuary powers with the Centre and not with the federating unit which is the State. This is essentially a legacy from the *Raj*, and not on the line of the August proposals.

Ambedkar, in introducing the Draft Constitution before the Constituent Assembly as Chairman of the Drafting Committee, said that 'the Draft Constitution can be both unitary as well as federal according to the requirements of time and circumstances. In normal times, it is framed to work as a federal system. But in times of war it is so designed as to make it work as though it was a unitary system'.[68] These would show that decentralization in terms of constitutional arrangement has not proceeded after independence. Gandhi, writing "Independence" in the middle of 1946, foresaw this when he said that 'I know on the contrary that many would have India become a first-class military power and wish for India to have a strong centre and build the whole structure round it'. (*CWMG*, 85-34).

7. How Gandhi related him to the Masses

Swaraj as the Primary Objective

We will examine here what Gandhi's primary objectives were after all. They were seemingly many. But when he said in *Hind Swaraj* that 'The Congress has always insisted that the Nation should control revenue and expenditure. It has always desired self-government after the Canadian model…All I have to show is that the Congress gave us a foretaste of Home Rule.', it was clear that already at this time he was demanding the independence of India (Canadian model meant Dominion Status, derived from the formation of Canada as the first Dominion in 1867). It was a logical conclusion from his whole argument in *Hind Swaraj*. His insistence on the independence kept growing afterwards. He aimed at the independence in order to assure his other objectives accomplished, which is also clear from *Hind Swaraj*. In this sense the freedom of the nation was his primary objective. Narayanbhai also told the author in an interview in October 2012 that independence was his primary objective.

S-T-S Model

This is where the masses come in within the context of NC/CD that we have discussed. Therefore his immediate objective with the masses was to awaken them. As Bipin Chandra says, his movement could be summarized by the formula S-T-S, or Struggle-Truce-Struggle.[69] These were the findings of collective research based on the interview of more than 1,500 persons and conducted together with Mridula Mukherjee, Aditya Mukherjee, and Sucheta Mahajan. Mahajan quotes the AICC resolution of 22 September 1945, which says that 'the guiding maxim of the Congress must remain: negotiations and settlement when possible and non-cooperation and direct action when necessary'.[70] There is a basic convergence of this resolution and the S-T-S formula.

We may notice the beginning of the relation between Gandhi and the masses in the sudden visit by a Tamil indentured labourer, Balasundaram by name, to Gandhi's office at Durban, whom he took care of legally as well medically. It did not take time for the story to be spread, and, as Gandhi wrote in his *Autobiography*, 'Balasundaram's case reached the ears of every indentured labourer, and I came to be regarded as their friend…. A regular stream of indentured labourers began to pour into my office, and I got the best opportunity of learning their joys and sorrows'. (*CWMG*, 39-126~7)

Rajkumar Shukla who ultimately took Gandhi to Champaran may be called Balasundaram's successor.

Even when there was no large-scale national movement, he had a variety of means of contact with the masses. For one thing he kept travelling in the country. Perhaps the Harijan tour of 7 November 1933 to 2 August 1934, including a visit to the earthquake-torn Bihar, to make the people familiar with the Harijan problem and invite donation from them, was the most important. It was, in his words, their 'vote of confidence' in his CD started by the Salt March a few years ago. The CD was not a resounding success in terms of the results, as is seen from the "Provisional Settlement", popularly known as the Gandhi-Irwin Pact of 5 March 1931(*CWMG*, 45-432~436), but he was not afraid of facing the masses, as he had endured his own sacrifice by imprisonment.

There were also his speeches after the prayer. Those speeches were rather late in his life to be introduced into his regular programme, as he must gradually have come to think that, in view of the rapidly changing situation, it was necessary to take such an opportunity to tell the masses in his own words what was taking place in the country. He said in "Speech at Prayer Meeting" in May 1946 that 'Silent prayer is the best prayer...It was only during my (recent) tours in Assam and Bengal that I started speaking after prayers'. (*CWMG*, 84-139) Judging from his itinerary in the *CWMG*, "Speech at Prayer Meeting" he gave at Sodepur, Calcutta, on 8 December 1945 was probably his first such speech, apart from some sporadic ones he had given before (*CWMG*, 82-189~190). This means that most of his speeches at prayer meetings were made in the two years of 1946 and 1947.

One may take it that his whole life was one of mobilizing or training the masses. We have seen several cases in which he emphasized the importance of the training of the participants in CD, as against NC. At the time of the Quit-India Movement, he wrote in "A Challenge" that '...twenty-two years are nothing in the training of a nation for the development of non-violent strength'. (*CWMG*, 76-232) This means from 1920, the year of the special Calcutta and Nagpur Sessions of the Congress, to 1942. The Resolution of 8 August also talks of 'all the non-violent strength it (the country) has gathered during the last twenty-two years of peaceful struggle' with which to launch a mass struggle. (*CWMG*, 76-461) One may wonder if the idea of training the nation was already on his mind when he left the shores of Africa for India in 1914.

It was his conviction that, in order to awaken the people, everything must be transparent, and explainable in easy language. This is why he avoided 'revolutionary', namely terrorist activities. Terrorism, on the other hand, stimulated him to think of a Non-violent alternative. Thus, the Salt March was conceived of as a means to contain political violence and communal violence. The INA was also thought to be difficult for the people to understand. He also wanted to make 'every pie' accountable. He thought that what was beyond the means of the masses was also a luxury for him.

During the Quit-India Movement and afterwards hundreds of workers went underground. One of them was Aruna Asaf Ali. Gandhi wrote on her in his "Statement to the Press" he issued on the occasion of the Royal Indian Navy (R.I. N.) Mutiny, that 'I had the pleasure of meeting her on several occasions while she was underground...I did not like her being underground. I do not appreciate any underground activity. I know that millions cannot go underground. Millions need not. A select few may fancy that they will bring *swaraj* to the millions by secretly directing their activity. Will this not be spoon-feeding?'. (*CWMG*, 83, 182~183) Here he was taking the side of the millions. Put it differently, he wanted to form a majority among the masses by his Non-violence and transparency. If at all Gandhi had got something in common with Marx, the idea of having to organize a majority by peaceful means, which Marx and Engels arrived rather late in their life, and expounded by Engels in the Preface to the 1895 Edition of Marx's *Class Struggle in France,* was one of such common points. We will see another common point between Gandhi and Marx in the Section on Machinery in Chapter Three.

Democracy of Gandhi's Conception

In order to know how Gandhi defined the new, independent India in terms of the masses, it would be worth studying a few letters he wrote around the time of independence. Put together they represent his concept of democracy. First is a reply to a friend, who complained about the moral deterioration in the Congress, titled "Are We Going Down?" dated 4 February 1946. There Gandhi wrote that 'the glow of *swaraj* in action must be felt by the illiterate millions of India. They must feel the vital difference between the present autocratic and ordinance regime and the orderly, democratic, non-violent regime under *swaraj*'. (*CWMG*, 83-84)

Then he said in "Talk with Workers" at Patna on 20 April 1947 that 'What they (the Ministers of Provinces) needed was...plain common sense, combined with the will to go down to the masses, share their lives, think in their terms and win their confidence...The masses will instinctively feel that the era of the common man had arrived'. (*CWMG*, 87-317) These were all new ideas at the time, and would show him to be a true democrat. They would also show that he believed in the building of a civil society in India. The masses here are not considered to be the mere object. This was also clear in "A Discussion" held almost at the end of his life, which said that 'the Congress had also to rebuild a new society based upon truth and non-violence—a society not so much dependent on the existence of a strong and centralized government as on the intelligent co-operation of the people organized on a voluntary basis and inspired by the ideals of justice, tolerance and truthfulness'. (*CWMG*, 90-506)

Also look at "An Indian Governor", written two days after independence at Calcutta where he spent 15 August 1947. This was the time the Britishers were being replaced by the Indians as Governors and in other high posts. In Calcutta Rajagopalachari (hereafter Rajaji) was sworn in as the first Indian Governor of the newly-created West Bengal State. Gandhi writes that an Indian Governor (1) 'should...be a teetotaller', (2) 'should represent hand-spinning as a visible token of identification with the dumb millions of India, a token of the necessity of 'bread labour' and organized non-violence'... (3) 'dwell in a cottage accessible to all'... (4) 'no caste or creed or colour distinction'... and (5) 'speak the language of the province...and Hindustani, the lingua franca of India written in the Nagari or Urdu script. This is neither Sanskritized Hindi nor Persianized Urdu'.... (*CWMG*, 89-53~54) One may feel that they were too rigid. But some of them may be of even more relevance today, some seventy years after the achievement of independence.

Even before the coming of independence, Gandhi tried to make politics, and the Congress itself, to be nearer the masses. One of such projects, almost a stroke of genius, was to hold the Annual Session of the Congress in the villages to make it more familiar to the villagers. This started with the Faizpur Congress at the end of 1936. It could not have been held without Gandhi's enthusiastic support, who, in "India in a Village" used such terms as 'a model village' or 'village India' on Faizpur, and advised that 'The (Reception) Committee must not aim at reproducing a city in the village. That would be doing violence to the whole conception'. (*CWMG*, 63-17) It is as if he was talking against the rapid industrialization today. And it is easy to see that he was familiarizing his 'village republic'. Faizpur in Maharashtra was followed by Haripura on the Tapti in Gujarat, Tripuri near Jabalpur in the C.P., and finally Ramgarh in Bihar before the Congress was banned because of the War.

A different, almost unexpected, sector where Gandhi tried to look after the interests of the masses was his strong criticism towards the end of his life of the continuation of the war-time control on consumer goods. He first took up this problem in "Speech at Prayer Meeting" early in November 1947, already after independence. He put the matter thus, 'Control gives rise to fraud, suppression of truth, intensification of the black market and to artificial scarcity. Above all it unmans the people and deprives them of initiative, it undoes the teaching of self-help they have been learning for a generation. It makes them spoon-fed'. (*CWMG*, 89-467)

In another "Speech at Prayer Meeting" in the middle of the same month, he said that 'I feel that continuing the controls is criminal…it is harmful for India. I am sure that there is no scarcity of food or cloth in the country. The rains have not betrayed us this year. There is enough cotton in our country and enough people to work on the spinning-wheels and the looms'. (*CWMG*, 90-44) He further argued in still another "Speech at Prayer Meeting" in December that 'decontrol means that instead of merely a few people in the Government the millions have to learn to be far-sighted'. (*CWMG*, 90-197)

Masses' Response

How then did the masses respond to Gandhi's 'call'? Here is an attempt to theorize it by an Indian scholar. Sociologist-cum-economist P.C. Joshi wrote in his *Mahatma Gandhi: The New Economic Agenda* that 'Gandhi's life-long endeavour to understand the problems of the masses and to be understood by them had distinguished him as a new type of social thinker and political leader who had emerged on the Indian scene through a long process of trial and testing by the masses themselves. Here was, therefore, the key to the understanding of the quality of Gandhi's thought which was constantly evolving in the course of lifelong encounter with the people and in response to the problems posed by social praxis'.[71] The author would like to look at it as an obituary to Gandhi, and as such it is one of the finest. Joshi's point of the masses themselves having selected Gandhi as the leader, and the latter having kept responding to them, is indeed remarkable.

A concrete example of the response to Gandhi by the masses is provided by Kamaladevi in her *Memoirs*. When she was arrested for her activities of salt making in Bombay, she was put in different jails and one of them was Hindalga Jail. There she found a number of very poor peasant women from the then Uttar Kannada District, who told their story to her in Kannada, her mother tongue. Kamaladevi records, 'Quietly over the long evenings they told me stories'. Gandhi's call reached them. 'He too was in prison to bring freedom for all. He too suffered like them, did not only ask others to suffer…We understand now that it is fear that makes us slaves…The Mahatma has made us free so we are not afraid…'.[72] We are reminded of a folk song 'We are not afraid today…' by Pete Seeger, who died while writing this book.

Incidentally look at what Kamaladevi wrote on Gandhi's centenary. It says, 'As one travels round in India, in towns and in villages one comes across stone and cement figures trying desperately to look like him (Gandhi). But one characteristic is common to all, be they fine or ugly, they invariably show him walking, on his march, the eternal quest.'[73] Kamaladevi has certainly criticized Gandhi in many ways, but the above is a superb obituary to him as much as the one by P.C. Joshi quoted above.

Amidst all this Gandhi himself felt, and told others, as he wrote in "Letter To P.C. Ghosh" in 1945 that 'It has been my experience so far that wherever I go and settle down, my presence gives the poor and destitute a sense of comfort'. (*CWMG*, 81-372) Vinoba was writing how the people trusted his words. He wrote that people trusted that what Gandhi said 'he said it from his heart. There is no second meaning in his words. What is clear is also clear in the same way in his mind…But for all those leaders (before him) people did not have such pure confidence that what they were talking was from their mind'.[74] When Gandhi died, he was convening a meeting at Sevagram in February 1948 in order to coordinate the various organizations under his leadership to adjust to the new environment of independent India. When Vinoba attended the meeting, actually held on 11 to 15 March[75], even he of thirty-two years of close association with Gandhi found many faces among the 'Gandhi family' assembled there new to him. But Gandhi remembered everyone of them.[76] Vinoba also wrote that 'when Gandhi died the people of India felt that it was as if a member of their families had passed away'.[77]

8. With the CWC, especially with Jawaharlal Nehru

Congress Organization

Between Gandhi and the masses there was the Congress organization at various levels. Since his attendance at the PCCs (Pradesh Congress Committees) is seldom on record, we may take it that his contact with the Congress was mostly by attending the Annual Sessions, AICC, and CWC. Very often his attendance gave the meeting that much more importance, or, rather, he selected important meetings to attend. Notable is the fact that those different levels of the Congress organization became standing ones by the new constitution of the Congress in 1920 in the drafting of which Gandhi played a major role. Therefore, these Committees themselves were symbolic of the arrival of the Gandhian era in the Congress history.

The CWC was the core organ. But before discussing it, it will be worth looking at Gandhi's relations with his co-workers in general. One of the outstanding characteristics of Gandhi as a leader was that he was quite naturally concerned with the health, other personal problems, and the family of almost each and everyone of his many hundreds of co-workers. This was what Vinoba pointed out in the above. That must have helped him to mobilize them when necessary. Yajnik wrote that after Gandhi's imprisonment in 1922, he was also arrested and was brought to the same quarters of the same Yerawada Prison. Gandhi had been there for more than a year already, but on seeing Yajnik he 'enquired about my health...'. Gandhi was already living on the diet of 'goats' milk and fruit'. While they were together for less than a year, this being Gandhi's longest prison term in life, Yajnik gradually took in some of Gandhi's daily routine at the latter's instance.[78]

We will show two more examples of his concern with the fellow workers. One was a "Letter to Kasturba Gandhi" of 29 March 1934, a letter from Gandhi who was touring in Bihar to his wife who was in jail (*CWMG*, 57-324~5). Originally written in Gujarati, it is hardly more than one page in English translation. But it contains concise information on as many as 44 of their associates and concludes with the immediate travel plan of Gandhi himself. Another was a "Letter to Kishorelal G. Mashruwala" of 4 November 1946. Also originally in Gujarati and a little less than one page in English translation, it gives messages to 14~15 workers at Sevagram, including such prominent workers as Asha Devi, Aryanayakam, Shankerrao Deo, Jajuji, Kumarappa, Vinoba and Kaka, and begins with 'Because you are the oldest person in the *ashram*, I am writing to you. Read this to all'. (*CWMG*, 86-73~74) Gandhi wrote this in Calcutta on his way to Noakhali, and was not destined to be back at Sevagram, or to see most of the above names, again.

Back to the Congress CWC, it consisted of the President, elected by the AICC, and about 15 other members nominated by the President. Many of them were almost permanent members as they served continuously with many Presidents from 1920s through 30s to the 40s. Sardar Vallabhbhai Patel, Rajendra Prasad, and Rajaji were typical of this type, representing Western India, North India, and South India, respectively. They were all different in personality, aptitude, and political beliefs. About Patel, for example, Gandhi said in "Speech at Gandhi Seva Sangh Meeting-II" in 1940 that 'he happens to be a born politician. Politics is in his blood. He is not born for the constructive programme...I was born for the constructive programme. It is part of my soul. Politics is a kind of botheration for me...This is the main difference between us'. (*CWMG*, 71-254) Temperamentally also, while Gandhi was all for the Harijan work in the jail, it did not interest Patel, who was in the same jail. He took to the making of envelopes out of whatever paper was available.

Those three, together with a few others, formed the solid Gandhian core in the CWC, called the Old Guard, and it would have been difficult to dislodge them. Abul Kalam Azad was also there representing the Nationalist Muslims after Ansari was gone. As for Nehru, Gandhi said at "Speech at Gandhi Seva Sangh Meeting, Hudli-III" that 'Obviously Rajendra Babu, Vallabhbhai, Rajaji and others are inclined in one way, Jawaharlal in another'. (*CWMG*, 65-120) This was in 1937 when Jawaharlal was President of the Congress. He was thought to be the representative of the educated youth, especially those leaning to the left. When Nehru was elected President in 1936 and chose his CWC, Gandhi wrote in "Letter to Agatha Harrison" that 'You see from the formation of his cabinet that he has chosen a majority of those who represent the traditional view, i.e., from 1920. Of course the majority represent my view'. (*CWMG*, 62-353) There were some Socialists after the formation of the CSP in 1934, but they were always in a minority.

Azad writes in *India Wins Freedom*, his autobiography, that when he was elected President at the Ramgarh Session in 1940 he had to constitute his CWC. Ten members had been in the previous one also. They were Sarojini Naidu, Patel, Jamnalal Bajaj (Treasurer), J.B. Kripalani (General Secretary), Gaffar Khan, Bhulabhai Desai, Shankerrao Deo, Profulla Chandra Ghosh, Rajendra Prasad, and Azad himself. Then Nehru who had been aloof was brought back, and Rajaji, Syed Mahmud and Asaf Ali were added. One more seat remained vacant.[79] It would be possible to detect the basic continuity of the Congress leadership in this composition.

Rajaji was deemed to be Gandhi's successor for some time. He was related to Gandhi by marriage. But in due course, in 1936 according to Narayanbhai, Nehru was nominated as such by Gandhi.

Strife in the CWC

Apart from the difference which came to the surface during the Second World War and after between Gandhi and the CWC, there had been two important previous splits in the CWC. One was the squeezing out of Subhash Bose as the President, mentioned above. At this time Gandhi himself talked of 'the old colleagues' (*CWMG*, 68-383), or 'the Gandhi-ites (to use that wrong expression—Gandhi)' (*CWMG*,

69-90) in the CWC. The other, earlier one was the split between the Gandhian 'No-changers' and the 'Pro-changers', also mentioned above.

There was a third one, similar to the case of Bose but on a smaller scale in which Gandhi was not directly concerned. It was when seven members of the CWC, Rajendra Prasad, Rajaji, Jairamdas Doulatram, Jamnalal Bajaj, Patel, J.B. Kripalani, and S.R. Deo, almost all of them of the Old Guard, were not satisfied with President Nehru and resigned from the CWC in June 1936. It was mediated by Gandhi without a difficulty. In the case of Bose, Gandhi did not play such a role.

Compared to these two or three earlier ones, however, the differences which occurred during the War and immediately afterwards were much more serious, as will be discussed in Chapter Four in more detail. They were so at least from Gandhi's point of view, as they showed him to be in a definite minority, almost alone, in the CWC.

On the part of the CWC shortly before the Partition, J.B. Kripalani, the 'Professor' as Gandhi used to call him, as Congress President sent a telegram to Gandhi who had just arrived in Calcutta from Noakhali on his way to Bihar, saying that 'We all consider your presence here next Working Committee meeting sixth (6 March 1947) essential'. (*CWMG*, 87-38, fn-1, 2) He did not indicate the subject matter of the meeting. Gandhi's "Telegram to J.B. Kripalani" said 'Regret Inability'. (*CWMG*, 87-38) The "Congress Working Committee's Resolution on the Punjab", thus passed without Gandhi's knowledge, said that it was now necessary 'to find a way out' of the Punjab situation, and that 'This would necessitate a division of the Punjab into two provinces, so that the predominantly Muslim part may be separated from the predominantly non-Muslim part'. (*CWMG*, 87-538) When Gandhi came to know this, he wrote in "Letter to Jawaharlal Nehru" that 'I would like to know the reason behind it...Kripalani said in answer to a question... that it was possible that the principle might be applied to Bengal also'. (*CWMG*, 87-124) So a crucial decision, though not of a division of the whole country, had been taken in Gandhi's absence, and this was the beginning of the widening gap between him and the CWC. Gandhi, moreover, was often not available at Delhi, as was seen from the chronology of his last fifteen months.

There is no evidence to show whether he would have supported or opposed the Resolution on the division of the Punjab. But it violated almost all the principles he supported in the Rajaji Formula, to be taken up in Chapter Four, especially the plebiscite. But it was supported by Nehru and Patel. Would Gandhi have gone against them? In fact, the "Speech at Congress Working Committee Meeting" shows that when the CWC met on 2 June 1947 to discuss the HMG's statement to be announced by the Viceroy the next day on the partition, 'He said that though he did not agree with the decisions of the Working Committee regarding the division of India, he did not want to take any step which would stand in the way of the Working Committee in implementing its previous decision'. (*CWMG*, 88-61)

Their relation was well reflected in a speech by Kripalani at the AICC which finally approved the partition plan forwarded by the CWC. Narayanbhai writes that on this occasion 'Acharya Kripalani recalled his association of 30 years with Gandhiji. He had supreme faith in Gandhiji. "Why then am I not with him?" the Congress President asked'.

Kripalani's own reply is quoted from Pyarelal's classic, *Mahatma Gandhi—The Last Phase,* dedicated to Mahadev Desai, his senior as Gandhi's Secretary. 'Because I feel that Gandhiji has as yet found no way of tackling the problem on a mass basis. When he taught us non-violent non-cooperation, he showed us a definite method which we had at least mechanically followed. Today he himself is groping in the dark. He was in Noakhali. His efforts eased the situation. Now he is in Bihar. The situation again has eased. But this does not solve in any way the flare-up in the Punjab. He says he is solving the problem of the Hindu-Muslim unity for the whole of India in Bihar. May be. But it is difficult to see how it is being done. There are no definite steps, as in non-violent non-cooperation, that lead to the desired goal. And then unfortunately for us today though he can enunciate policies, they have in the main to be carried out by others, and these others are not converted to his way of thinking'. 'It was', continues Narayanbhai, 'in these painful circumstances, concluded Acharya Kripalani, that he had supported the division of India'.[80] This would show how there was a virtual parting of ways between Gandhi and the CWC.

Just fifteen years afterwards Kripalani stood for the Lok Sabha in the then Bombay Northeast Constituency, against the sitting official

Congress candidate, V.K. Krishna Menon, the Defence Minister in the Nehru Cabinet, calling himself a close associate of Gandhi.

According to N.K. Bose, however, rather contrary to what Kripalani said on the above occasion, or what Kamaladevi told us, as we will see later, Gandhi had not given up and was biding time. He said in his lectures *Gandhi in Indian Politics* that '...there is clear evidence that he was also thinking of some new plan of action'. Bose did not mention exactly when it was, but from the context it seems that Bose was talking about the time of the AICC Session mentioned above, in other words the time when the partition of India was taking root in the minds of the people. Bose continued that, asked what the alternative would be, Gandhi said, 'Another movement...the British are leaving not because of any strength on our part but because of historical conditions and for many other reasons. If we utilize this opportunity in order to rebuild the Congress organization, and bring order out of this chaos, the transfer of power would be worthwhile. Otherwise, the kind of freedom which will come will not be freedom of the masses...in a few months' time, people will begin to realize that they had not very much of real power. When this realization came, his idea was to tour round the country, feel the pulse of the nation, and decide upon some new plan of action...Gandhiji thus lay low; he wanted to wait until India would begin to feel that enough power had not come to her, and she wanted a change'.[81]

What Pyarelal writes amounts to almost the same thing. He says that Gandhi told Sushila Nayar, his sister, shortly before his death, that 'Finally, he would undertake an all-India tour to awaken the masses to the grand opportunity that had opened out before them to take their destiny in their own hands and mould it according to their wish'.[82] This could have been his fourth nation-wide *satyagraha*, and this time against the independent Government of India itself. But what really could Gandhi have done even with his *satyagraha*, when he had hardly any comprehensive set of policies except the Constructive Programme, with no design of redistribution of property, and when even Nehru and Patel would have then united against their *Guru*.

Gandhi-Nehru-Patel

Among the CWC members it was Nehru and Patel Gandhi came to depend on even to the exclusion of others. When he was coming to Delhi in September 1947, which turned out to be his last such trip, he wrote in "Letter to Manibehn Patel", Patel's daughter, that 'Sardar and Jawahar will decide what I should do next'. (*CWMG*, 89-160) His journey itself was in response to Nehru's telegram of 2 September saying that 'I feel sure now that you should come to Punjab as early as possible' (*CWMG*, 89-134, fn 1), and an earlier one of 21 August requesting his 'healing presence' in the Punjab (*CWMG*, 89-75, fn 3) These would show that even Nehru's mass appeal was less, perhaps much less, than that of Gandhi, and Nehru knew it. The "Statement to the Press" Gandhi issued on reaching Delhi talked about 'The Central Government, the ablest, the most courageous and the most self-sacrificing team that the Union could produce', which was under the leadership of the two. (*CWMG*, 89-167) But from time to time Gandhi could not see eye to eye with them. On those occasions he used to say, as in "Speech at Prayer Meeting" on 28 September that 'I know nobody listens to me these days' (*CWMG*, 89-255), or, as in "Speech at Prayer Meeting" on 2 October (his last birthday in life), that 'But today nobody listens to me'. (*CWMG*, 89-275) According to Narayanbhai 'nobody' meant neither Nehru nor Patel.

But even these two were not always sure of themselves in the difficulties immediately following the Partition. As Gandhi said frankly in "Speech at Prayer Meeting" only several days after his arrival in Delhi, 'The Sardar always used to walk with his head high, but I tell you today he walks with his head bent. And Jawaharlal, that brave and courageous Jawaharlal who used to fly in the air, is today sitting helpless'. (*CWMG*, 89-181~182) But Gandhi was sure, as he said in "Speech at Public Meeting" at Panipat in December, that 'The two make an inseparable pair. Neither can do without the other'. (*CWMG*, 90-157)

That was perhaps how he wanted to believe, as the relationship between them deteriorated subsequently. On 30 January 1948, the last day of his life, Gandhi was meeting Patel who came at 4 pm as appointed. Nehru was coming at 7 pm after the prayer. According to "Talk with Vallabhbhai Patel", 'Although he had previously expressed his view, Gandhiji told the Sardar, that one of the two—either the Sardar or Pandit Nehru—should withdraw from the Cabinet, he had since come to the firm conclusion that the presence there of both of them was indispensable. Any breach in their ranks at that stage would be disastrous. He further said he would make that the topic of his post-prayer speech in the evening'. (*CWMG*, 90-534) Of course there was no such speech any more.

Nehru as the Heir

The assassination of Gandhi helped to put the two more closely. But even then, as Meghnad Desai points out in an article on "Communalism, secularism and the dilemma of Indian nationhood", 'most of Nehru's Congress colleagues were religious and held orthodox social views. Was it common to the Gandhites and was it due to Gandhi having a say in their selection? This meant that Nehru had to fight a constant battle with his own party members—Patel, Pant, Prasad, Tandon, Kripalani—in the first decade after 1947 to assert secularism as a positive philosophy and as a code of behaviour in public life'.[83] Did it not mean that Gandhi himself was 'religious and held orthodox social views'? And was Nehru's fight not what Gandhi had anticipated? If so was it not the very reason why Gandhi chose him as his heir? Rajaji was there whose name is not in the above list, but Nehru was much younger and much more dynamic. Even so, Desai continues, 'During 1947-1951', when Nehru was not yet in total command of the Congress, 'he accepted a shoddy compromise over the issue of Babri Masjid. Pant (UP Chief Minister) and Patel (Union Home Minister) had made only half-hearted gestures to prevent the installation of the idols of Ram in the periphery of the Masjid, and Nehru did not insist on their removal—a decision which would come back to haunt India in 1992'.[84] And ever since.

Another indirect evidence of why Gandhi chose him as his heir has been provided by journalist Inder Malhotra in his *Indira Gandhi*. He writes, 'In June 1975 after Indira's refusal to step down despite the Allahabad judgment but before the imposition of the Emergency, I had taken a straw poll of prominent and thoughtful individuals in Bombay. My question was, "What would Nehru have done in identical circumstances"? All 36 of my respondents were unanimous that he would have "resigned in thirty seconds flat". This arguably is the most important of the reasons why, in comparison with her father, Indira will always come second. Moreover, while Nehru built the institutions to sustain democracy, Indira found it expedient to let them decay and did nothing to repair them'.[85]

Earlier, journalist Raj Thapar wrote in her memoir, *All These Years*, that 'Indira herself avoided Parliament like the plague, unlike Nehru who had tried to nurture it with love and patience, aware that democracy was a new plant in our polity and unless tended with care would collapse at the first onslaught. We were to discover later how right he was.'[86]

These will speak for themselves. Gandhi must have trusted Nehru's institution building capacity for the democracy in India. The dismissal of the Communist Government in Kerala in 1959 would loom even larger in this light as the victory of Indira over Nehru, of institution-destroying over institution-building.

We will see that there were several fields where Nehru did not quite speak Gandhi's language. We will see one such field here, that of mass organization. Bipan Chandra broadly compares the two in this way. 'A critical weakness of Nehru's effort at socialist transformation flowed from non-adherence to the Gandhian strategy in one crucial aspect, i.e., its emphasis on the mobilization of the masses and on the organisation of mass struggles though non-violent in character'.[87] Then there was nothing left for Nehru to depend upon except bureaucracy, which was bound to expand under such circumstances.

Nehru-Gandhi Correspondence

We will see the relation between Gandhi and Jawaharlal a little further. An exchange of letters between them in early 1928 is a good material for this purpose. On 11 January of that year Nehru wrote a long "Letter from Jawaharlal Nehru" to Gandhi. He had just returned from Europe, where he had visited the Soviet Union also, and had been highly impressed by the rapid industrialization there.

In this letter Nehru frankly poured his all-out impatience with Gandhi, perhaps expecting explanation, or even consolation from him. In the first-half of it he wrote critically about Gandhi's interpretation of the Madras Session of the Congress at the end of the previous year, and Gandhi's negative attitude on the Independence Resolution moved by Nehru himself and passed by the Session.

In the second half of the letter, Nehru was even more outspoken and wrote that 'I hardly agreed with anything that some of your previous publications—*Indian Home Rule* (*Hind Swaraj*), etc.,—contained. I felt and feel that you were and are infinitely greater than your little books.' He criticized *khadi* work. He went on to say further that 'You misjudge greatly, I think, the civilization of the West and attach too great an importance to its many failings…It is the opinion of most thinkers in the West that these defects are not due to industrialism as such but to the capitalist system which is based on exploitation of others.' Finally he said that 'You do not say a word against the semi-feudal zamindari system which prevails in a great part of India or against the capitalist exploitation of both the workers and the consumers' (*CWMG*, 35-540~4). One finds here almost everything that composed what later came to be called 'Nehruvian' thinking. Probably at the time of India's independence Nehru held those same ideas intact. The difference was he did not criticize Gandhi again in so candid terms, but he did it by not speaking 'Gandhi's language'.

What is surprising was Gandhi's reply dated 17 January. There he wrote that 'The differences between you and me appear to me to be so vast and radical that there seems to be no meeting-ground between us. I cannot conceal from you my grief that I should lose a comrade so valiant, so faithful, so able and so honest as you have always been; but in serving a cause comradeships have got to be sacrificed…I suggest a dignified way of unfurling your banner.' (*CWMG*, 35-470). What was on his mind at the time of writing this is not clear. Nehru's letter, though sharply-worded here and there, was logical, candid, and by no means discourteous or hostile to Gandhi. It is difficult to think that it angered him. Then was Gandhi' letter a bluff? But that is not very much like him. Probably he was hurt when he thought that he was classified together with the exploiting classes, or he found that his *Hind Swaraj*, which was so dear to him, was so severely criticized.

Equally surprising was Nehru's reply dated 23 January. He at once surrendered, if we may call it that way. But how can we call it otherwise? He wrote, 'I have no particular banner to unfurl nor had I thought of the possibility of any warfare between you and me...No one has moved me and inspired me more than you...But even in the wider sphere am I not your child in politics...?... Perhaps you may have been led to think that I am going to start some kind of a campaign against your ideas and it was desirable that before doing so some kind of statement should be issued. I have no such intention...Please do not trouble to answer this letter. There is nothing to answer'.[88]

We know that he had by this time been deeply attached to Gandhi, as was shown in the above letter, and he knew it himself. But he would have been welcome by a large number of the educated and dissatisfied young people if he had parted with Gandhi politically and intellectually. The rise of these young people was already seen at the Madras Session of 1927. The surprise is that it did not seem to occur to Nehru at all to 'unfurl his own banner' as distinct from Gandhi's.

Perhaps the time was too early for that. The year 1934, when the CS Party was formed, would have been more suitable to do so. But even then he remained loyal to Gandhi, and became Gandhi's foremost lieutenant in keeping the socialists to the Congress. Gandhi kept telling socialists to consult and follow Nehru, and the advice was heeded to. For instance, he wrote on Nehru in "Letter to Narendra Deva", Chairman of the CSP, early in August 1934, that 'We are both labouring under a heavy handicap in that Jawaharlal, who has given us the *mantra* of socialism, is not in our midst (because of imprisonment), and I consider him to be the natural wearer of the Congress crown of thorns when I and other elderly men and women have been permitted to take well-deserved rest'. (*CWMG*, 58-275) He was already giving a hint here that Nehru would be his successor.

Another wonder on 1928 was that, in spite of the surrender on the part of Nehru, he did not revise his views, and did not speak Gandhi's language, especially on industrialization, or on constructive programme. Gandhi complained in "Letter to Jawaharlal Nehru" in September 1933 that 'I notice one gap in your letter. You make no mention of the various constructive activities of the Congress'. (*CWMG*, 55-429) Mark the words 'of the Congress', as Gandhi apparently thought it would be more appealing to Nehru's loyalty to the organization.

But Gandhi probably accepted him after the surrender. Perhaps this exchange in 1928 marked the beginning of their real cooperation which continued through thick and thin till the underlying differences appeared to the surface during the war years, as will be discussed later. At the Congress Session at Karachi in 1931, for instance, as M. Chalapathi Rau, who was in a position to know Nehru intimately, tells us in his *Gandhi and Nehru,* there was complete agreement between the two on the main Resolution which was achieved by 'a thorough exchange of views' during the 'early morning talks' of the two in February and March of that year.[89] He says that it is wrong to look at Nehru simply as Gandhi's 'nominated heir', as Nehru himself 'had to fight strenuous battles within the Congress and without, in Gandhi's time and after...'.[90] This supports what Meghnad Desai pointed out in the above. It played some part in all this that Nehru's Soviet enthusiasm gradually declined as the trials and mass executions became known to the world. Nehru incorporated Gandhi's above letter of 17 January 1928 *in toto* in his *A Bunch of Old Letters*[91] without a comment.

It is about this event that journalist M.J. Akbar writes in his *Nehru* that 'Apart from that burst of rebelliousness that provoked him (Jawaharlal) to ignore Gandhi in the first flush of his return in December 1927, and which resulted in a severe rebuke from the Mahatma, Jawaharlal never stepped out of the Gandhi line again, but it was equally true that there was a distinctive Nehruvian thrust to the policies he now espoused'.[92] Judith Brown's *Nehru A Political Life* points out on the relation between the two that 'Each needed the other...But the price was a constraint on his radicalism...and he would feel profound ambiguity in his relations with the more radical politicians, such as the Bengali Subhash Bose, who would in a sense have been his natural political allies...'.[93] Reena Nanda also refers in her *Kamaladevi Chattopadhyay A Biography* to 'Jawaharlal Nehru's habitual hesitation when confronted with a clear choice on socialist issues'.[94] This ambiguity or hesitation would not have been explainable without Gandhi's overwhelming presence. It must have been different, however, for the still younger generation. Economist V.K.R.V. Rao, for example, writes in *The Nehru Legacy* that 'To those like myself who were brought up on the Nehru magic and the Nehru traditions, socialism was an integral part of the freedom...'[95]

In "Speech At A.I.C.C. Meeting" at the beginning of 1942, Gandhi said that 'I have always said that not Rajaji, not Sardar Vallabhbhai, but Jawaharlal will be my successor. He says whatever is uppermost in his mind, but he always does what I want. When I am gone he will do what I am doing now. Then he will speak my language too...Ultimately he will speak my language. Even if this does not happen, I would at least die with this faith'. (*CWMG*, 75-224) Then in April the same year Gandhi said, in explanation of what he had said on the above occasion, in "Question Box" (subtitle, Guerrilla War) that 'That means that he will take my place when I am gone. He has never accepted my method in its entirety. He has frankly criticized it, and yet he has faithfully carried out the Congress policy largely influenced, when it was not solely directed, by me. Those like Sardar Vallabhbhai who have followed me without question cannot be called heirs. And everybody admits that Jawaharlal has the drive that no one else has in the same measure. And have I not said also that when I am gone he will shed the differences he often declares he has with me'. (*CWMG*, 76-51~52) This was a few months before the 'Quit-India' Movement and Gandhi probably wanted to make it beyond doubt where his wishes were before a crucial struggle would start. Narayanbhai told the author in October 2012 that Nehru was the natural choice because Patel was the only other candidate.

9. Gandhi and the Princely States

Gandhi, the States, and the British

Gandhi may also be said to have put a restraint on the aspiration of the State peoples, just like on that of the left-leaning educated youth. But he was quick to notice that the movement by those peoples had come up more or less to the same standard as in the British India, and also that, as he said in "States and the People" in November 1938, there came 'The almost simultaneous awakening in the various States'. (*CWMG*, 68-151) Perhaps because of this awakening, the British were also shrewd enough to notice that the Princes should be made use of as a political force against the Congress. The move was already manifest at the RTCs to which a number of Princes/their subordinates had been invited.

The British intention became clearer after the breaking out of World War II. The CWC requested the British in its "Working Committee's Manifesto" of 14 September 1939 'to declare in unequivocal terms what their war aims are in regard to democracy and imperialism…in particular, how these aims are going to apply to India…'(*CWMG*, 70-412).

The "Viceroy's Declaration", the reply that came a month later, practically said nothing except that, for the present, 'the establishment of a consultative group, representative of all major political parties in British India and of the Indian Princes…'(*CWMG*, 70-418), and, for the future, 'at the end of the war they (HMG) will be very willing to enter into consultation with representatives of the several communities, parties and interests, in India, and with the Indian Princes…' (*CWMG*, 70-417). Obviously not only the Princes but also the Muslims, or rather the Muslim League, and perhaps the Untouchables also, have been given attention here. Gandhi wrote about this in "Statement to the Press" the next day that 'The long statement made by the Viceroy simply shows that the old policy of divide and rule is to continue…The Congress asked for bread and it has got a stone'. (*CWMG*, 70-267) He also said in March 1940 in "Letter to Agatha Harrison" that the Princes and the League were the obstacles but 'The Princes are a new creation. They were never before brought into the picture'. (*CWMG*, 71-332)

It was in this background that the above CWC Manifesto ironically said that 'The Working Committee have noted that many Rulers of Indian States have offered their services and resources and expressed their desire to support the cause of democracy in Europe. If they must make their professions in favour of democracy abroad, the Committee would suggest that their first concern should be the introduction of democracy within their own States in which today undiluted autocracy reigns supreme'. (*CWMG*, 70-411)

One remarkable thing here is that Gandhi, perhaps because of his own Princely-State background, said that the new independent India would have a lot to learn from the States by way of their administrative know-how. In "Discussion with Rajendra Prasad" in June 1947, when the independence was just round the corner, he said 'I am sure they will be able to give us much that we lack and need. Congressmen know how to give fight, fill jails, but they lack the art of government, never having had any experience of administration. The States can provide us with all that if we know how to tap and utilize it'. (*CWMG*, 88-72) May be as an example of 'the art of government', Gandhi in "Speech at Meeting of M.P.S" (*sic*) at the time of the RTC said, 'The Hindus and Muslims are living more in peace in what is called Princes' India than in British India'. (*CWMG*, 48-59)

One may well wonder here if, had he lived longer, together with his opposition to land redistribution, and his theory of Trusteeship, the merger of the Indian States would have been delayed to some extent. We may read the signs of this in, for instance, "Letter to Premabehn Kantak" of 1935 in which he says that 'it is difficult to say anything today with certainty about the Indian States. But in a general way it can be stated that the *swaraj* Government will do nothing to impede the growth of their strength' (*CWMG*, 60-432), or, in "Travancore" of 1939 where he said that 'There is room, in my conception of an independent India, for States with Princes as constitutional trustees, as in Aundh'. (*CWMG*, 68-414) Aundh was a small Princely State in Satara District in Maharashtra, but even as late as in 1939 it was the only State out of five hundred strong that Gandhi could call a constitutional monarchy. Even in his "Speech at A.I.C.C. Meeting", the second of the three Quit India speeches he made on 7-8 August 1942, he said that 'I have kept a place for the Princes and the zamindars in India that I envisage'. (*CWMG*, 76-393) The inevitable question we are led to ask here is, was he after all on the side of the rich, or the poor. In the next chapter we will see show Jaiprakash Narayan's proposal for abolishing the rulership was objected to by Gandhi.

Notes

1. *Writings of Bipan Chandra*, 397~8.
2. Indulal Yajnik, *Gandhi as I Know Him*, 1~2.
3. *Ibid.*, 234.
4. Narayanbhai, *ibid.*, II, 385.
5. Vinoba, *ibid.*, 407.
6. Yajnik, *ibid.*, 57.
7. Gene Sharp, *Gandhi as a Political Strategist*, 25~39.

8. Narayanbhai, *ibid.*, I, 483, II, 5~6, 176, 211, 265, 429, III, 403, 457.
9. Sharp, *From Dictatorship to Democracy*, 20.
10. Hampton and Fayer, *Voices of Freedom*, 453~474.
11. H.Yamaguchi, "Some Issues Latent in Hind Swaraj", *Journal of Gandhian Studies,* January 2012, 1~21.
12. Narayanbhai, II, 644.
13. Arthur Herman, *Gandhi and Churchill*, 178.
14. B.R. Nanda, *Road to Pakistan*, 78~9.
15. Vinoba, *ibid.*, 412.
16. Vinoba, *ibid.*, 417.
17. G.P. Pradhan, *Lokamanya Tilak*, 135.
18. *Ibid.*, 134.
19. *Ibid.*, 57.
20. *Ibid.*, 151.
21. Narayanbhai, II, 602.
22. Thomas Weber, *Gandhi, Gandhism and Gandhians*, 5~18.
23. Narayanbhai, II, 576.
24. Narayanbhai, II, 137.
25. Judith Brown, *Gandhi*, 233.
26. N.K. Bose, *Studies in Gandhism*, 255.
27. Kamaladevi, *Memoirs*, 149~151.
28. Tendulkar, *Mahatma*, I, xiv~xv.
29. Narayanbhai, II, 653~665.
30. Yajnik, *ibid.*, 495.
31. *Ibid.*, 514.
32. Yajnik, *ibid.*, 288(d)~(e) (*sic*).
33. *Ibid.*, 154.
34. *Ibid.*, 148.
35. Sucheta Kripalani, "Leader and Teacher of Women", S. Radhakrishnan, ed., *ibid.*, 222.
36. Tridip Suhrud, *Reading Gandhi in Two Tongues and Other Essays*, 129.
37. N.K. Bose, *My Days with Gandhi.*
38. Pyarelal, *Mahatma Gandhi—The Last Phase*, 2 vols.
39. Sushila Nayar, "This I Saw", S. Radhakrishnan, ed., *ibid.*, 273.
40. Judith Brown, *Gandhi*, 248.
41. Narayanbhai, II, 676.
42. Bernard Imhasly, *Goodbye to Gandhi*, 170-1.
43. Vivek Pinto, *Gandhi's Vision and Values*, 141.
44. *Ibid.*, 146~51.
45. Samar Guha, *The Mahatma and the Netaji*, 135.
46. *Ibid.*, 148.
47. Narayanbhai, III, 450.
48. Joan V. Bondurant, *Conquest of Violence*, 45-104.
49. Shriman Narayan (Agarwal), *Gandhian Constitution*, 63~4.

50. *Ibid.*, 95.
51. *Ibid.*, 135.
52. Address for Defence by Bhulabhai Desai, Bimal Prasad ed., *Towards Freedom*, 857.
53. Vinoba, *ibid.*, 417.
54. Dietmar Rothermund, *Mahatma Gandhi*, 60~1.
55. Narayanbhai, III, 68.
56. *Ibid.*
57. Narayanbhai, III, 69.
58. Vinoba, *ibid.*, 417.
59. Shriman Narayan, *Gandhian Constitution*, 109.
60. *Ibid.*, 112.
61. Rajmohan Gandhi, "What If Gandhi Had Lived On?", *Outlook*, 23 August 2004, 32~3.
62. Rajmohan Gandhi, *Mohandas*, 675.
63. Pyarelal, *Mahatma Gandhi—The Last Phase*, II, 758.
64. Rothermund, *ibid.*, 117.
65. Yajnik, *ibid.*, 424.
66. *Report of the Committee appointed by the (All Parties) Conference to determine the Principles of the Constitution for India (Nehru Report)*, 105.
67. Yajnik, *ibid.*, 358.
68. *Essential Writings of Ambedkar*, 479.
69. *Writings of Bipan Chandra*, XX, 7, 31~2, 34, 76-fn, 145.
70. Sucheta Mahajan, Amit Kumar Gupta, ed., *Myth and Reality*, 64.
71. P C Joshi, *Mahatma Gandhi*, 46.
72. Kamaladevi, *Memoirs*, 175.
73. Kamaladevi, "Gandhi and Indian Socialists", S. Radhakrishnan, ed., *Mahatma Gandhi 100 Years*, 57.
74. Vinoba, *ibid.*, 394.
75. Suhrud, *ibid.*, 158.
76. Vinoba, 457.
77. *Ibid.*, 424.
78. Yajnik, 295~8.
79. Azad, *India Wins Freedom*, 33.
80. Pyarelal, *The Last Phase, II*, 256, Narayanbhai, *ibid.*, IV, 393.
81. N. K. Bose, Bose and Patwardhan, *Gandhi in Indian Politics*, 50~3.
82. Pyarelal, "India after Bapu", Radhakrishnan, ed., *ibid.*, 294~6.
83. Meghnad Desai, Michael Leifer, ed., *Asian Nationalism*, 93.
84. *Ibid.*, 112.
85. Inder Malhotra, *Indira Gandhi*, 189.
86. Raj Thapar, *All These Years*, 310.
87. *Writings of Bipan Chandra*, 155.
88. S. Gopal, ed., *Selected Works of Jawaharlal Nehru*, Vol. 3, 18~20.
89. Rao, *Gandhi and Nehru*, 98, 112.

90. *Ibid.*, 48.
91. Nehru, A Bunch of Old Letters, 56~8.
92. M.J. Akbar, *Nehru*, 187.
93. Judith Brown, *Nehru*, 87~8.
94. Reena Nanda, *Kamaladevi Chattopadhyay*, 74.
95. V.K.R.V. Rao, *The Nehru Legacy*, 53.

THREE
Gandhi's Socio-Economics

'To those who are hungry and unemployed God can dare reveal Himself only as work and wages as the assurance of food'. "Work Instead of Alms".

. —25 February 1939, *CWMG*, Vol. 68, p. 447.

1. Gandhi and the Current Trend in Poverty and Unemployment

Employment Question in India

As Gandhi got familiar with the condition of India after returning from South Africa, particularly of rural India he came to call the '700,000 villages', he began to say, quite often, that the peasants were in the state of unemployment for four to six months in a year. Either they did not have enough land, their own or other's, to work throughout the year, or, even if they had, did not have the necessary means of production like the irrigation facilities to put the land to productive use. As in the case of Anantpur village in Sagor District in CP, he said in "What I Saw in Anantpur" at the end of 1933 that 'The villagers are occupied not more than four months in the year'. (*CWMG*, 56-333)

During the tour of Orissa in 1934, for example, he said in "Interview to Associated Press of India" that 'I have always considered Orissa to be the poorest of our provinces. That impression was strengthened by intimate contact with the villages visited during the tour. The enforced idleness among people is appalling'. (*CWMG*, 58-67) The 'enforced idleness' was the term Gandhi often used.

We will take a brief look at how the situation on employment has, generally speaking, deteriorated after independence, with the help of two tables given below, from *The Hindu* of 11 April 2008, originally from pp. 23 and 24, respectively, from *Report of the Expert Group on Agricultural Indebtedness*, Finance Ministry, 2007. From Table 3.1, we notice that the number of operational holdings has doubled for the generally shrinking total area operated. The increase was phenomenal in the 1981-91 decade, the period of Indira Gandhi's and Rajiv Gandhi's Prime Ministerships. There has been a correspondingly sharp decline in the average area operated.

In Table 3.2, it is noteworthy that not only the ratio of the marginal holdings increased tremendously, as was to be expected from Table 3.1, the ratio of the large and medium ones decreased very rapidly. So there was no polarization but the general impoverishment in the agricultural sector, at least in terms of operational holdings, and one does not get the idea where the marginal farmers or the landless labourers would get employment. Therefore, there is all the more need for a food-for-work scheme like NREGA (National Rural Employment Guarantee Scheme, now MGNREGA with Mahatma Gandhi added to it), though it is essentially a stop-gap measure and does not amount to creating lasting employment.

Table 3.1: Operational Holdings

	1960-61	*70-71*	*81-82*	*91-92*	*2003*
No. of Operational Holdings (lakh)	508	571	710	935	1013
Area Operated (lakh ha)	1335	1257	1186	1251	1077
Average Area Operated (ha)	2.63	2.20	1.67	1.34	1.06

Source: The Hindu, 11 April 2008.

Table 3.2: Percentage of Operational Holding by Size

	1960-61	*2003*
Marginal	39.1	71.0
Small	22.6	16.6
Semi-medium	19.8	9.2
Medium	14.0	4.3
Large	4.5	0.8
Total	100.0	100.0

Source: *Ibid.*

As for land redistribution, V.K. Ramachandran quotes *Annual Report of the Ministry of Rural Development 2006-7* that, while 4.89 million acres of land had been distributed in the past sixty years, 63 million acres could have been distributed even under the per family ceiling of 25 acres.[1] Interestingly the latter figure is comparable, quite by accident, to what Vinoba set as the target of the Bhoodan Movement of 50 million acres. The enormous disparity between the two figures concerning land redistribution would amply show that the land redistribution, or land reform, have been difficult to achieve in the post-independent India, and remain to be so. It will show the deep rootedness of the 'vested interests', a term we will come up with again shortly in connection with the education of India after independence.

In an interview with Ram Dayal Munda, together with Vijay Upadhyay, both senior anthropologists, in Jharkhand in 2007, the author was told that in a one-crop area totally dependent on the rainfall like that, in the dry season a number of young men were put in trucks by the contractors and sent to their working places the whereabouts of which were known only to the contractors. When asked if the situation of the rural unemployment then was the same as in the days of Gandhi in the sense of 4-6 months of unemployment in a year, his reply was 'yes'. Indeed, the size of the internal migration in India, estimated on the basis of the latest 2011 National Census, amounts to '400' million persons, comprising one-third of the total population.[2] Economist C.H. Hanumantha Rao writes, referring to a study in 2004, that 'The decline in the relative contribution of agriculture to GDP is leading to out-migration of male labour resulting in feminisation of agriculture'.[3] Under the circumstances the voting ratio of 66 per cent the Indian voters have achieved in the latest 2014 Lok Sabha Elections must be remarkably high.

One of the causes of such a huge migration is undoubtedly the flood and drought which destroy the production system in the countryside. The year 2010 may not be a normal year, but some figures about the lack of rains are useful. By 16 August the Chief Minister of Bihar had already declared 28 out of the 38 Districts drought-afflicted, but the remaining 10 also were so declared on this day.[4] *The Indian Express* added that 26 Districts in Bihar were in the same drought condition the year before, and in the months of June and July that year there was only 392.8 ml of rain compared to the normal fall of 508.5 ml. The latter said also that the Eastern U.P. from Mirzapur District eastward, about a third of the State, had a rainfall of 319 ml as compared to the normal figure of 559 as of 13 August.[5] The point is that there are no other water-providing facilities in the case of rain failure.

We will borrow some figures from the NREGA to look at the situation from a different angle. *The Hindu* on 2 April 2008 writes that the Scheme was to be expanded from the then 330 to all the 604 Districts from April 2008 onwards. It had been launched by the Prime Minister in a village in Ranga Reddy District in Andhra Pradesh on 14 November 2004, Jawaharlal Nehru's birthday. It was to cover the 150 most backward Districts first and to concentrate on works like water conservation, drought-proofing, land development, road connectivity and such other infrastructural building.[6] In 2007-8, in the year before the expansion, thirty-one million households wanted to have work under the Scheme, and 30.8 million of them got it. So the ratio was very high. But those who got 100 days or more of work as stipulated amounted to only 3.226 million, barely 10 per cent of those who wanted it. The figures would suggest the presence of widespread unemployment.

The budget for 2008-9 was slated to be Rs. 16,000 Cr. The programme actually started with 200 Districts on 2 February 2006, expanded to 330, and then to the present 625(the latest total). It is, according to *India A Reference Annual 2012*, 'the flagship programme of the Government that directly touches lives of the poor and promotes inclusive growth'. The last but one Lok Sabha Elections were held in 2009. A prominent political scientist of India said then that NREGA was the only piece of good governance and the then Ruling coalition was to fight the Elections almost on the strength of it alone. Incidentally the budget for Defence was going to exceed Rs. 100,000 crore for the first time in the fiscal 2008-9. The figure for 2014-5, made known on 10 July 2014 by the Finance Minister's speech, is Rs. 229,000 crore, which is near $ 40 billion.

At the end of the first week of July 2013, the Government of India decided to subsidize food (grains) to the 75 per cent of the rural, and 50 per cent of the urban population who are considered to be poor. Put together they amount to 800 million, two-thirds of the total population. It takes $23 billion every year to subsidize food on this scale. NREGA is not a programme for subsidy, nor simply for food for work, but for payment in cash for building productive capacities in the countryside which are so much in need, and as such was something new. It picked up some elements from the Gandhian ideas of labour, discussed in Chapter 1. The new subsidy plan suggests that the NREGA is not succeeding. But in the eyes of Gandhi the new proposal would have a much larger element of living on relief, or on alms, instead of earning one's relief and livelihood, that Gandhi so much used to warn against for the millions of refugees, and even some ex-INA soldiers, as we have seen. He used to say, for example, that 'Let each suffering individual earn his relief by working for it'.

Arjun Sengupta Commission

The National Commission for the Enterprises in the Unorganized Sector (Arjun Sengupta Commission) published its *Report* in 2007, said to be the first and the most detailed of the sort. It said that '...the whole approach to planning in India should change. Only maximizing economic growth should not be the aim...The normal market mechanism benefits only the middle and the higher income groups, for the rest it is the government's job to ensure economic development...the disadvantaged groups that constitute an unbelievable 836 million people or 77 per cent of the population. For the remaining over 235 million, they are in a position to take care of themselves'.

The *Report* further says that the contrast between the above two groups is one of 'shining India' and 'downtrodden India'. The latter of these two is sub-divided into four groups by the per capita consumption per day, into (1) extremely poor, with up to Rs. 9 per day, (2) poor, up to Rs. 12, (3) marginal, up to Rs. 15, and (4) vulnerable, up to Rs. 20, meaning at this time $ 0.5, the World Bank standard of poverty. Out of their total of 836 million, 82 per cent are Dalits, Scheduled Tribes, Other Backward Classes (hereafter OBCs), and poor Muslims. 79 per cent of them are in the unorganized sector. The *Report* said that India now had the first Government committed to the upliftment of the poor, and recommended that the NREGA, which was successful, should be extended to the whole of

India and the limit of 100 days of work a year should be done away with. (*The Hindu*, 5 September 2007)

Disparities in Education

The *Report* also said that the average number of years of education of those poor people was three years and a half. This is the most staggering figure in the *Report.*[7] We will take this opportunity of looking a little into the disparities in education in India. Shashi Tharoor wrote that 'Today, an IIT degree is held in the same reverence in the West as one from MIT'.[8] He is of course right, and the man who laid the foundation of these superb facilities is rightly being held in high esteem, at least in certain quarters. Historian Ramachandra Guha writes, for instance, that 'To explain the rise of the software sector...perhaps the story should really begin with Jawaharlal Nehru's government, which had the foresight to set up a chain of high-quality engineering schools, and the wisdom to retain English as the language of higher education and of interest and intranational communication'.[9] Without retaining English the growth of tne technological education would have been unthinkable. However, the point is how the growth of these Indian MITs and of the whole higher education on one hand, and the meagre three and a half years of schooling for the great majority of the people on the other, have been compatible so far. The government policy seems to be a continuing emphasis on the IITs, Central Universities and other institutions of higher education. It speaks of the universalization of the secondary education but not of the primary education. Is the gap going to be still wider? The answer seems to be 'yes'.

The author is reminded of what a knowledgeable couple from Jaisalmer, Rajasthan, told him early in 2008. They said that apart from the four biggest cities, Bangalore, and Ahmedabad, there are no facilities for the training of the youth in India for the world standard. We will discuss Gandhi's educational views elsewhere. But this much of the widening gap is what he did not quite foresee in his days.

The findings by G. Balatchandirane are very interesting in this connection. He said that in India after independence 'thc higher education sector got more than what would be considered a fair share in the context of a country at the initial stages of modernisation'.

Two reasons exist. One was there were 'vested interests' who wanted good higher education for their families. Indeed the comparative growth of higher per unit of population education in terms of the number of the institutions and the students in different Indian States would be largely explained by the presence or otherwise of such vested interests who could exert pressure on the educational policies. The other was the economic model India was following needed well-trained professionals.

Balatchandirane then writes. 'This invariably slowed down the spread of elementary education and hence the overall economic development of the country. If there had been less investments in higher education in the beginning, perhaps India would not have had world class institutions like the IITs by the 1950s itself, but there would have been equitable distribution of wealth as a large share of the population would have had equitable access to elementary education. India may not be in the news for the waves it is currently making in the IT sector; but then it would not be so far behind China in manufacturing if it had a large section of the population literate early'.[10] A very exciting view to say the least.

In an article titled "The India Model" in *Foreign Affairs*, Gurcharan Das put the matter in this way. 'They (many Indians) wonder fearfully if India is going to skip an industrial revolution altogether, jumping straight from an agricultural economy to a service economy'.[11] But even in the service economy, Jean Dreze and Amartya Sen wrote under the title "Putting Growth in its Place" several years later that 'One indication that something is not quite right with India's development strategy is the fact that India has started falling behind every other South Asian country (with the partial exception of Pakistan) in terms of social indicators, even as it is doing so well in terms of per capita income.'[12] It may be of interest to refer here to a study by Hirashima Shigemochi on the implication of the educational history of modern Japan for her agricultural development.[13]

Gandhi in *Hind Swaraj* denied, or rather underestimated, the significance of literacy as such. He later changed his mind, and told so to some of the co-workers. His *Nayee Talim* (New Education or Wardha scheme of education) was one shape his ideas developed into. Gandhi, if alive today, would be in two minds of whether to take Nehru's policy or to go for Arjun Sengupta's and

Balatchandirane's thinking. But there is no doubt that the latter would be much closer to him. Rothermund says that Gandhi saw the evolution of the Atomic Bomb in the progress of science and technology.[14] Vinoba notes similarly. It implies that in Gandhi's view there is an element of violence in science and technology.

2. Some Developmental Scenarios

Gandhi and Development

We will consider what Gandhi would do given the present conditions of employment and education, or would have done under similar circumstances. But first it may be worth asking if Gandhi himself showed the way to the creation of employment in the villages, by, say, introducing multiple cropping, building irrigation and other infrastructural facilities, or calling attention to other means of increasing productivity like better seeds, better cattle, better implements. There are signs that he was interested in better seeds or better cattle, but generally the answer is 'no'. For a man who said so much about the peasants being unemployed, he did not put forward any systematic idea to mitigate the situation, above all to create employment in the villages, except in *khadi* and village industries. On the major aspects of agricultural activities, he always pleaded 'ignorant'. Neither do we see that there was any agricultural expert among his immediate co-workers, perhaps apart from a few like J.C. Kumarappa. Who was there to integrate, systematize and theorize the ideas Gandhi seemed to throw at his co-workers whenever they occurred to him from time to time?

Were there any prominent politicians before or after independence known for their interest in agriculture? Before independence there was hardly any, as they were busy achieving the freedom of the country. But not so after independence, and one of them was the subject of an article "Jagjivan Ram and inclusive agricultural growth" by M.S. Swaminathan.[15] It says that Ram served twice as Union Minister of Agriculture, 1967-70 and 1974-77, both under Indira Gandhi. Shortly after coming to the office, he took up the new agricultural strategy which C Subramaniam, his predecessor, had started in 1964. He demanded that the spread of the High-Yielding

Varieties be tackled with utmost attention, and Swaminathan himself, an agro-scientist, was requested to give him a monthly briefing. It came to be known that the wheat production would reach a record high of 17 million tonnes from the previous 12 million by the beginning of 1968. Ram played a catalytic role in the spread of HYV wheat. He also took care of providing credit and inputs to small farmers. Ever since he resigned from the Bihar Assembly over the irrigation cess he remained interested in the environmental issues also, practicing organic farming himself. He was also keen on the income diversification, dairy, fishing, and agro-industries.

Would it be possible to compare Gandhi to Jagjivan Ram? In December 1945, Gandhi visited R.G. Casey, the last but one British Governor of still undivided Bengal. Casey writes in his memoirs *Personal Experience: 1939-46,* that 'In December and January, I was to see him many times...In my many talks and correspondence with Gandhi, there was one subject which clearly dominated his mind—the encouragement of cottage industries to absorb the great deal of idle time of the tens of millions of the Indian peasantry. He was impatient of any proposals for irrigation schemes to enable them to grow more crops, or of industrialization to absorb redundant labour. Home cotten growing, home spinning and weaving, and the like (encourage the cultivator to grow his own clothes—Casey) filled his mind and he talked and wrote to me at great length about it'.[16] From this, we will have to conclude that at that later stage also Gandhi's mind was closed to wider agricultural or industrial development. It is all the more remarkable as Bengal had just suffered a great famine owing to the war, around 1943, when tens of lakhs of people had perished or become refugees.

We will recall that the *Arjun Sengupta Report* said, 'the whole approach to planning should change', and 'for the rest (low income groups) it is the government's job to ensure economic development' (rather than to be entrusted to the market). We may call such an idea broadly an alternative path of development here. We may see that some such thinking has emerged by now and some of it had already been provided in Gandhi's lifetime. We may take a look at some of them to see if these ideas have had any legacy of Gandhi's thinking, or alternatively have had any impact on his thinking. It will help us to examine how Gandhi is relevant in this age.

Some Alternative Thinking on Development

1. M. Visveswaraya's *Planned Economy for India*, 1934. This will be discussed in detail in Section (6) of this chapter.

2. A letter by Sam Higginbottom, Director of the Agricultural Institute, Allahabad, to Gandhi, proposing a programme for the training of village workers who were, in his opinion, very much short in India. It says, 'The details of the programme will include proper use of all village wastes for soil enrichment; the prevention of erosion; the right system of rotation of crops; the selection of better seed, methods and implements; cattle improvement through selective breeding and proper feeding; co-operation for purchasing and marketing of village products, for road improvement; development of existing village industries that process village products and, wherever necessary, the introduction of new village industries to round out the village life'. (*CWMG*, 60-110~111) This was a scenario for all-out development of agriculture. Gandhi recommended this programme in "His Economic Faith" early in 1935. It is not clear if he tried to incorporate them into his own Constructive Programme.

3. E.M.S.'s "Minute of Dissent to the Kuttikrishna Menon Committee Report on Malabar (the British-ruled part of Kerala) Tenancy Reforms 1939".[17] E.M.S. Namboodiripad (an Indian communist from Kerala, hereafter E.M.S.) was a member of the Malabar Tenancy Reforms Committee appointed by the Congress Government in the then Madras Province where he was a member of the Provincial Council. He submitted the longest minute of dissent, in which he wrote that the landed in Malabar leased out most of the cultivated land to the tenants, got a total net rent of Rs. 2.5 crores from it a year, 'If the payment of this amount goes in hand with some social service rendered by the landlords as a class, it would be quite justified', but 'it (landlordism) gets its rent for no service rendered to society, that therefore it is parasitic in nature, and that any scheme of economic planning should include its abolition'.

E.M.S. claims that he was speaking not as a socialist or communist, but for the 'development of capitalism'. If the landlordism was abolished without compensation, out of the rent the peasantry was paying, Rs. 137 lakhs would remain with them 'for the actual consumption of the peasant. With more food for himself, his family and his cattle, he will become a sturdy and independent peasant...Children will flock to the schools and sick ones will be properly attended to'. But it is not the peasant alone who stands to gain by it. Industries, large and small, will also get their share with the improvement of the countryside... Special mention should be made of the textile and tile industries, because the first thing that the peasant would, perhaps, do is to house himself and clothe himself better'.

This is a far-sighted scenario for inclusive development based on a drastic land reform which includes the related development of agriculture, industry, and the social sector. E.M. S., however, said, in "Talking about Kerala" with V.K. Ramachandran in 1992, that a major constraint in Kerala is that 'people here have been taught to think that development means only the development of social services; they don't think that industry and agriculture should be developed'.[18]

It would be exciting if some economic calculation can be made along similar lines for the whole of India now. Does not the highly developed IT industry interested in drawing such a blueprint? The above Minute provided the basis for the policies of the first E.M.S. government in Kerala in 1957-59, although what was achieved was, naturally, far less than he had envisaged in the Minute. There is no evidence that Gandhi had an opportunity to see it. E.M.S. later said that 'This minute of dissent was the starting point of my study of socio-economic conditions in Kerala'.[19]

4. Jayaprakash Narayan's draft resolution as quoted in Gandhi's "Jayaprakash's Picture". When the Congress Session was meeting at Ramgarh in March 1940, Jayaprakash Narayan (hereafter JP) sent a draft resolution to Gandhi for the CWC to consider. According to "Discussion At Working Committee" Gandhi recommended it saying that 'It will place before the country a picture of the kind of freedom we aim at...', but dropped it because of opposition (*CWMG*, 71-337). JP's draft said, among other things, that 'The life of the villages shall be reorganized and the villages shall be made self-governing units, self-sufficient in as large a measure as possible. The land laws of the country shall be drastically reformed on the principle that land shall belong to the actual cultivator alone, and that no cultivator shall have more land than is necessary to support his family on a fair standard of living. This will end the various systems of landlordism on the one

hand and farm bondage on the other'. No other proposal in the Congress circles has ever gone as far as this on abolition of landlordism and land redistribution. Gandhi said that 'As an ideal to be reduced to practice as soon as possible after India comes into her own, I endorse in general all except one of the propositions enunciated by Shri Jayaprakash'. The exception was what JP wrote on the Indian States toward the end of his draft which read 'there shall be complete democratic government established...there shall not be any titular heads of the States in the persons of Rajas and Nawabs'. Here JP talks of the abolition of the Rulers, but not of the Indian States as such. Gandhi explained the difference between the two in this way. 'Perhaps Shri Jayaprakash has no faith in the Princes automatically surrendering their autocracy. I have'. (*CWMG*, 71-422~425)

5. Gandhi's own programme for Village Swaraj, written on 18 July 1942 and published in *Harijan* of 26 July under "Question Box". (*CWMG*, 76-308~9) These dates are significant for the reason mentioned above. Gandhi wrote that 'My idea of village *swaraj* is that it is a complete republic...Thus every village's first concern will be to grow its own food crops and cotton for its cloth...it will grow *useful* money crops...It will have its own waterworks, ensuring clean water supply...Education will be compulsory up to the final basic course...There will be no castes such as we have today with their graded untouchability...The government of the village will be conducted by a Panchayat of five persons annually elected by the adult villagers, male and female...'. This little paper thus touches many different aspects of village life and can be seen as one type of development scenario. It should be noted that he had adopted the idea of universal suffrage, even for the villagers. Swiss scholar Gilbert Etienne said that Gandhi's idea was close to that of Charles Metcalf's argument of 'little republics', which was not true to historical reality.[20] It is Henry Maine's *Village Communities* that Gandhi mentioned in the Appendices to *Hind Swaraj*.

He has discussed many other things related to this note at different places though in a piecemeal manner. He for example discussed the high child mortality in India, and the 'heavy expenses' for a girl's wedding, in "Child Mortality" (*CWMG*, 16-468~471) and "Infanticide of Girls" (*CWMG*, 24-381), as early as in 1920 and 1924, respectively. He is also concerned in his "Awfulness of Child-Marriage" that almost

40 per cent of the girls in the age group of 10 to 15 are married according to the Census of 1931. (*CWMG*, 62-122) For the previous Census of 1921, Gandhi quoted Sir Ganga Ram in his "Enforced Widowhood" to show the already many, and increasing, number of widows up to 15 of age in the Indian society. (*CWMG*, 31-262~263) A long time afterwards he wrote in "A Letter" on the widows in Hindu society that 'Hinduism has denied to women the right to remarry…if they (men) must remarry, let them select as their partner a widow…'. (*CWMG*, 88-104).

As a social reformer he should have said categorically that Hindu women should be allowed to remarry and the taboo be removed. Only a few months before his death he wrote in "Fragment of a Letter" that 'In no other country are widows insulted as much as they are in our country'. (*CWMG*, 90-31) We have discussed his general idea of the status of women in Chapter One. On the women in the struggle, he says in his "Fragment of Letter to Chhaganlal Joshi" in September 1930, after the Salt March, that 'It is good indeed that women have come out'. (*CWMG*, 44-146) He also wrote a few months later on 'the women of India' in 'the last decade' in his "Interview to the Press" in January 1931 that 'They have brought *swaraj* nearer. They have added several inches to their own height and that of the nation'. (*CWMG*, 45-129) He did not fail to praise Kasturba after her death. A couple of months before his own death, Gandhi wrote in another "Fragment of a Letter" that 'whatever place our women achieved today is due to Kasturba's courage, purity and steadfast faith'. (*CWMG*, 90-121).

He was careful about water throughout, which comes from his interest in health. He wrote, for example, in "Letter to Maganlal Gandhi", the then Manager of Sabarmati Ashram, early in 1924 that 'Is not the water to blame for so much illness there?' (*CWMG*, 33-7) In connection with health, in "Wells and Ponds" on 12 January 1930, not long before the Salt March, he wrote 'Many of the villages have only one pond, where the cattle drink and people bathe or wash, cleanse utensils and wash clothes, and people fetch the water for drinking and cooking from the same pond'. His advice was 'Never should utensils be cleansed or clothes washed in a pond from which drinking water is drawn'. (*CWMG*, 42-390~391) On the village health he said in "Diseases in Villages" at the end of 1929 that 'It has been the experience of all my colleagues who have lived in villages that fever, constipation and boils are the most common ailments'. (*CWMG*, 42-281) When sickness became prevalent at Segaon (later Sevagram) in its early days, he wrote, 'The illnesses at Segaon have set me thinking. I feel that as long as the water there does not improve, the place should be abandoned...'(*CWMG*, 68-85) A little more than a year later in "Letter to Sharda G. Chokhawala" from Segaon he wrote 'Here the place has almost been turned into a hospital'. (*CWMG*, 71-75, see 93 also) Even in Noakhali in 1947 he called the attention in "Discussion with Members of Chandipur-Chandirgaon Gram Seva Sangh" that the villagers were using the water of the same tank for various purposes, therefore, the water was not clean, and offered some suggestions. (*CWMG*, 86-310) He also warned against the villagers' spitting and clearing their noses as the causes of many diseases (*CWMG*, 86-439)

For the philosophical side of keeping health, he wrote in "Letter to Premabehn Kantak" in 1932 that 'If the body is not yours, but is a trust given to you by God, you should certainly give some time for keeping it fit'. (*CWMG*, 50-307) He himself gave as his motto, in "Speech at Sevagram" in 1945, 'prevention is better than cure'. (*CWMG*, 79-124) A couple of years later he wrote in "Letter to a Naturopath" that 'The true function of the medical profession, as I conceive it, is not to prescribe cures...but to prevent illness by teaching the people to observe the rules of health'. (*CWMG*, 88-24)

Toward the end of his life he increasingly leaned on the idea of nature cure. He said at "Speech at Prayer Meeting, Bombay" in March 1946 that 'If once we decide that what cannot be shared by the millions should be taboo for us, we are driven to nature as the only cure...'. (*CWMG*, 83-263) But he admits that there is a difference of opinion among the believers of nature cure. He writes in "Letter to Dinshaw K. Mehta", his nature cure doctor, early in 1946, 'I don't have any faith in vaccination', but Dinshaw had it. (*CWMG*, 82-349) Incidentally, with the progress in age, Gandhi lost all, or almost all, of his teeth. Decayed teeth cannot be left to nature cure. One thing which has not been written about so far is if any dentist or dentists attended to them. Or could he have been his own dentist in any way?

About the leprosy patients, he said in "Discussion with Dr. Chesterman" early in 1939 that 'I have visited many mission hospitals, seen the wonderful work of the missionaries among lepers. This work may be called their monopoly and speciality, for practically no one else has come in to take it up'. (*CWMG*, 68-419) The activity of the non-missionary Indians was yet to be seen then. But he was paying a minute attention to the emergence of its signs. At the end of 1944, he visited Dattapur Colony near Sevagram and wrote some praising words for Manohar Diwan, Vinoba's disciple, for his 'pioneering work in this field' as "Remark in Visitors' Book". (*CWMG*, 78-387) When two leprosy relief workers from the South visited Gandhi early in 1945 he wanted them to make a detailed plan in "Advice to Leprosy Relief Workers" (*CWMG*, 79-114) There he also said that 'My interest in leper work is as old as my residence in South Africa'. As he said in "Speech at Prayer Meeting" on 23 October 1947, 'A small conference is being organized at Wardha very soon through a committee. People engaged in this work will be meeting there on the 30th of this month'. (*CWMG*, 89-394) He must have been very sorry that he could not go. It would have been his home-coming since August 1946 also.[21]

The author had an opportunity of interviewing Dr. Ma Haide (George Hatem) who, as Advisor to the Minister of Health of the Chinese Government, was in charge of the leprosy relief work in China. One of the things he told the author, on 30-31 March 1985, was that while in China the presence of leprosy patients was gradually being confined to the two southern Provinces of Yunnan and Hainan, in India that stage was yet to be reached. He had visited India by then.

On still different subjects, in "Letter to M.I. David" in 1931 Gandhi was expressing a hope for bee-keeping (*CWMG*, 46-349) He is asking 'What is the lowest yield required from a cow to make her self-supporting?' in "Letter to T. Titus" in 1933 (*CWMG*, 54-305). He was of the opinion that the greatest loss during the Second World War years was that of the cattle wealth, and 'Lakhs of cows and bullocks were slaughtered by the (foreign) army for food'. (*CWMG*, 85-330) After years of comparison, he reached the conclusion, as he said in "Speech at Prayer Meeting" in 1947, that 'Buffalo's milk is not as good as cow's milk'. (*CWMG*, 87-359) In "A Note" he was giving the average quantity of milk a cow gives per day in India with that of several other countries. (*CWMG*, 89-79) He was interested in fishing in Travancore (*CWMG*, 85-350), and in East Bengal (*CWMG*, 86-388).

On education, we have seen how Gandhi would have looked at today's science and technology. On literacy, he called the attention to the fact that 'there is more illiteracy in India today than there was fifty years ago' in "Pertinent Questions" in 1924 (*CWMG*, 24-564). On literacy, however, he was not all for it. In *Hind Swaraj* he cites an example of a peasant who 'earns his bread honestly. He has ordinary knowledge of the world. He knows fairly well how he should behave towards his parents, his wife, his children and his fellow-villagers. He understands and observes the rules of morality. But he cannot write his own name. What do you propose to do by giving him a knowledge of letters? Will you add an inch to his happiness?'(*CWMG*, 10-54) This was his starting point. In "Letter to P.N. Rajbhoj" in 1933 he wrote that 'We have had hundreds of saints, they were not all learned men. Jesus, Mahomed and others were unlettered. It should not at all be taken to imply that I am opposed to formal learning but the importance given to it today is beyond proportion'(*CWMG*, 55-52) It would be possible to think that Kasturba was a model for him of an illiterate but virtuous person, a female version of the above peasant.

In this connection it would not be widely off the mark to reproduce a letter the author wrote to the Editor, *Outlook*, and was printed in its 12 July 2010 number in full. It will speak for itself. It reads, 'I've been impressed by the glittering expansion of India's professional colleges (June 28). However, it is difficult to avoid the feeling that they are overwhelmingly urban-oriented, probably more so with the passage of time, in the sense that they are there to help create employment in urban areas. Some of the figures from the *India Labour Report* 2009, referred to in the article, would testify to this. This applies to those colleges located in rural districts, too. Why is it that one hardly finds any colleges in the fields of agriculture, dairy, forestry or fishing? Will this glittering expansion be of help toward the solution of such problems as drought? I am reminded of Mr. Gandhi who used to say that in independent India, cities should come to the help of villages. Is he no more?'

The author heard a presentation on the condition of higher education in a prosperous rural area at a seminar organized by CRRID (Centre for Research in Rural and Industrial Development) at

Chandigarh in 2006. A professor from a university in Punjab told us that although they reserved 5 per cent for the students from rural families it could not be filled. In an agriculturally prosperous State where 66 per cent of the population lives in rural areas, only 4 per cent of the University students are from them and the ratio is still lower in the medical or engineering colleges, he said.

Back to Gandhi, on what we call ecological question today, in his "Speech at Public Meeting, Noakhali" in 1925, said to have been attended by over 25,000 people, most of them Muslims, he reportedly talked about the danger of erosion by the rivers in addition to the usual Hindu-Muslim relations, untouchability, and *charkha*. (*CWMG*, 27-97~98) More than twenty years later, he would make a pilgrimage on foot from village to village in this area in search of Hindu-Muslim reconciliation against heavy odds.

On the forest cover, he said about his own Kathiawar in "Plea for Voluntary Federation" that 'no common waterworks will answer the purpose (of a proper supply of water even in dry years) for all time unless there is a long-view scheme of afforestation…The Princes and the people have to combine to plant trees on an extensive scale'. (*CWMG*, 70-118) In "Speech at Prayer Meeting' shortly before independence he said on the importance of the trees that 'Where trees are in abundance, rainfall too is abundant…It is a law of nature that where there are no trees there is no rainfall and the land soon becomes a desert'. (*CWMG*, 88-425)

Finally on spinning, an interesting letter has been addressed to Gandhi by someone who was studying the All-India Spinners' Association, and was partly reproduced in his "How I Discovered the Spinning—Wheel" in 1928. It said, 'Nothing is more wrong than to think that you have asked India to spin and that India has begun to spin driven to do so by you. The truth is rather that the millions in the villages have driven you to it—to be their agent for disposing of all their yarn'. (*CWMG*, 37-287) Its tone has got much in common with a paragraph from P.C. Joshi's book quoted already. Just in passing, Yajnik writes that when he visited Gandhi at his Kocharab Ashram as early as in 1916, he found him 'weaving on a small hand-loom'[22], the spinning-wheel not having been discovered by then.

From the above, it would be clear that a lot of what Gandhi said and thought is still valid today, although similarly a lot has lost its contemporary significance.

6. Shriman Narayan Agarwal's *The Gandhian Plan of Economic Development for India*, 1944, with Gandhi's Forward (*CWMG*, 78-200). This was written by Gandhi's close and young disciple. He also wrote *Gandhian Constitution for Free India* fairly soon afterwards, and *Vinoba—His Life and Work* some time later. Both are discussed elsewhere in this book. This one was written after Visveswaraya's Plan, National Planning Committee's work, and the Bombay Plan by eight industrialists, to place Gandhi's ideas before the public in a systematic manner.[23]

It says that the 'four corner-stones' of Gandhian Plan/Gandhian Economics were simplicity, non-violence, sanctity of labour and human values, (*CWMG*, 15~29), and the Village Communism/Gram Panchayats would be placed on these bases. Part Two of the book discusses main sectors of the economy in some detail. Interestingly the industries are classified in three different categories. First, the 'Allied Industries to Agriculture' include Animal Husbandry, Dairy Farming, Tanning and Leather Work, Fruit, Vegetable, and Forest Industries. Second is the 'Cottage Industries' including Khadi, Paper Making, Oil Extraction, Paddy-husking, and fifteen 'miscellaneous industries' such as Gur, Bee-keeping, Soap, Poultry, Carpentry, Smithy, Match, Pottery, Tiles and Brick-making. Finally come the 'Basic Industries' which include Defence, Power, Mining, Machinery and Machine Tools, Heavy Engineering, and Chemical. It is not clear if Gandhi really acknowledged the establishment of those industries in the third category.

J.C. Kumarappa's *Economy of Permanence* may be grouped in the same category. It is also with Gandhi's Foreword (*CWMG*, 81-145), where Gandhi calls Kumarappa 'This doctor of our village industries'. It was in 1945. Kumarappa added Part II on planning shortly before Gandhi's murder.

7. Radha Kamal Mukerjee's *Planning the Countryside, First Report*, 1946. A well-known economist in the Lucknow School of Social Sciences, he wrote this as the Economic Advisor to the Maharaja of Gwalior. He stressed the coordinated development of agriculture, dairy farming, forestry, cooperatives, tenancy reforms, literacy, public health, and village industries for an integrated rural development in the then Gwalior State. Probably no other such proposal came forward from the Indian economist before

independence.[24] As P.C. Joshi, himself trained in this School, wrote in his paper "Founders of the Lucknow School and Their Legacy", 'At one of his (Radha Kamal's) lectures "On Agriculture and Industrialism" delivered at St. Stephen's College, Delhi on November 27, 1917, Mahatma Gandhi presided. In his concluding remarks on RK's address, Gandhi upheld Mukerjee's institutional approach and observed that "the principles of Western economics could not be applied to Indian conditions in the same way as the rules of grammar and syntax of one language would not be applicable to another language". Gandhi eloquently appealed to students "to read economics out-of-doors, in the fields, cottages and workshops, in relation to actual facts and conditions instead of cramming Western economics heedless and forgetful of the phenomena around them"'.[25] This is not in the *CWMG*. P.C. Joshi told the author in an interview at Delhi on 18 August 2003 that RK had reached a point logically which Gandhi 'intuitively' came to grasp, the lecture was arranged by Principal Rudra of St. Stephens who knew Gandhi, and Gandhi said afterwards that if Radha Kamal was there, there was no more need of him!

8. Gandhi's support to the All-India Compost Conference planned by Mirabehn, about a month before his death. He said in "Speech at Prayer Meeting" that 'fertilizers are required (for food production) for the import of which we have to spend crores of rupees. The fertilizers cause erosion of the soil…It (the Conference) recommended ways to make compost and what is called organic manure' (*CWMG*, 90-264). He also said in "Compost Manure" that 'The task undertaken by Mirabehn is of immense magnitude'. (*CWMG*, 90-271) Much earlier he published "Cowdung Cakes or Manure" in 1929 where he said that 'Cowdung is mostly used for making cakes for fuel…(but) To make full and good use of cowdung is to use it as manure…'. (*CWMG*, 42-170~171)

9. Chipko Movement. Sunderlal Bahuguna and his wife, Vimla, the initiators of the Movement, say that 'The (Chipko) movement went on from 1973 to 1981'. It started because the felling of trees by the government 'created landslides and the drying up of water sources', and the villagers protected the trees by hugging them. Their slogan was "What do the forests bear? Soil, water, and pure air." Because of this Movement 'Many women went to jail. But they did

not yield.' Sunderlal, by the way, had met Gandhi on the day before the assassination. He said that in the course of the movement 'I have walked from Kashmir to Kohima, from the western side of the Himalayas to the eastern side, a distance of 4,870 kilometres and spread the message of the Chipko movement'. Then the construction of the Tehri Dam over Ganga started and 'We launched a non-violent movement against it'. One sifnificant characteristic of these movements was they 'spread through folk songs. In a people's movement the appeal is not to the head but to the heart'.[26] Ishizaka Shinya followed the birth and the growth of the anti-Tehri Dam Movement, and analyzed the Gandhian influence, including that of Bahuguna's, upon it.[27]

The Chipko Movement spread to some other parts of the country as, for example, the Appiko Movement in northern Karnataka from 1983. Shortly before its start Bahuguna himself had visited the area.

The Chipko Movement is an example of NGO activities which have been mushrooming in India in recent decades. The Anna Hazare Movement together with the other two referred to by Vivek Pinto in Chapter Two also belong to this category. So does the Narmada Bachao Andolan (NBA). NBA was started by a number of activists, whom we may call Gandhians at least to some extent, to protect land, forest, water and the tribal people who depend on them for their life in the Narmada Valley in Western India. The Narmada is the longest river in India flowing westward into the Arabian Sea, which originates in a Central Indian Highland called Amar Kantak. We will also cite an example of the Ekta Parishad here, an NGO of mostly young workers with an eye on the rural development in its various aspects, with its Headquarters at Bhopal, Madhya Pradesh. One might even place Vinoba's Bhoodan Movement here, but that is taken up separately later in this Chapter.

10. *Mandal Commission Report (Report of the Backward Classes Commission)* 1980. This is not a general development scenario. It, however, stresses land reform as most important for uplifting the backward classes, and is not simply a set of recommendations for reservation for government schools and the government posts, as is often supposed to. It says in its Recommendations that 'until the stranglehold of the existing production relations is broken through radical land reforms, the abject dependence of under privileged classes

on the dominant higher castes will continue indefinitely. In fact there is already a sizable volume of legislation on the statute books to abolish zamindari, place ceilings on land holdings and distribute land to the landless. But in actual practice its implementation has been halting, half-hearted and superficial...It is the Commission's firm conviction that a radical transformation of the existing production relations is the most important single step that can be taken for the welfare and upliftment of all backward classes'. (First Part)[28]

The Recommendations also include expansion of the reservation for the OBCs. What about women? The Indian society seems to be moving toward making reservation for women. But some quotations from Kamaladevi may be worth listening to. She was against fixing a quota for women. She said, 'They (women workers in the pre-independence days) never sought reservations for women in any sphere... They claimed and struggled forcefully for equality but the claim was on merit and not on sex alone which they felt cut at the very foundation of the principle of equality and betrayed a lack of self-confidence... (but after independence) all the old dynamics have melted away...women have since begun to seek the path of the weak and the defeated'.[29] She was also against any reservation not based on merit. As Shakuntala Narasimhan, one of her biographers, quotes, Kamaladevi says in *Of Reason Fragmented*, 'To accommodate minorities and weaker sections, the Constitution of India is mutilated from time to time...Every single citizen is forced to think of himself or herself as a member of a certain socio-economic group, and no more as an Indian, proud of being a citizen of a great country. Whole groups, under some social label or other, now strive to become 'backward''.[30] Would Gandhi have approved of it? It seems he would. But as Reena Nanda writes in her own biography of Kamaladevi, she was also against Nehru's linguistic reorganization of the States, the idea Gandhi had originally proposed, on the ground that it would fortify 'ethnic identities' and strengthen 'linguistic chauvinism'.[31]

11. Comprehensive Land-Use Management Programme (CLUMP) by the Karnataka Government, 1989. It could very well have been one of the very few pro-poor, State-level, village-based, and coordinated development programmes in independent India, if it had not met a premature demise before it even got started. Fifteen Mandals from five Districts in the State representing different

agro-climatic conditions were to be selected for the programme. The author had a privilege to be involved in a small way in its programming stage in 1989, visiting different places in Karnataka and having discussions with officials and villagers.

It would not be off the mark to note here a private discussion this author had the pleasure of having with a former Government of India official. The author's small NBT book *Japan* came out in 2006, in which he expressed his opinion that Japan's ODA to the Asian countries was mostly used to build large-scale engineering—oriented economic infrastructure like power generation and transport-power to India and transport to China—and left such tasks as poverty alleviation to be taken care of by the trickling-down effects. This is in fact how Japan has developed herself. Suppose put CLUMP and the Delhi Metro together, would it be too much to say that the Metro can wait for some time in favour of the CLUMP type development? Would it not mean for the cities to come to the help of the villages, which Gandhi emphasized so much for independent India? Without having the CLUMP type programme how would you plan to create employment in the villages, thus to stop migration from the villages to the cities? Lastly this is how the Japanese public would like to see the assistance used, not for the big projects but for the sake of the common people's welfare. The above official, however, expressed the view that Japan had rightly concentrated the use of her ODA in the sectors in which she was most experienced and at her best, which had been in the best interest of both. As the result he had not heard of 'a single scam' in connection with the Metro. In the decentralized projects like CLUMP that would not be assured, he said.

12. A series of works by Jean Dreze and Amartya Sen on Indian economy, beginning with their co-authored *India: Economic Development and Social Opportunity*, 1995.[32] Dreze is sometimes described as the driving force behind the NREGA. Their target seems to be to train the people of India into healthy and educated workers of both sexes who would be capable of making use of the new economic opportunities emerging by liberalization and deregulation.

The author may be allowed to present two instances in which he was an active participant.

13. Japan International Cooperation Agency (JICA)'s country study report *Nepal*, 1992.[33] Basically it is a proposal for external

assistance to Nepal. It says that the main direction of the assistance should be shifted from its tarai region, which has been its main recipient so far, to the hill area, which has been largely neglected and is increasingly becoming unable to sustain the population. Thus it hoped to be a new breakthrough in the development thinking. As the means of doing so the report recommended nurturing a network of multi-purpose 'local townships' as the nuclei for providing public hygiene and medical care, education, administration, and entertainment for the general public, supporting economic activities like mini-hydros instead of large dams, roads for man and cattle and not highways, lodges for trekkers in place of modern hotels. All these are not meant to bring urbanization to the villages but to make the hill area more habitable and ecologically resilient. The existing small towns in the hills may be developed into these townships by gradually taking over these functions. The privilege of submitting the report to JICA, and through it, to the Governments concerned fell upon the author.

14. An 'interaction' the author had the pleasure of having with the students of Jain Vishva Bharati University, Ladnun, Rajasthan, on 25 February 2008, under the auspices of Pratibha J. Mishra, Head of the Department of Social Work of the University. Compared to the other programmes mentioned above this was on a minute scale, but was very instructive to the author. The students were engaged in regular field work in some rural and urban communities in the region within the framework of six subjects of health, education and literacy, environment including tree-planting, employment, non-violent families with no domestic violence, and self-employment. The author was taken to observe a couple of villages and spent hours in each of them a few days before.

In the 'interaction' he presented a development scenario he thought fit to the local conditions. It consisted of a dozen items. These were: (1) to induce the villagers regularly to visit the rather chaotic-looking Primary Health Centre in the village to have their blood pressure measured, to begin with, (2) to make use of cow-dung and other materials for organic fertilizer in view of the semi-desert conditions, drink boiled water for prevention of diseases which was more important than cure, (3) to find the kind of trees to suit the local sandy soil, (4) cautious transition to the cattle-based, milk-based and fodder-based economy together with the improvement of the cattle, (5) fishing in the ponds to supplement the nutritious conditions of the non-vegetarians, (6) to maintain and improve ecological conditions in terms of soil, water and plants, which will contribute to the cause of peace in the communities also. The watertable in this semi-arid area is said to be 300 feet. (7) any way of securing and teaching how to use a sewing machine to relieve women from hard work? (8) any possibility of young men and women now organized separately in youth groups to work together so that both will be better motivated, the students being already co-educational, (9) any possibility of setting up of a cooperative for sales, buying, and credit-giving, (10) to teach villagers some sports after the students have learned them, almost any, say, table-tennis or volleyball, and cricket and soccer (and running) according to the availability of the field, (11) to read aloud story books to the small children who may gather at the village library, and (12) how to do with the drops-out, or those who take the midday meal home. The presentation was followed by keen exchange of views for which the author is thankful to the students.

Any such list is bound to be tentative. Any number of similar programmes may be added. If we draw some common elements from them, we may say that, apart from the land and the accompanying employment problem which will be discussed shortly, the most important ones would be education, safe drinking water, prevention of diseases, protection of forestry and soil, organic fertilizer, and irrigation depending upon the availability of water. These may be broadly classified as the Basic Human Needs which will constitute the core of the poverty alleviation of our time.

3. Constructive Programme

Gandhi A Superb Volunteer

If we compare these scenarios with Gandhi's Constructive Programme, we find that the latter, even in its most up-to-date form of the 'thoroughly revised' 18 points, 1945, is not much more than a patchwork. The 18 points are: (1) communal unity, (2) removal of untouchability, (3) prohibition, (4) khadi, (5) other village industries, (6) village sanitation, (7) new or basic education, (8) adult education,

(9) women, (10) education in health and hygiene, (11) provincial languages, (12) national language, (13) economic equality, (14) kisans, (15) labour, (16) adivasis, (17) lepers, and (18) students. The list is capable of being expanded easily and Gandhi was fully aware of it. This is in a sense the style of Gandhi as he was a kind of a volunteer, always ready to catch something new to work upon.

When, for example, the refugees from West Pakistan were flowing into Delhi with practically no clothes to put on, and the climate was getting into the cold season towards the end of 1947, he publicly started collecting blankets and quilts, even newspapers, to cover them at night, saying, as in "Speech at Prayer Meeting" on 4 October, that 'We have to provide blankets to lakhs of people'. (*CWMG*, 89-283~284) Another "Speech at Prayer Meeting" a week later began with 'Today also quite a few blankets have been received', and went on thus, '...it may not rain during the winter, but the dew is inevitable...Those who get the quilts can protect themselves against the dew if they spread newspapers on the quilts. Then the dew will not pass through'. (*CWMG*, 89-327) That is why people said that if you went to him looking for some work, there was always something he would give you. Indeed, if we look at his life, we would find a number of things he had accomplished as a volunteer. In a way his whole life, even the Salt March, was a volunteer's work. This is why Vinoba said that 'He has given the work of achieving independence the form of service to man'.[34]

Back to the Constructive Programme, he founded over the years a number of specialized organizations to help the work in those specific fields. In "Address To A.I.S.A. Trustees" at the end of 1944 he was talking of 'all our five constructive programme institutions (Charkha Sangh, Gram Udyog Sangh, Hindustani Talimi Sangh, Harijan Sevak Sangh, Goseva Sangh)'. (*CWMG*, 78-370) In the "Draft Constitution of Congress" which he completed on the last day of his life and became known as "His Last Will and Testament", those five are all listed in that order as the autonomous bodies the newly conceived Lok Sevak Sangh would affiliate. (*CWMG*, 90-528) In that sense those five remained Gandhi's hope till the last. There is no such organization for the Hindu-Muslim unity, which comes at the top of the Constructive Programme. It may be interpreted to mean that it was a duty for everyone to hold to the Hindu-Muslim unity.

If we set aside prohibition, which seems to be of less significance, the three topmost items in the Programme are Hindu-Muslim unity, untouchability, and *khadi*. The Hindu-Muslim unity became with the passage of time the most important issue for India and for Gandhi himself. We will go into it in Chapter Four. The untouchability issue, to which Gandhi devoted about a year and a half whole-heartedly, starting from the fast against the Communal Award in September 1932, then the untouchability work in prison, and the nine-month long Harijan tour from November 1933 onward, will be taken up later in this Chapter. It was already discussed to some extent in Chapter One. What about *khadi*?

Khadi vs. ***Agriculture***

Khadi was Gandhi's principal weapon to cope with the under-employment. But why was it that, as we discussed before, he did not make agriculture itself, by far the main means of livelihood in the country, also his main means of coping with this problem? Surely that would have provided millions of peasants and landless labourers some work. And the advice by Higginbottom and others were at Gandhi's disposal.

Broadly there were two reasons for his inability to do so. One was the land relations at the time, which made it impossible for him to act as he wanted, even if he had wanted to do so. This question will be discussed in the next Section. Another reason was his lack of interest in, and knowledge of, agriculture. This was decisive. He himself admitted this when he wrote in "Letter to Premabehn Kantak" on the last day of 1934 that 'The small size of landholdings is a big problem...Even small plots can be profitable if they are cultivated intelligently...But our own superficial knowledge in this field is a handicap. That is why we do not take up directly problems relating to agriculture. Our present aim is to popularize such crafts and industries as we can think of and as would be easy for the villagers to learn...'. (*CWMG*, 60-37) This will open the way to village industries, and craft-based village education, but not directly to the agricultural development. He also said in "Interview to the Press" ten days afterwards that 'I dare not think of land improvement and improvement in the methods of agriculture, for I know my limitations...'. (*CWMG*,

60-72) Was he then, as he often called himself, a calculating *bania*? If his limitations were so serious why not bring up others around him?

In the series of "Discussion with Shrikrishnadas Jaju", just below, there seemed to appear some significant change, or its germ. It came too late, but it is interesting in evaluating him. Gandhi said on agriculture that 'I am rather ignorant in this respect for I have no personal experience'(*CWMG*, 78-162), but that 'The time has now come for us to pay attention to agriculture. Till now I believed that improvement in agriculture was impossible unless we had the administration of the State in our own hands. My views on this are now undergoing modification. I feel that we can bring about improvements even under the present conditions, so that the cultivator may be able to make some income for himself from the land even after paying his taxes'. (*CWMG*, 78-179)

Here he is talking of the possibility of improving agriculture and increasing income from there, though without making a reference to the land system. But it is difficult to see how the change in thinking has produced any concrete results. In "Answers to Questions" at the end of November 1945, when asked why he laid more emphasis on spinning than on agriculture, Gandhi said that 'One of the reasons why I have not laid stress on agriculture is that even my knowledge of it is almost nil'. (*CWMG*, 82-133~134)

Discussion with Jajuji

Shrikrishnadas Jaju was one of Gandhi's main lieutenants in the field of *khadi* work. His son, Narayan Jajoo, told the author about his late father in an interview at Wardha on 11 November 2004, that Krishnadas' family originally migrated from Bikaner hundred and twenty-five years ago (as of then) as it was a dry area and the family had to earn something on their own. Krishnadas began practicing law from about 1905, but left the practice in 1920, and at the instance of Jamnalal Bajaj joined the work of popularizing *charkha*. For a week from 7 to 14 October (except 9) 1944, Gandhi had "Discussion with Shrikrishnadas Jaju" every day and on many things concerning *khadi* and other related matters. Its record covers 30 pages of the *CWMG* (78-156~198). Gandhi said in the above "Address" that 'Shri Jajuji, the General Secretary of the (Charkha) Sangh, has discussed with me the future policy of the Sangh in all its aspects for seven days devoting one hour daily to it'. (*CWMG*, 78-369)

What they discussed were four questions.

(1) Gandhi said that 'now I feel that *khadi* alone cannot revive the villages. Village uplift is possible only when we rejuvenate village life as a whole, revive all village industries and make the entire village industrious' (*CWMG*, 78-187).

(2) For that purpose Gandhi thought that such 'other village crafts' as bullock oil-press, hand-made paper, grinding stone (for flour and rice), and the cattle wealth should be taken up (*CWMG*, 78-161~162),

(3) Whereas Jaju said that 'Today all the *khadi* that may be produced can easily be sold...most of the *khadi* is sold in the cities...It is *khadi* alone that can in a large measure relieve unemployment among the poor. But there is little scope for earning money through *khadi* produced for self-sufficiency...Otherwise we cannot succeed in providing relief to those underemployed villagers who have work only for part of the year' (*CWMG*, 78-177~178), Gandhi thought that '*Khadi* should not be for sale but for self-consumption', which was his idea of decentralization. (*CWMG*, 78-190) Jaju replied that 'Most of the spinners in the countryside spin only for wages, scarcely for their own use...About three lakhs of people are employed in *khadi* work...Requiring people to spin for self-sufficiency, we would reduce it to no more than thirty thousand'. (*CWMG*, 78-192~193) What Jaju said was more logical, and it is difficult to say if he was convinced at the end. But Gandhi wound up by insisting that 'We shall see what difficulties we come across in working the programme of self-sufficiency. Commercial *khadi* may continue for a time, but the essential programme of the A.I.S.A. hereafter must be that of self-sufficiency...'. (*CWMG*, 78-198)

(4) One more topic was what Gandhi thought to be the 'top-heavy' machinery of the AISA, which in his view should be decentralized. He said that 'My view is that we should let as many provinces as wish to be free to develop their work as they desire'. (*CWMG*, 78-174~175) Here he placed the Provinces at the centre of the picture. It may have been in tune with his idea of the linguistic Provincial Congress Committees or the linguistic States. It may have been also in tune with the demand for a federal and decentralized India as was expressed in the 'Quit-India' Resolution.

Need for a More Integrated Plan

We may ask why, apart from the patchwork called Constructive Programme, there has been no Gandhian programme for alternative development, which is pro-poor, integrated, with at least some idea on the land problem, employment creation industrial or otherwise, infrastructural building such as NREGA, public health with prevention as the core, education Wardha type or otherwise, and environmental protection. These are the items which should have been put together into a more or less cohesive programme. India's urban population is expected to increase by 404 million by 2050, according to a UN report published on 10 July 2014, and their needs should be coped with, or, better, their migration itself should be deterred by making the villages more sustainable.

One may say that his 'village republics', as we have seen, do include all these and more. About his image of the village, he wrote in "Village Industries", that 'Today the villages are barren and desolate and are like dung-heaps. Tomorrow they will be like beautiful gardens and it would be difficult to deceive the people there'. (*CWMG*, 86-59) He also said in "A Note" in April 1947 that 'we must make the whole village a health resort. The hospital has no place in it. We must be satisfied with what little we may be able to do in the prevention of disease'. (*CWMG*, 87-370) But the idea lacks the basic thinking on land or employment, and is, therefore, not clear how the whole system can be pro-poor. His villages also give the impression of stagnant villages, lacking the idea of change, of dynamics, to sell themselves to the present generation.

S.S. Gill points out that 'In Gandhian *swaraj* there is no provision for the production of social surplus'.[35] This is a serious challenge. It sounds as if Gandhi is satisfied with the flow, without taking care of the stock.

Educating the Brain by Hand

Education is one area where Gandhi's thinking was breath-taking. Ever since *Hind Swaraj*, he gave the impression that he rather valued being unlettered. Gandhi knew this as he wrote in "Notes" (subtitle,

What about Literacy?) in 1937 on 'a grievance a learned correspondent has made of the neglect of literacy of which he imagines I have been guilty'. (*CWMG*, 66-80) But he had second thoughts. In a couple of "Talk with Mirabehn" six years afterwards, he said 'Three R's have a value all their own', and 'As a matter of fact it was only yesterday that I fully realized the value of the three R's. In the past, I have often expressed indifference to them'. (*CWMG*, 77-102, 103) This does not mean that he shifted his whole emphasis to the literary education. He wrote in "Notes" (subtitle, Adult Literacy) that 'Give the villagers village arithmetic, village geography, village history and the literary knowledge that they must use daily, i.e., reading and writing letters, etc...They have no use for books which give them nothing of daily use'. (*CWMG*, 72-180~181) He was keen on developing the scheme of education he called 'basic national education', 'Wardha scheme of education' or *Nayee Talim*. This was aimed, as he wrote in "A Step Forward" after the Educational Conference on 22 October 1937, at 'imparting full primary education including the secondary course less English through a vocation'. (*CWMG*, 66-279)

As he said in "Discussion with Teacher Trainees" in 1939, his idea was 'The brain must be educated through the hand'. He continued, 'The old idea was to add a handicraft to the ordinary curriculum of education... To me that seems a fatal mistake. The teacher must learn the craft (spinning, carpentry, etc.) and correlate his knowledge to the craft, so that he will impart all that knowledge to his pupils through the medium of the particular craft that he chooses'. (*CWMG*, 68-372~373) This was a stroke of genius even though there had been some input of the idea by, for instance, an Italian lady whom he met on his way home from the RTC. The *Nayee Talim* (new education) was probably one of the areas where his thinking had changed most over the years, together with intermarriage and non-armament.

N.K. Bose wrote that Gandhi 'was indeed trying to convert all the people of India, particularly its children, into intelligent, well-trained labourers'.[36] Bose also pointed out that Jinnah opposed the system, sensing instinctively that it would lower the barrier among the communities.[37]

Gandhi Unfamiliar in his Own Country

How to characterize Gandhi's Constructive Programme is not a simple industrialization or no industrialization problem. There is more to it. This may well be a part of what Gandhi often called his conflict with the educated classes of India. He did not write or speak about it in length. But it has got a lot in common with Gandhi-or-Nehru problem. Let us look at it in a somewhat different way, and see, for example, what economist Sukhamoy Chakravarty said in his *Development Planning—The Indian Experience*. He says that there was very little, at least till then (1987), that both the mainstream economists and their leftist opponents had learned from Gandhi, and only recently ecologically minded scholars began to take interest in him.[38] Gandhi was thus unknown, so to speak, among the intellectuals of his own country, for the independence of which he strove so hard.

A different expression of the question of Gandhi and the educated classes of India would be Gandhi's repeated call to the latter to come forward and participate in the Constructive Programme. Gandhi, for example, wrote in "U.P. National Service" that 'Indeed our ideal should be to have at least one worker to everyone of the seven hundred thousand villages. But apart from the A.I.S.A. we have hardly a worker even for every district'. (*CWMG*, 42-260) This was written toward the end of 1929, hardly ten years since the start of the Constructive Programme. But he kept issuing the call for years to come. Within a month, he wrote in "Hindi in the Congress" that 'very few Hindi speaking people are available for national work'. (*CWMG*, 42-364) In "Letter to Vinoba Bhave" in late 1932, he was talking of the difficulties of getting village workers but also was giving some cautions to them in living a village life. He said, 'Wherever they go, they should boil water for their use and drink only that...They should sleep in the open, accepting if possible a *charpoy* to keep themselves, so far as is humanly possible, safe from the danger of snakes, etc., I am giving all this advice without experience of course...I realize very well how exceedingly difficult it is to go into the villages. However, despite the difficulties, we must go. I, therefore, very much like the beginning you are making'. (*CWMG*, 51-293) Vinoba had already settled down in a village near

Wardha. Gandhi also wrote in "Letter to F. Mary Barr" in 1933 that 'You must not get malaria...Smear the uncovered limbs with paraffin oil... The mosquitoes keep away from paraffin". (*CWMG*, 54-209~210)

Still continuing, in "Some Questions" in September 1933 he writes that 'workers are very few compared to the magnitude of the task before the reformer, and, the majority of workers being town-bred, they are disinclined to go to the villages and settle there'. (*CWMG*, 56-1) In "Letter to Premabehn Kantak" in 1937 he wrote that 'Only a handful of workers are willing to go to villages, and they, too, are inexperienced'. (*CWMG*, 64-342) On July 1940, at the beginning of the rainy season, Gandhi wrote in "To Sevagram Workers" that 'I hope everyone drinks only boiled water...As a protection against malaria everyone should apply kerosene oil to hands and feet...We should protect ourselves against the sun...' (*CWMG*, 72-234) In "Speech at Prayer Meeting" in December 1947 he advised the woman worker that 'Most women workers we have are from the cities. We could find a few in villages and even these had some connection with the cities...A woman worker from a town should not carry to the villages the atmosphere and the ways of towns...All I have to say is that the women workers who truly want to serve, not to exploit, must have a sense of propriety and take to the villages only the things that it would be appropriate to take'. (*CWMG*, 90-201~202)

The 1,500 or more persons interviewed in the research by Bipan Chandra and his collaborators were presumably from this category of people. He writes about them, 'They were the whole-timers of the national movement...They made life long sacrifices. Many took a vow not to marry till freedom's day. They sat all their lives in jails, or *ashrams*, or Khadi Bhavan, or in trade union and Kisan Sabha offices...They were the 'standing army' of the national movement'.[39] The 'standing army' was the words by an interviewee in 1985. He also told a story of great significance. While engaged in some political work back in 1931, a peasant came and asked him if he was married. He said 'no'. The peasant then asked if he had a father to support him. When he said 'yes', the peasant said, 'That explains your readiness to carry on with the struggle. If you had a family of your own and had to feed them, you would talk a very different tune'.[40]

Employment Created through Khadi

All this of course does not mean that the organizations for the Constructive Programme were idle. Gandhi said in "Speech at Federal Structure Committee" at the RTC on 15 September 1931 that 'today the Congress, through its organization, the All-India Spinners' Association, is finding work for nearly 50,000 women in nearly 2,000 villages, and these women are possibly 50 per cent Mussalman women. Thousands of them belong to the so-called untouchable class'. (*CWMG*, 48-16) In "Interview to the Press" a few years later, he gave some new figures by saying that 'The Spinners' Association had distributed one and a half crores of rupees among 160,000 people of which 120,000 were spinners, 24,000 washermen, and the rest weavers'. (*CWMG*, 60-73) In "*Khadi Jagat*" published in May 1941, he wrote that 'At present it (A.I.S.A.) provides employment to 224,421 spinners, of whom 167,996 are Hindus and 56,425 are Muslims, along with 20,643 other artisans, such as ginners, carders, dyers, weavers and washermen'. (*CWMG*, 74-59) Toward the end of the next year 1941, in an overall interpretation of "Constructive Programme: Its Meaning and Place", he wrote that '275,146 villagers, including 19,654 Harijans and 57,378 Muslims, scattered in at least 13,451 villages, received, as spinners, weavers, etc., Rs. 34,85,609 in 1940. The spinners were largely women'. Gandhi was deeply dissatisfied with this much of twenty years' result and continued that 'Yet the work done is only one-hundredth part of what could be done if Congressmen honestly took up the *khadi* programme.' (*CWMG*, 75-151)

In the discussion with Jaju mentioned above, Gandhi said that the Sangh's work now covered 15,000 villages where it distributed four and a half crores of rupees to the poor (*CWMG*, 78-157), and as we saw, Jaju said that there were three hundred thousand workers employed in *khadi* work. In "Discussion with a Friend" in the middle of August 1946, Gandhi said that 'During that period (twenty-five years of A.I.S.A.) it distributed over seven crores of rupees as wages among four and a half lakhs of the poor spinners and weavers, principally spread over twenty thousand villages of India'. (*CWMG*, 85-170) Probably these were the last figures he showed himself.

We may see that Gandhi, towards the end of his life, was not at all happy about the situation of *khadi* in the country. In "A Note" he wrote on 17 November 1947 that 'I find that talk of *khadi* and village industries does not interest people any more... (but) How long will you feed them (refugees) without giving them any work? I am sure everyone will remember this old man one day when it is realized that India has no alternative except to develop village industries'. (*CWMG*, 90-57) In "Speech at Prayer Meeting" a month later he again said that 'Today we have forgotten the *charkha*...Only a few lakhs of people can be employed by the mills. What occupation shall we provide for the hundreds of millions?'. (*CWMG*, 90-233~234)

The above figures of employment may not be very large by his standard, but they would show that Gandhi's rural programme is largely targeted on the Muslims and untouchables. One may wonder if the economic benefit accruing to the Muslims in this way was not enough to prevent the Muslim masses from turning anti-Congress. One may also wonder if the economic benefit accruing to the Harijans in this way, coupled with the Temple-Entry Movement, to be discussed shortly, was not enough to prevent them from turning away from Hinduism and going the way of conversion. On 14 October 1935 the Bombay Presidency Depressed Classes Conference 'passed a resolution urging complete severance of the Depressed Classes from the Hindu fold and their embracing any other religion which guaranteed them equal status and treatment with the other members of it'. (*CWMG*, 62-37, fn. 2) They finally selected Buddhism.

To Modernize Gandhism

If we put together all the elements of alternative development which may have existed in Gandhi's mind, are they enough to cope with the socio-economic problems India, or the world, faces now?

While thinking this, we were attracted by what Sheela Reddy wrote in the "New Gandhi" special in *Outlook* in its 11 September 2006 number, which falls on the centenary of that memorable Empire Theatre meeting to mark the start of Gandhi's first ever *satyagraha*. Reddy says, quoting one activist, that 'Young people may not be able to relate to a *dhoti*-clad Gandhi with his *charkha*...But tell them how he was a millionaire London-returned barrister who threw away everything to fight for justice and equality, and they begin at once to appreciate him'. This 40-year old Gandhian was himself 'in shirt and trousers', and, unlike the old school, 'laughs a lot'!

She quotes another activist who says the same thing in this way, '*Khadi* and *charkha* are outdated symbols. We need to now climb on Gandhi's shoulders and look ahead'.[41] All this implies that the Gandhian movement should examine itself and be modernized. Then, it would find itself speaking to a wider audience. That is the way to make Gandhism competitive in this age. In other words it can be still competitive and relevant. To talk of 'non-violence and truth', and to talk of them alone, as some of the author's respondents seem to be doing, would not quite meet those standards.

4. Land and Property

Gandhi's Satyagraha Pledge

Why is it that Gandhi was not able to formulate a coordinated scenario for development, or social change, of his own? Here we come to the crux of the matter.

On 24 February 1919, when the storm of the Rowlatt Bills was about to threaten the country, Gandhi, together with his close associates said to have numbered about 20, Yajnik says 24, from Ahmedabad and Bombay, signed "The Satyagraha Pledge" (in English) at Sabarmati Ashram. It said that if the Bills became Acts, the signatories would 'refuse civilly to obey these laws...'. This may be by NC, but probably more by CD. It also said that 'we further affirm that in this struggle we will faithfully follow truth and refrain from violence to life, person or property'. (*CWMG*, 15-101~102) It is noticeable that Gandhi consolidated his and his friends' determination by an oath. Now, 'life' and 'person' are easily understandable. But why 'property'? Where does the idea come from? Although in letters it was limited to the anti-Rowlatt Bills struggle, it was binding upon him as it was a pledge. In spite of all his genuine sympathies with the poor, this is what did not make him really pro-poor. When E.M.S. talked of 'This ability of his (Gandhi's) to rouse the masses and yet to check them'[42], he meant substantially the same thing.

In this sense his non-violence was a double-edged sword. It was capable of facing and overcoming violence. As such it is a treasure of mankind. On the other hand, it is capable of restraining, for example, legitimate demands of the *kisans*, as we will see. Therefore a fundamental contradiction is possible, and is bound to occur, between his two essential messages of peace on one hand and poverty alleviation on the other.

In order to prove this point of Gandhi being not necessarily pro-poor on land and property, let us see what he had to say on the land question over the decades.

We will begin with the "Working Committee's Resolutions at Bardoli" of 12 February 1922, said to have been drafted by Gandhi (*CWMG*, 22-377, fn. 3). The Resolutions were primarily to suspend the impending mass CD because of the incident at Chauri Chaura. But they also say in Item 6 that 'Complaints having been brought to the notice of the Working Committee that ryots are not paying rents to the zamindars, the Working Committee advises Congress workers and organizations to inform the ryots that such withholding of rents is contrary to the resolutions of the Congress and that it is injurious to the best interests of the country'. Then Item 7 continues that 'The Working Committee assures the zamindars that the Congress movement is in no way intended to attack their legal rights, and that even where the ryots have grievances, the Committee's desire is that redress should be sought by mutual consultations and by the usual recourse to arbitrations'. (*CWMG*, 22-378) Would it be difficult to see that the draftsman's sympathy here lies more with the zamindars than the ryots?

Gandhi's Eleven Points

After an interval of eight years, Gandhi published the Eleven Points in "Clearing the Issue", about a month and a half before the Salt March. We have seen this already. The third item is 'Reduction of the land revenue to at least 50 per cent...'. Although Gandhi claimed a week later in "Some Implications" that '...in formulating the eleven points, I have somewhat and to the extent of my ability given a concrete shape to their (masses') feeling' (*CWMG*, 42-451), this and the next, on abolition of the salt tax, were the only items having a direct bearing on rural India. The "Provisional Settlement", known as the Gandhi-Irwin Pact, concluded early in March 1931, moreover, states that 'nor are they (Government of India) able, in the present financial conditions of the country, to make substantial modifications in the Salt Acts', except loosening some of their rigidities (*CWMG*, 45-436). Even otherwise it is difficult to find much in the Pact which is likely to bring benefit to the masses. It is all the more shocking because, as Rothermund points out, the prices of wheat and then millets dropped sharply in the summer of 1930, thus creating a situation that did not exist at the time of the March. So, 'No-tax and no-rent campaigns spread like wild fire. This gave an entirely new dimension to the campaign which had not been related to agrarian problems at all…'.[43]

Karachi Resolution

We will move to the "Resolution on Fundamental Rights and Economic Changes", passed by the Congress Karachi Session on 31 March 1931, shortly after the above Pact. It was moved by Gandhi himself by "Speech on Fundamental Rights, Karachi Congress", presumably to heal the injury the Congress had suffered during the CD campaign. The twenty items of the Resolution include one on the 'Substantial reduction in agricultural rent or revenue paid by the peasantry', and another on the 'Control of usury'. (*CWMG*, 45-371) In explanation of the Resolution, Gandhi said that his Eleven Points 'have been made more comprehensive' here (*CWMG*, 45-372). He also said that the control of usury meant 8 per cent of maximum interest. (*CWMG*, 45-373) But, as the Resolution says, these measures were 'to enable the masses to appreciate what *swaraj*…will mean to them', in Gandhi's words to show 'the broad features of *swaraj*', and not the immediate policies of the Congress. There was nothing on land redistribution. The Congress Election Manifesto in 1936, on the eve of the first Provincial elections under the new Government of India Act, gave a summary of the Karachi Resolution as its economic programme 'Pending the formulation of a fuller programme', (*CWMG*, 65-461) suggesting that there was little progress in that direction at least in those five years.

Gandhi said at "Interview to '*Madras Mail*'" in December 1933, during his Harijan tour, that 'I do think, however, that the actual cultivator should have a title in the soil, and a larger share of its produce. At present, in many places, he gets far too little'. (*CWMG*,

56-383) This was probably the first time that he said something which was definitely on the side of the tenant. A little later, however, when the CSP was formed and Narendra Deva sent its Draft Programme, Gandhi, in reply, wrote in his 'Letter to Narendra Deva' of 2 August 1934, already referred to in relation to Jawaharlal Nehru, that on the property relations 'I do not contemplate the elimination of the princes and the landlords nor do I contemplate redistribution of land to peasants. I aim at reformation of the princes and the landlords. It is possible, without a violent redistribution of land, to secure for tenants rights which virtually amount to ownership'. (*CWMG*, 58-275)

This is a very important statement on land and more generally on property question. It would be too harsh to say that he was against any redistribution. But it was conditional. Non-violence was an absolute prerequisite. He is not talking of the possibility of non-violent distribution here. To him redistribution meant violent redistribution. People would have to wait till there occurs a change in the mind of the propertied classes. Again on whose side was he?

In the then United Provinces (UP), Gandhi pointed out in "Duty of the United Provinces" in 1929 that 'U.P. is the home of so many big landlords and *talukdars'* (*CWMG*, 41-501), and in "Letter to Sir Malcolm Hailey" in 1931 that 'The chief difficulty in U.P. as it seems to me is the evictions already obtained and the evictions that are still continuing. They may all be lawful but there is something wrong in the system which allows of so many evictions'. (*CWMG*, 47-371)

Congress Governments and the Kisan

Friction began to be manifest, after the Congress formed provincial governments in seven Provinces in 1937, between those governments and the peasantry. As early as September 1938, "Draft of Resolution for A.I.C.C.", drafted by Gandhi himself, was passed, which said that 'the Congress will...support measures that may be undertaken by the Congress Governments for the defence of life and property'. (*CWMG*, 67-368) It uses almost identical terms with the *satyagraha* Pledge of 1919. On the other hand Gandhi said that if these governments are not able to run without the help of the police and the military, they should 'give up office'. Those are the two sides of the coin of his Non-violence.

It was in Bihar that the friction surfaced most intensely. Gandhi once said of Bihar in "Letter to Vallabhbhai Patel" in 1934, the year of the earthquake, that 'If it is possible anywhere in the country to fight elections without money and solely on the prestige of the Congress, it is in Bihar'. (*CWMG*, 58-368) His confidence at this time went back to his and his co-workers' effort for the peasants in Champaran, Bihar, in 1916~17. The same Gandhi, however, said in "Answers to Questions at Gandhi Seva Sangh Meeting, Brindaban-I" in May 1939 that 'We do not have the same hold among the peasants of Bihar as we used to'. (*CWMG*, 69-210)

On the adjoining UP in the same period of 1937-39, historian B.R. Nanda writes in "A Biographical Sketch" of Govind Ballabh Pant, then the Premier, that 'The most notable achievement of Pant's ministry during the next two and a half years was a tenancy bill which assured tenants security of tenure, fixation of rents by a government agency, and abolition of vexatious restrictions'. He continues, 'The bill was carried in the face of stubborn opposition from the Muslim League which turned this, as indeed most other issues, into a communal issue'.[44] This was after the coalition talk between the Congress and the League of 1937 broke up. Nanda also writes in his *Gandhi and his Critics* that there was an anxiety in the U.P. Congress in 1937 that if a coalition ministry with the League came into being it would not be possible to formulate an agrarian programme, and as a matter of fact there was a stubborn opposition by the League in the U.P. Assembly to the land reforms during 1937-46.[45]

After the independence, Nanda goes on in "A Biographical Sketch", the U.P. Zamindari Abolition and the Land Reforms Act was passed by the Legislative Assembly and became effective in July 1952 supervised by Pant as Chief Minister. As the big peasants were dominant in the Assembly, however, there was not as much a progress in the land reforms part of it as in the Zamindari Abolition part.[46] So in reality it was not a communal issue.

The "A.I.C.C. Resolutions" of June 1939, again drafted by Gandhi, included a clause which read that 'no Congressman may offer or organize any form of *satyagraha* in the Administrative Provinces of India without the previous sanction of the Provincial Congress Committeee concerned'. (*CWMG*, 69-367)

Around this time Gandhi said in "Internal Decay" that 'Kisans of Bihar are supposed to be Congressmen. Their leaders are Congressmen. Bihar Ministers live in perpetual dread of *kisan* risings and *kisan* marches'. (*CWMG*, 68-321) He wrote in "Red Tape" at the end of 1938, as we saw, that 'If...they (the Congress Ministers) find that they cannot run the State without the use of the police and the military, it is the clearest possible sign, in terms of non-violence, that the Congress should give up office and again wander in the wilderness...' (*CWMG*, 68-195). Here he did not specifically mention Bihar. But he came back to this Province without particularly mentioning the name in "Speech at Public Meeting, Brindaban" (in Champaran) when he said that 'It pains me to hear the *kisans* resorting to violence...If you want to abolish zamindari, it is well and good. Do so through non-violence'. (*CWMG*, 69-241) This was in May 1939. In 1947, as the independence was coming near, the Bihar government prohibited holding any kind of a special day like the Punjab Day or Pakistan Day, and as Gandhi told in "Speech at Prayer Meeting" at Patna in March, they 'had banned the *kisan* rally also'. (*CWMG*, 87-141)

Through all these vicissitudes, Gandhi was certainly not hostile to the *kisans*. In 'Letter to Sahajanand' of January 1945, he wrote to Swami Sahajanand Saraswati, the Bihar-based President of the All-India *Kisan* Sabha, that since Andhra-based N.G. Ranga wanted to approach the Congress in Andhra in connection with his *kisan* movement, 'I had no hesitation in approving of his project', and 'You would please put yourself in touch with the Bihar Congressmen'. (*CWMG*, 79-51) This move could be interpreted to be an attempt on the part of Gandhi to reconstruct both the Congress and the mass movement from the damage of the war years.

But Gandhi did not conceal his anti-class war attitude. In "Answers to *Zamindars*", July 1934, said to be a conversation with Congress-supporting nationalist *zamindars*, he said that 'You may be sure that I shall throw the whole weight of my influence in preventing class war...Wipe out the injustice that you may have been consciously or unconsciously guilty of and shed all fear of the Congress and Congressmen'. (*CWMG*, 58-248~249) He also said in "Letter to Agatha Harrison" quoted above that 'I would strain every nerve to prevent a class war'. (*CWMG*, 62-353) Would it not be justified to call him an Indian *Narodnik,* or has someone already called him that way?

E.M.S. had this to say in his *The Mahatma and the Ism* (*hereafter Ism*) on Gandhi's 'Quit-India' speech on 8 August, in Hindi which was followed by another in English, that 'It is significant...that Gandhi's two-hour speech at the AICC session contained not a word addressed to the workers or the peasants: A major part of the speech was devoted to an exposition of his and the Congress' attitude to the Hindu-Muslim question; then...special appeals to the journalists, to the princes, to the government servants, to the soldiers, and to the students...The overwhelming majority of the people, i.e., the workers and peasants, did not come into Gandhi's picture at all'.[47] Both of the speeches Gandhi gave on that day after the passing of the Resolution, and one more on the previous day before the Resolution had been put to the vote, were basically nationalistic in nature. For instance, in the last one, concluding with the famous 'I have, therefore, pledged the Congress and the Congress has pledged herself that she will do or die', (*CWMG*, 76-401) he said, 'I want Englishmen, Europeans and all the United Nations to examine in their heart of hearts what crime India has committed in demanding independence today'. (*CWMG*, 76-399) However, E.M.S. was also right in his criticism. For, Gandhi said in that speech, for example, that 'I have kept a place for the Princes and the *zamindars* in India that I envisage' (*CWMG*, 76-393), but nothing on the *kisans*. Why not?

On the Eve of the Sunrise

Somewhat later, in January 1946, Gandhi said, in "Answers to Questions at Constructive Workers' Conference, Madras", that 'As for the present owners of wealth, they would have to make their choice between class war and voluntarily converting themselves into trustees of their wealth'. (*CWMG*, 83-27) 'Trusteeship' was one of the key Gandhian concepts. He came to make much use of it toward the end of his life, presumably because he found that he had to be more critical of the wealthy classes.

We will also look at Gandhi's responce to the Tebhaga Movement in East Bengal demanding to lower the landowner's share from half to one-third. In his "Talk to Representatives of Krishak Samiti (peasants' committee)", during his pilgrimage in Noakhali in January 1947, he admitted his ignorance of the Movement, but when requested his blessings for it, he said, 'Yes, yes, all good movements have my blessings'. He was also asked 'Can we not build up Hindu-Muslim unity through a concrete programme?'. This was a very important point, and if Gandhi had been able to do something about the tenancy or rural debts in such a way as to give relief to both the Hindu and Muslim peasants simultaneously, and also to create employment in the villages, the communal situation could have been very different. (*CWMG*, 86-388)

In 'Speech at Prayer Meeting' a week later, he said, also in connection with the Tebhaga Movement, that he would even support the idea of 'the entire produce to the tillers of the soil', and 'He further believed that no one who did not till the land had any claim to the produce. Only those who toiled should have a share in the output…But he warned the people against the use of compulsion or violence'. (*CWMG*, 86-413)

The Tebhaga Movement and the communal disturbances of Noakhali were both taking place in East Bengal, shortly before the Partition of India, at places not far away from each other. One wonders what has separated one from the other. Historian Sumit Sarkar writes in his *Modern India: 1885-1947* that the worst affected areas by the great war-time famine were south-west Bengal and the Districts of Dacca, Faridpur, Tippera and Noakhali.[48] The disturbances in Noakhali were apparently under its influence. He also points out on the Tebhaga that 'North Bengal became the storm-centre…Muslims did participate in considerable numbers in the *Tebhaga* bases, despite (the religious disturbances of) Calcutta and Noakhali…But throughout south-east Bengal…remained untouched…'.[49] Noakhali belonged to this latter category.

Another interesting point was that Gandhi was at first ignorant of the Tebhaga Movement. It would be of significance to know if such other movements existed elsewhere in the country that had not been originally under his or the Congress' guidance, what their relations were with the Congress and its governments, and to what extent they could overcome communalism.

Gandhi sometimes even took the side of the landlord, and said, 'What can the poor *zamindar* do when they (actual cultivators of the soil) say that they will simply not work the land unless they are paid enough to feed and clothe and educate themselves and their children in a decent manner?' Here he talked about a rather unlikely event of the peasant resorting to NC to overcome the landlord. But what kind of the peasants was he talking about? We may say that in the pre-independent India's hierarchical tenancy system, generally the upper tenant was close to the landlord in status, was not the actual tiller of the soil, was belonging to the higher castes, and was supporting the Congress, while the lower tenant was its opposite on all these points.

For example, E.M.S. was writing on the *kanamdars* and *verumpattamdars* as the 'two main classes of tenants in Malabar' in his *A Short History of the Peasant Movement in Malabar*. This paper is unique in that it was dedicated, first of all, 'To the *kisan* family of a father, a mother and six children who sheltered me for twenty months of my underground life…'.[50] He writes that 'Many of the *kanamdars* are themselves not cultivators, but lease their lands to *verumpattamdars* for cultivation, while most of the *verumpattamdars* are actual cultivators'.[51] As for the relationship of the Congress and these two strata of tenants, he says that 'Most of them (Gandhite Congressmen) belong to families of *kanamdars* themselves and move in that circle'.[52] On Gujarat at the time of the Salt March also, Thomas Weber writes that the greatest support to the March were from 'the middle peasant *Patidars*'. Seven from among them took part in the March, and the 'major stopping places' on the route were also their villages.[53]

Gandhi towards Agrarian Radicalism?

Gandhi himself did not conceal his opposition to the land redistribution, at least of the non-compensation type. Therefore, it is difficult to believe, as Bipan Chandra, for example, says, that 'The most remarkable development was his shift towards agrarian radicalism'.[54] He placed it in a larger context of Gandhi's life, and said that Gandhi was constantly changing and the direction of the change was 'invariably, in more radical directions'.[55] It is true that Gandhi changed his opinion on issues like intermarriage, armament or education, sometimes radically, as seen above. Vinoba put it in somewhat stronger terms and said that Gandhi was changing every day, was *viksit* (developed) at every moment, and was, therefore, a *vikasshil* (developing) person.[56]

With all the respect to Bipan Chandra and his scholarship, however, the author is not able to bring himself to accept 'agrarian radicalism' as characterizing Gandhi's thought. True, Gandhi said that he would like to see non-violent redistribution. But he said several times that he was against the class struggle, and would oppose it as much as possible. He did not always look kindly at the organized peasant movement, or for that matter any organized movement, and always tried to keep it under his control. When he wrote in the middle of 1947 under the title "Question Box" (subtitle, How to Combat *Himsa*), for example, that 'The present power of the *zamindars*, the capitalists and the *rajas* (the three components of India's ruling elites of his conception) can hold sway only so long as the common people do not realize their own strength. If the people non-co-operate, what can a *raja*, a *zamindar* or a capitalist do?' (*CWMG*, 88-2), he was writing something of great importance, but more as a treatise on NC than as a theoretical backing for an agrarian revolution.

This Section has been mainly on Gandhi's thinking on the question of land. But we may also see what Yajnik had thought of his relations with the labour movement. He wrote that, except in Ahmedabad, Gandhi 'had never cultivated any acquaintance or relations with organized Labour in the whole of India…there was hardly a prominent political leader in the Congress then who had ever led any Labour struggle in any part of the country.'[57] He also wrote that the general strike in the Bombay mills continued for nearly six months in 1928, but they met 'the cruel apathy of the Congress party' during that period.[58]

5. Trusteeship and the Bhoodan Movement

Vinoba Transcending Gandhi

Gandhi often explained his trusteeship in very plain terms. He wanted to put it in everybody's mind, and as such it became a part of his training of the nation. He even said in "Speech at Prayer Meeting" at Noakhali in February 1947 that 'He wished it (trusteeship) became a gift from India to the world' (*CWMG*, 86-420). But it was also difficult to achieve. On the day before his life was taken away, in "Interview to Margaret Bourke-White" he was asked 'Did he know of any industrialist who lived up to that ideal (of a trustee)?'. He said, 'No, though some are striving in that direction, my host, G.D. Birla, for instance'. (*CWMG*, 90-521~522) If Jamnalal Bajaj had been alive Gandhi would probably have put his name first.

Here we will see Vinoba's Bhoodan (land donation) Movement as an outstanding, though in the end unsuccessful, example of promoting trusteeship and land redistribution in post-independent India. By so doing Vinoba really went several steps ahead of his *Guru*. But it was not a pre-planned action. It began quite accidentally.

Some landless Harijan peasants came to him in Pochampalli, a Nalgonda, Telangana, village in April 1951, and said, as Shriman Narayan's wife who was there with Vinoba told her husband later, 'We are very poor. We are also unemployed and, therefore, unhappy. Please help us...We want only work and nothing else. Please give us some land so that we may work hard on it to eke out our livelihood'. They said 80 acres was needed for forty landless families there.

Vinoba did not know what to do. His programme for the villagers then was only common (group) spinning. The Harijans were thus unconsciously pointing out the limitation of *khadi* work. Then an idea struck Vinoba. He asked the assembled villagers if they could donate some land. Thereupon one of the peasants, Ramchandra Reddy by name, offered to donate 100 acres for the landless, and Vinoba was saved. He coined the word '*bhoodan*' when he reached the next village. Soon *Gramdan* (donation of a village) Movement was born out of it. He could also have praised the Harijans for asking for land to work upon instead of begging. The episode at the Telangana village clearly showed that Gandhi's rural reconstruction programme did not have a plan to distribute land to the tiller.[59]

Thus started, Vinoba's '*pad yatra*' for Bhoodan continued from 8 March 1951 to the end of 1967 except from 1959~60 when he was ill. The places he visited and the distance he moved in miles have been recorded in the *Vinoba Sahitya* (Vol. 20). He must have written many letters during the *pad yatra*, but only seventy-three of them, written from 1951 to 66, have been incorporated in the *Vinoba Sahitya* (Vol. 13). Gautam Bajaj, the Editor of the 21-volume *Vinoba Sahitya,* told this author on 12 November 2004 that Vinoba was not interested in keeping his papers and burnt a lot of them himself. Most of these seventy-three were written in the earlier years of the *yatra*, and, therefore, were full of hope. Not many of them were written in the later years. So it is not clear if he was able to keep up the hope he had entertained in the beginning. In 36th letter, for instance, he wrote that they should 'win over the landlord and the moneylender with love'. Did he hold to the idea till the end? He settled down in his ashram at Paunar, near Sevagram, from 1970 and passed away there in 1982. From Gandhi's point of view it was a retirement. It would not have been possible for Gandhi to retire, although he said that many people advised him to retire to the Himalayas in his later life. Unlike an activist like Gandhi, a scholar like Vinoba could have led a retired life. Narayan Jajoo told the author on 11 November 2004 that Vinoba was a man who accepted Gandhi's thinking only so far as he was convinced, thus keeping the independence of his mind.

Some years ago, P. Sainath, Editor, Rural Affairs, *The Hindu*, contributed an essay titled "Nine Decades of Non-Violence".[60] Baji Mohammed, nearing 90 in age, hails from Navrangpur, then in Koraput District of Orissa. In 1930s he reached Raipur by cycle and then took a train to Wardha to meet Gandhi. 'My run was his walk', he said. He was also told, '*Jao, lathi khao*'. In the 'Quit-India' he was duly arrested on 25 August and spent five years in jail. More than a thousand went to jail from Koraput, of whom more than 100 became martyrs. Many of his co-fighters became MLAs in the 1952 Elections, the first after independence.

But he never contested, and joined the Bhoodan Movement, donating fourteen acres himself. 'I was more *sewa dal* than *satta dal*, more service oriented than power seeking', he said. The only regret is that his vision of what we should be as a nation is still not realized, added Sainath. Although a small episode, the story shows the internal connection between the freedom movement and a post-independent socio-economic movement like the Bhoodan. It also shows that at least some, probably many, of the freedom-fighters got into the state machinery after independence, thus proving the fatal accuracy of what the Reader in *Hind Swaraj* told the Editor on the succession of the *Raj* by the Indians. Gandhi himself repeatedly said that many Congressmen were writing to him expressing their wishes to enter the Constituent Assembly or to become MLAs. He of course did not like it, and this led to the idea of the Lok Sevak Sangh at the end of his life. That ideal itself was soon buried. The episode of Baji Mohammed is also important as it is the story of a Muslim.

The episode reminds the author of the village called Panimora in Bargarh District of Orissa. When he visited it, the population was about 6,000, all-Oriya, a fairly large village, with Gandhi's bust at the entrance. It became famous at the time of the 'Quit-India' as thirty-two villagers went from here to take part in it. Four of them were still surviving as of December 2007. Of these four, two happened to be in the village on that day, aged 83 and 96 respectively, and they could be interviewed. Vinoba visited the village in 1963. The villagers expressed the opinion that the Government was doing very little for the poor folks.

To come back to the Bhoodan, Vinoba set the donation, and the distribution, of one-sixth of the landlords' property as the target of the Bhoodan. It was based on a discussion he had with the constructive workers at Sagar on the Gandhi Jayanti in 1951. It was calculated that if there were 10 million landless families in the country, and the five members of those families needed one acre each, that would come up to fifty million, one-sixth of all the agricultural land in the country then. He was going to accomplish the donation and the distribution by non-violence. He also fixed 1957 as the deadline.[61]

He was on his way to Delhi then to discuss the First Five-Year Plan at the invitation of Prime Minister Nehru. During the three days' conference with the Planning Commission there were two things he stressed. One was 'achieving self-sufficiency' (in foodgrains). The other was 'to provide work for all'. As for the Bhoodan itself, it seems that he thought his action was a stop-gap measure till the government launched a full-scale land distribution plan by legislation.

According to Shriman Narayan, 'The real intention (of Vinoba) was to create the right atmosphere so that progressive land reforms could follow'.[62] But that was not to be. Vinoba himself used words like creating *hawa* and *vatavaran* (atmosphere) for the reform, and achieving *jitna* (winning over the people). Thus he tried to tackle what Gandhi himself did not dare to do. Therefore, Vinoba said that 'I have a conviction that Bapu will be feeling satisfied with my work from whatever corner of the Universe he may be in'.[63] This was in spite of the fact that he was of the opinion that 'even Gandhi's thought, as developed by him in his lifetime, cannot solve our contemporary problems'.[64] If he and his co-workers had been more careful in attending to the details of the actual distribution, and if they could have the substantial support of the administrative machine of the government, things may have been different. In the mean time the number of the landless families has shot up so rapidly, that it became no longer manageable for a volunteers' group like the Bhoodan Movement before long.

Vinoba, however, left a couple of extremely important pieces of advice. One was on the approach to the poor. This was when he was involved in discussing the Draft Second Five-Year Plan. He said that the theory of 'percolation', meaning the trickling-down theory, failed, and 'We must endeavour to reach the weakest segments of our population directly through specific schemes of development at the grass-roots'.[65] We may recall that the *Arjun Sengupta Report* was written on exactly the same line.

The second was on decentralization. His view was that 'He is of the definite opinion that full-fledged panchayats should be established only in those villages where land has been redistributed either through Bhoodan or legislation…In the absence of these economic reforms, village Panchayats…may well turn into engines of social and economic oppression and exploitation'.[66] He also said it was Gandhi's idea that '…every village should have the power to decide what goods will be brought in from outside and what will be sent outside'.[67]

He continued that Gandhi saw the danger of the concentration of power and property owing to science and technology. His declaration of village self-government, of decentralization, was in opposition to this. If India on the contrary goes toward centralization, *himsa* is necessary to consolidate it and defend its interests. 'This idea of decentralization and village self-government is Bapu's singular gift to the mankind'. It is 'the only way for the mankind'.[68] Vinoba is thus analyzing from his own angle why Gandhi was and had to be opposed to the machine age.

Even before his retirement around 1970 to Paunar, Vinoba's movement had been seriously disturbed by the political situation in the country. As Bipan Chandra writes in his *In the Name of Democracy*, 'the Sarvodaya movement (led by Vinoba) was a major victim of the conflict between the JP movement and the Congress and Mrs. (Indira) Gandhi'.[69] In the early years of the Bhoodan Movement, JP sometimes accompanied Vinoba and the two made a joint appeal for land donation. K.V. Kesavan told the author in one of our conversations that in his youth he was once taken to one of Vinoba's speech meetings where JP was also present and gave a speech more forceful than Vinoba's for land donation. But as Bipan Chandra stresses, 'The dependence of the JPM on the RSS-Jan Sangh became clearly visible when later on 25 June 1975 Nanaji Deshmukh, the organizing secretary of Jan Sangh and one of the top RSS leaders, was made the movement's chief organizer...'.[70]

Vinoba 'would not let the Sarvodaya movement become a part of the JP movement, and, when he found that a majority of the Sarvodayites were determined to do so, he split the movement. This did not save the movement, which became virtually defunct...'[71] Why did many of the Sarvodaya workers join JP in this way? It was because he, and also his wife, had been close to Gandhi for many years, a social worker himself, and was considered by many as a true Gandhian. We have seen that Gandhi once spoke on JP's behalf at a CWC meeting. When, therefore, the author asked some people if JP was a Gandhian, some of the respondents were astonished at the question itself. But in the opinion of some others, including Bipan Chandra, although JP was close to Gandhi he did not really understand Gandhi, and his political behaviour in the years leading to the Emergency was cited as its evidence. It would seem that E.M.S. was closer to the first view. In his *ism*, he writes that 'Vinoba Bhave acted as the high priest of the authoritarian Indira Congress, while the tallest two of the other Sarvodaya wing—Kripalani and Jaiprakash—acted as the godfathers of the Janata opposition'.[72] He seems to say that JP was 'against authoritarianism' and was, therefore, defending democracy.[73] The author himself supports the second view.

After Bhoodan

There is some severe criticism of the Bhoodan Movement. Journalist Tavleen Singh provides one such example. She says in her *Lollipop Street* that 'Vinoba Bhave had spent years walking around the Indian countryside persuading landlords to give up their land to the landless.

It may have, at the time, seemed like a truly Gandhian way of making the poor better off. But in the end it made not the slightest bit of difference to anyone since the areas through which he took these long walks remained pretty much as poor as ever while Punjab, where capitalist farming came in with the partition, boomed.'[74]

How is the present situation in Indian villages after Vinoba left the scene in 1982? P. Sainath's talk at Delhi in August 2011 on "Twenty Years After—The Countryside and Two Decades of Reforms" struck the author on at least two points. One is that after twenty years of the reform 46 per cent of the children in India are malnourished. The ratio is higher than in the Sub-Sahara region, and 'this single indicator is not something for you to be proud of'. Second is that most of the farmer suicides are of cash crop farmers. His book, *Everybody Loves a Good Drought, Stories from India's Poorest Districts,*[75] published in 1996, is not at all out of date. He investigated two Districts each from Tamil Nadu, Bihar, Orissa, Madhya Pradesh and Uttar Pradesh. Since he did it during the 'off-agricultural seasons' he could see what the poor people were doing during the '200~240 days'. The off-agricultural season means so many days? But it tallies well, too well, with Gandhi's forced idleness of the peasants during 'four to six months' a year.

One of his earlier pieces entitled "When farmers die" is also worth being quoted here.[76] The suicide of the farmers had been continuing for seven years even in 'better-irrigated regions', he wrote, and discussed 'unbelievable sums' of input into water and other outlay and 'incredible levels of debt', all accompanying the transfer to the cash crops. He concludes, 'Almost every sector of Indian democracy failed the Andhra Pradesh farmer; the Government and the political class; the tame intellectuals and planners. The human rights groups and a once-activist judiciary. And a media...'

6. Employment and Industrialization

Gandhi's Changing View of the Machines

Gandhi made devastating comments on the machinery in *Hind Swaraj*, and said that 'I cannot recall a single good point in connection with machinery. Books can be written to demonstrate its evils'. (*CWMG*,

10-59) Thereafter he repeatedly said that the ideas he had expressed there, and that not only on the machinery, had not changed. Thus, on the future of industrialization in India, he said in his "Speech at Indian Majlis" at Oxford, when he was in Britain for the RTC in October 1931, that '... if the future of industrialism is dark for the West, would it not be darker still for India?' (*CWMG*, 48-225) This was in the midst of the world depression. Also he wrote for the "*Khadi Jagat*" in May 1941 that 'The bloody massacre going on in the present war is probably a demonstration of the fact that industrialism will lead the world to destruction in the end. Enlightened revival of handicrafts alone can save it'. (*CWMG*, 74-59) This was when the phony war in Europe was turning into a hot one.

We, however, notice that his antagonism to the machinery was gradually mitigated with the passage of time. He began to say increasingly that his opposition to the machinery was to the extent that its use squeezed out men from employment. His "Letter to J.M. Sen Gupta", in June 1928, was probably its beginning, in which he wrote that 'I am not against machinery as such, but I am opposed to machinery that may be designed to displace the masses without giving them any adequate and satisfactory substitute'. (*CWMG*, 36-446) Later on he also said in "Notes", in 1946, that 'My opposition to machinery is much misunderstood. I am not opposed to machinery as such. I am opposed to machinery which displaces labour and leaves it idle'. (*CWMG*, 85-239~40)

His opinion of the machinery also began to have still another shade. In his "Interview to Capt. Strunk" in 1937, he said, 'my opposition to machinery, railways, etc., does not mean that as soon as we are independent we should uproot all of them. They will be used for the benefit of the nation...'. (*CWMG*, 65-361) In "Alternative to Industrialism", written on the train from Sevagram to Delhi on 25 August 1946, which proved to be his last journey from the ashram, he said 'I do not believe that industrialization is necessary in any case for any country. It is much less so for India...At the same time I believe that some key industries are necessary'. (*CWMG*, 85-205~6) This will fit in with what Shriman Narayan wrote in *The Gandhian Plan of Economic Development for India*, seen above. Gandhi went a step further and wrote in *Hindu Pani* and *Muslim Pani* in October 1946 that 'As I have often said in these columns trains and steamers are the best media for the practical education of the millions of travellers in spotless cleanliness, hygiene, sanitation and camaraderie between the different communities of India'. (*CWMG*, 85-449) The author is not aware if he has 'often' written this sort of message before, but this passage is unique in that Gandhi recognized, probably for the first time and probably by his own experience, the inevitable function of the modern means of production and transport. This may well be the spot in his whole writings that is closest to the thinking of Marx, together with the idea of acquiring the majority of the masses by non-violence, discussed above.

There is another spot closely related to it. In "Speech at Bilaspur" in 1933 delivered at the B.N. Railway Labourers' Federation, he said that 'I know that labourers do observe the distinction between Harijans and non-Harijans. I expect labourers, more than all others, to efface these distinctions. It has been my deep faith that we shall some day achieve communal unity through labourers. I consider labour to be a powerful unifying agent. It is a great equalizer. It should be a matter of shame to have communal divisions among labourers, who all earn their bread by the sweat of their brow and, therefore, belong to one vast brotherhood' (*CWMG*, 56-282).

The author once had an opportunity of attending a study meeting in Tokyo back in 2000, when a South Korean scholar presented his analysis on the railways under the Japanese rule over Korea, 1910~45. It was the Japanese who constructed most of the railway network in Korea, with their own interests foremost in mind. As the result, the distance between Japan and the Chinese northeast (later Manchukuo) by railways was minimized at the expense of the local industries. The areas where the network was built earlier had been kept under close Japanese bondage, in a way until quite recently. Railways themselves became something very repulsive to the common people. In his childhood it was said that he was a bad person who travelled by the railways. And the fact that the trunk line was running north to south meant that the division of the Peninsula into the North and the South gave a great damage to the unity of the economy. We may wonder if Gandhi's experience at Pietermaritzburg soon after his arrival in South Africa did not have a similar meaning to him on the railways which died very hard.

DP on Gandhi

Dhurjati Prasad Mukerji (hereafter DP), who, together with Radha Kamal Mukerjee, was the founder of the Lucknow School, presented a paper on "Mahatma Gandhi's Views on Machines and Technology" in Europe in 1953. He said that 'The views expressed in 1924 seem to mark a departure from those of 1908 (should be read 1909)... All this appears to be a move away from the uncompromising position taken up in the *Hind Swaraj*". The year 1924 refers to a conversation between Gandhi and Ramchandran, a student from Santiniketan. Then DP gave Gandhi's idea of machinery a very unique position as, in his view, 'Technological values are usually associated with nationalist values, particularly in the eastern countries in the period of their anti-imperialist struggle...and also in the period of economic advance which is held to be possible only with the help of technology'. This will bring us back to what was discussed in the Introduction and at the beginning of Chapter Two.

But it is different with Gandhi. It is his idea that 'Hindu social organization is built on the principle of obligations which Gandhiji insisted on resuscitating in all social and economic spheres of activity...Only in the sphere of political struggle against foreign rule would he allow the exercise of the western sense of rights, and these too hedged in by the sense of social obligations, which was one vital significance of non-violence'. DP goes on that Gandhi's idea of machines and technology become clearer once we take '*aparigraha*, non-possession, or wantlessness and *srama* or labour', though the latter is not quite an Indian value but the former is, into perspective. DP's conclusion is that 'Gandhiji's views have to be carefully studied before any scheme of technical assistance and large-scale technological development is initiated'.[77] DP thus reached a similar point as Rothermund or Vinoba by a different route.

Origin of Gandhi's Anti-Machine View

Gandhi often said that Manchester destroyed India's village industries. Of course it was true. But his criticism of the machinery as such, it seems, originated not in the knowledge of India's economic history, but more from the influence of a certain school of thought in the

West itself, which was skeptical not only of the machinery, but the Western civilization in general. Ruskin belonged to this stream, and so did Tolstoy, whom Gandhi respected most. He said in "Interview to Evelyn Wrench" in 1931 that Ruskin 'made me decide to change my whole outward life' and Tolstoy 'affected the inner being'. (*CWMG*, 48-180) On being asked what world figure has exercised the greatest and best influence upon the twentieth century, in "Interview to Edmond Demeter" in 1931, he simply said, 'Tolstoy. He alone'. (*CWMG*, 48-387~8) In his Preface to *Hind Swaraj*, he writes that 'The views I venture to place before the reader...are also held by thousands of Europeans'. (*CWMG*, 10-7) In the book he says, 'Several English writers refuse to call that civilization which passes under that name'. (*CWMG*, 10-19) Among the twenty recommended books for perusal in its Appendices, as many as eighteen are by the Western authors, six of which are by Tolstoy, and two each by Thoreau and Ruskin. The two exceptions are by Indians, Dadabhai Naoroji and R.C. Dutt. (*CWMG*, 10-65) Out of the eighteen Western books Gandhi valued Henry Maine's *Village Communities* highly. In "What It Means" in 1939, he wrote, 'Mayne (*sic*) has shown that India's villages were a congeries of republics'. (*CWMG*, 71-4)

So there is nothing like the clash of the Eastern and Western civilizations here, as Gandhi may have thought. The Eastern civilization could not have had any treatise on the machinery in the old days. It was a school of thought born within the West, and different from socialism, that appealed to Gandhi.

Gandhi travelled widely in India for more than three decades after he came back to India, either by train or by car. This could not be justified simply by calling those means of transport 'a necessary evil' (*CWMG*, 57-495) as he used to say. Calling it that way does not solve the problem and is even hypocritical. His use of telegrams was also fairly frequent, as seen in the *CWMG*. A telephone was introduced in the Sevagram Ashram on or before 21 October 1940, the day when Gandhi was reported to be making a call (*CWMG*, 73-119). Telegram and telephone were the most advanced means of communication at his time. Would he have used internet if he were here? The UNICEF, Sweden, has sent a virtual story of Jesus, Mother Teresa and Gandhi having a dinner together on the Christmas of 2013, and, when shown the internet, Jesus clicked a wrong banner, Mother Teresa showed no interest, but Gandhi tried and clicked the right one! (http://www.fb.se/work/unicef/the-good-guys-christmas)

The use of those machines should have been theorized and made more convincing by Gandhi himself. One way of doing so was to justify the use of machinery as long as it does not displace humans. We will also have to consider what N.K. Bose said, that in *Hind Swaraj* Gandhi was mixing up 'industrialism as such' with 'the capitalistic form of industrial civilization'.[78]

Visveswaraya, and the NPC

It was M. Visveswaraya, Gandhi's contemporary, engineer, civil servant both in British India and Mysore State, later Dewan (Prime Minister) of Mysore, who strongly made the case for industrialization in Gandhi's time. In his book, *Planned Economy for India*, 1934, Visveswaraya wrote, in the same vein as Gandhi, that in the villages there was employment only for four to six months a year and it was important to build village industries. But he also said that if India started manufacturing machinery, like cars and railway wagons, she would not have to export scarce food to import such merchandise. As to the relation of the use of machinery and employment, he said it would take India twenty years more before she comes to the point where more use of machinery would displace employment. The use of machinery and power will increase employment till such a point is reached.

Visveswaraya goes on that India as a nation must have a ten-year development plan, and a Central Economic Council to supervise it. According to him, the key points of such a plan are to decrease the number of people dependent on agriculture from the present 250 million to 200, to increase employment in organized sector from 1.5 million to 10 million, and to increase literacy from 8 to 50 per cent. Here the literacy is ingrained in the bringing up of industrial manpower.[79]

The Congress in a few years constituted a National Planning Committee under the Chairmanship of Nehru. It was more or less of the type that Visveswaraya thought of in his book. E.M.S. wrote in his *Ism* that this committee was 'the first effort to translate into practice the glorious vision that had been placed before the country by Sir M. Visweswarayya in his book on Indian planning'.[80] When the first attempt was thus made by the Congress to have a long-term planning, it was based not on Gandhi's but on a non-Congressman's thinking. Gandhi himself wrote in a "Letter to M. Visvesvarayya" of 10 December 1934 that 'My objection comes in when such machinery displaces human labour without providing displaced hands with a substitute at least as good as displaced labour'. (*CWMG*, 59-435) The July 1939 number of the *Gram Udyog Patrika*, the AIVIA's monthly bulletin, contained what Gandhi called 'an interesting article on national planning' in "Mills *vs*. Charkha", which said that 'Any planning in our country that ignores the absorption of labour wealth will be misplaced'. (*CWMG*, 70-74) Gandhi himself wrote soon afterwards in "Letter to Jawaharlal Nehru" that 'I have never been able to understand or appreciate the labours of the (National Planning) Committee'. (*CWMG*, 70-86)

Such a process created a tradition of bypassing Gandhi's thought in India's planning without studying it carefully, for better or for worse. This takes us back to what Sukhamoy Chakrawarty said on Gandhian economics, quoted above. Again did not Nehru speak his language? We wonder, however, if Gandhi could not have been attracted by the concept of 'Appropriate Technology', thus making his constructive programme more technologically advanced and more broadly acceptable.G. P. Pradhan writes in *Pursuit of Ideals*, his autobiography, that it was Ram Manohar Lohia's original idea to evolve an agro-industrial society by creating employment on a wide scale with the appropriate technology.[81]

Interestingly the question of industrialization or no industrialization was, in a sense, given a decisive word sixty years after Gandhi's death. On 6 March 2008, the then Governor of West Bengal, Gopal Krishna Gandhi, a grand-son of Gandhi, said in the Legislative Assembly of that State that it was 'considered necessary to consolidate our success in agriculture and move towards rapid industrialization for the overall growth of the economy of the State and to create job opportunities'.[82]

E.M.S., in concluding the second edition of his *Ism*, wrote that though there was a fundamental difference between Marxism-Leninism and Gandhism, 'on specific issues where it is possible to develop joint actions, the opportunity should be fully utilized'.[83] This was written in 1981. Judging from the context, it seems he was not that positive on such 'joint actions' at this time. It would be interesting to ask which of the two, the leftists or the Gandhians, will take the initiative if such joint actions are at all possible. And what would be the position of other forces, like, say, *dalits* or tribals, in this equation. Shriman Narayan writes that E.M.S. admitted that 'the Gramdan Movement provided an alternative to their (the Communists') own policy in respect of the land problem'.[84] This was at 'a historic Gramdan Conference' at Yelwal, Karnataka, in September 1957 which both he and Vinoba attended besides Nehru and others. He was the Chief Minister of Kerala then. This is an interesting comment, and if it is correct, the Communists' policy could also have been an alternative to the Bhoodan and Gramdan Movements.

Still later, Ramachandra Guha wrote down his impressions when he saw three school boys in rural Karnataka who had apparently played the roles of Ambedkar, Visveswaraya and Gandhi, respectively, at a shool function. His impression was 'The vision of those young boys was capaciously inclusive…the boys understood what partisans and scholars do not—that our country today needs all three….. What I saw that day was a spontaneous, magnificent illustration of the idea of India.'[85]

Incidentally, Guha, toward the end of his recent work *Gandhi before India*, criticized E.M.S.'s discussion of Gandhi in his *Ism.* He writes that the *Ism* was written in the mid-1950s, but 'The image of Marxism took a battering in subsequent decades. News of the Gulag, the purges, the brutal suppression of minorities, and the mass famines induced by Communist regimes, have made it less easy to hail Marxism as 'progressive' while dismissing Gandhism as 'reactionary''.[86]

What Guha says here on the USSR may be perfectly true. The author, however, would have hoped that E.M.S. or any other person should have been criticized not by what happened outside their country on which they had no control, but by whether they have become independent of the Soviet influence, and standing on their own.

7. "Untouchables"

Assimilation, and Not Multi-Culturalism?

We have already argued in Chapter One that Gandhi dealt with the Harijans as a Hindu problem. His strong opposition to allowing them a separate electorate was one aspect of it. His policy was essentially one of assimilation, of leading them to abandon certain customs which he did not consider appropriate for Hindus. Gandhi expressed his idea on this point in some detail perhaps for the first time in his "Speech at "Antyaj" Conference, Nagpur" at the end of 1920. There he said, 'Hindus say that the *Antyajas* drink, that they eat anything and everything, that they do not observe rules of personal cleanliness, that they kill cows...(so) they should give up drinking and eating beef or, at any rate, killing cows...If anyone offers you left-over food...you should refuse to accept it and ask him to give you grains instead. Be clean in your habits. When you have finished your work of cleaning latrines, change your dress'. (*CWMG*, 19-153)

He himself made it clear, as we have seen, that his object in his Harijan work was 'their assimilation into the Hindu fold'. Has his idea prevented him from having for the future of India an image of a multi-cultural society ? In the case of Ramachandra Guha's 'idea of India' concept mentioned above, pluralism was apparently one important component of it. Chapter Six of his previous book, *India After Gandhi*, on the Constitution-making in independent India, was also so entitled, though he did not give it a clear definition.

True, Gandhi grew increasingly tolerant of inter-caste and inter-religious dining and marriage. Even in the midst of the Khilafat Movement, he wrote in his "Hindu-Mohammedan Unity" in the beginning of 1920 that 'I hold it to be utterly impossible for Hindus and Mohammedans to inter-marry and yet retain intact each other's religion'. (*CWMG*, 17-46) Conversion was out of question for him, and this itself remained throughout. In his "Interview to "Deshabhimani" " in 1921, when he was asked 'Are you for caste... in regard to inter-dining and inter-marriage?', his answer was 'I am against both on hygienic and spiritual grounds'. (*CWMG*, 21-187) This was his initial position. But he did not remain at the same position. As Vinoba said, 'He was changing everyday, was developed every moment...So we should not think in terms of what he would do or would not do if alive today'.[87] In "Letter to Haribhau Phatak" in October 1932, he said, 'Inter-dining and inter-marriage are not an essential part of removal of untouchability root and branch. These two form a separate reform and must come one day for all sections of Hinduism'. (*CWMG*, 51-199) Thus he had come around to the view that they would sooner or later be put on a programme, at least for the Hindus including Harijans. When Indira, Jawaharlal's daughter, was engaged to Feroz Gandhi, a Parsi, he wrote in "Notes"(subtitle, Indira Nehru's Engagement) in March 1942 that 'I have been, and I am still, as strong an opponent of either party changing religion for the sake of marriage…In the present case there is no question of change of religion…As time advances such unions are bound to multiply with benefit to society'. (*CWMG*, 75-375)

Therefore one would make a mistake in judging Gandhi by his view on Manilal's case of 1926 alone, or on Indira's case of 1942 alone. On the marriage of Abha, daughter of Amrita Lal Chatterjee, a Bengali, and Kanu Gandhi in 1944, Gandhi wrote in "Letter to Shantikumar N. Morarjee" that 'Is it not our wish that this inter-caste and inter-provincial marriage should prove to be ideal in every respect?'. (*CWMG*, 78-239) Abha was to be one of the few Bengalis among Gandhi's entourage at Noakhali in 1946-47 and was of great use. Then he wrote in "Letter to Narahari D. Parikh" of May 1945 that 'I would encourage them (inter-provincial marriages) and they ought to be encouraged', then 'we should unhesitatingly accord the highest importance to marriages between Ati-Sudras and caste-Hindus', and then 'Where parents are wise, there should be no difficulty even about marriages between persons of different religions'. Gandhi concluded this letter by saying that 'This will give you a glimpse of my latest thinking. This is an important letter'. (*CWMG*, 80-77~78)

One of the points he arrived at was, as he wrote in "Note to Munnalal G. Shah" in 1946, 'my blessings are given only when one of the parties to the marriage is a Harijan'. (*CWMG*, 84-56) Roughly at this time he wrote in "Marriages between Harijans and Non-Harijans" that 'at present the marriage of a caste Hindu girl to a Harijan is better than that of a Harijan girl to a caste Hindu'. (*CWMG*, 84-389) Again at this time, on inter-dining also, he said in "Talk with Members of Harijan Sevak Sangh" that 'At one time I did say that interdining was not an essential part of the campaign for the removal of untouchability…Today I encourage it'. (*CWMG*, 84-25) Moreover, he said in "Speech at Prayer Meeting" in Noakhali early in 1947 that, 'he had come to the conclusion long ago, that an inter-religious marriage was a welcome event whenever it took place…There was no question in this of conversion. Hence the marriage ceremony would be performed by priests belonging to both faiths'. (*CWMG*, 87-5) A very original idea. Did he then come to embrace multi-culturalism? It seems so, at least to some extent. He said in the above talk with the Harijan Sevak Sangh that 'My mind, I hope, is ever growing, ever moving forward'. (*CWMG*, 84-24)

Incidentally Ambedkar in his "Annihilation of Caste" says that the inter-caste dining is not enough for the abolition of caste, and 'I am convinced that the real remedy is inter-marriage'.[88] He practiced it himself.

A similar question may be asked on his attitude toward what sociologists call Sanskritization. Its idea was fully developed by M.N. Srinivas in his *Social Change in Modern India,* especially in its first chapter entitled "Sanscritization". Sociologist N. Jayaram defines it by quoting from Srinivas' another book[89] in this way. '…the process by which a low caste or tribe or other group takes over the customs, ritual, beliefs, ideology and style of life of a high and, in particular, a 'twice-born' (*dwija*) caste.'[90] It is an attempted move for upward mobility in the caste system itself and is not likely to wreck the system as such.

At another "Speech at Prayer Meeting" in Noakhali in February 1947, most of the discussion was about the Namashudras. It was presumably because they occupied a large part of the Hindus left behind after the riot in the previous year, as Gandhi himself was writing elsewhere. Because of the child marriage there were many young widows among the Namashudra women. A question arose that 'Among one section of that caste widow-marriage was prevalent. But in imitation of another section which was looked upon as superior, the former is giving up that practice'. This was typical sanskritization. Gandhi said that 'he advocated widow-remarriage for all young widows', and said that he was averse to child-marriages, was against the system of dowry, and would advise them to abolish all caste distinctions amongst themselves. (*CWMG*, 87-11)

Gandhi's Criticism of the Outcaste System

Even in his own framework of Hinduism, however, he kept criticizing the way the Depressed Classes were so classified. He went through the Hindu scripture himself, or through the eyes of his trusted co-workers like Vinoba, and came to the conclusion that there were no such categories of people described in them. Perhaps he put this idea for the first time in his "Speech at Tinnevelly" in 1921. He said that 'I dare tell the whole of this audience that there is no provision for untouchability in the whole of our *shastras*'. (*CWMG*, 21-191) It would have taken a great deal of moral courage to do so.

He put his doubt in a more systematic way in the form of ten questions in "Questions for Shastri Parishad" toward the end of 1932. They were, '(1) Define untouchability according to *shastras*. (2) Can the definition of untouchables given in the *shastras* be applied to the so-called untouchables of the present day? (3) What are the restrictions imposed by *shastras* on the untouchables? (4) Can an individual free from untouchability in his own lifetime? (5) What are the injunctions of the *shastras* regarding behaviour of the touchables with the untouchables? (6) Under what circumstances will the *shastras* permit temple-entry by the untouchables? (7) What are *shastras*? (8) How is authoritativeness of the *shastras* proved? (9) How will the differences arising over the definitions or interpretations of *shastras* be decided? (10) What are your conclusions?'. (*CWMG*, 52-265)

Just around this time, he wrote in "Letter to Mathuradas Trikumji" that 'I am being visited by a great number of *shastris* these days…It has become difficult to learn anything from them…". (*CWMG*, 52-269) He also said in "Statement on Untouchability (I)" a little earlier in 1932 that 'I find no warrant for untouchability' even in the *Gita* (*CWMG*, 51-345), or in "Letter to V.S.R. Sastri" of March 1933 that 'it has been a matter of very deep grief to me that in the contact I am having with so many learned *sanatanists*, hardly anyone of them has touched the fundamental points I have raised', which are for example 'Where is the authority in the *Vedas* for regarding them (untouchables) as such? And if there is none in the *Vedas*, can the later *shastras* impose disabilities or create classes not contemplated by the *Vedas*?'. (*CWMG*, 53-476)

Gandhi was writing from prison, as even in prison he was, in the words of the Government of India addressed to Bombay Government on November 1 1932, 'allowed complete freedom in regard to visitors and correspondence on matters strictly confined to removal of untouchability and that there should be no restriction on publicity'.

(*CWMG*, 51-290 fn. 1) Such an extraordinary measure on the part of the Government of India was probably intended to change the direction of CD, nominally still going on at this time, from the movement for independence to that of social reform, to let Gandhi take over a most difficult task in the field of social reform, if possible to press a wedge between caste Hindus and untouchables. In "Statement to the Press" in 1934, after the Harijan tour, he himself said that 'Many think that it was a profound error for me to have disturbed the course of the civil resistance struggle by taking up the (*Harijan*) question in the manner and at the time I did. I feel that I would have been untrue to myself, if I had taken any other course'. (*CWMG*, 59-6) Gandhi certainly diverted the CD Movement. He knew it. But perhaps he could not have lived without doing so.

After he was released, he started a '*Harijan* tour' at Wardha on 7 November 1933 and concluded it at Benares on 2 August 1934. The tour was a continuation of his diversion. Still the people showed their confidence in him by coming to hear him in strength. Before the start, he explained Vinoba's studies in "Speech to *Harijans*" and said that 'Vinoba has made a thorough study of the scriptures. He says that nowhere has God enjoined that some are high and others low, some touchable and some untouchable'. (*CWMG*, 56-189) During the tour he made a great number of speeches. What he wrote in "An Adi-Dravida's Difficulties" during the tour shows his basic attitude towards religions. He said, criticizing *Manusmriti*, 'Therefore I have suggested to seekers after Truth the only safe rule for their guidance in studying *shastras*, namely, that they should reject whatever is contrary to truth and *ahimsa*, the true foundations of all religions' (*CWMG*, 57-355) He received a large number of deputations, memorandum and so on. In "Our Shame" in 1934, for instance, he gives a summary of an eighteen-point list of disabilities submitted to him by 'Adi-Hindus of Tamil Districts'. In what Gandhi called 'a formidable catalogue', the disabilities included no access to schools, wells, and temples, making it a crime to hold umbrellas and wear sandals, closure of public pathways and so on. (*CWMG*, 57-259~261)

Even more original than the analysis of the scriptures was his study of the lists of those classes from the *Census Reports*, for example, from Bengal. He compared the list of 1931 with that of 1921 in "Human Manufacture (-II)" of May 1933, and said that 'In the British districts only of Bengal, 1,801,712 persons who were included in the list of 1921 have been excluded from that of 1931 and the number belongs to eight castes...Similarly there are some groups who have been for the first time included in the list of 1931...'. (*CWMG*, 55-118) He concluded that the untouchables was 'a human manufacture' by the arbitrary judgement of the British authorities. Probably also basing his argument on the 1931 Census, he said in "Notes" in March 1933 that there were eighty-six 'exterior castes' in Madras Presidency, and 'The more one studies these figures, the stronger will grow the conviction that this untouchability is purely man-made'. (*CWMG*, 54-45)

He has also reached a conclusion on his own in his "Our Delusion" in 1929 that 'If untouchability were a part of religion an untouchable of one province would be treated as such in every other province', but the reality is very different from that. (*CWMG*, 42-243) When he said 'we are forcing them (untouchables) to resist us', which is the reflection of ourselves, he was completely true and honest. Still, he did not go far enough to denounce the caste system as such. This was probably one example that he lacked moral and political courage to do, together with the land redistribution, and the widow remarriage.

Temple-Entry vs. *Socio-Economic Measures*

One question which claimed more of Gandhi's attention than anything else about the Untouchables was that of their entry into Hindu temples. Probably its earliest written manifestation was "A Letter" of 14 October 1932, where he wrote that 'Temple-entry is the crux of the movement for eradication of untouchability'. (*CWMG*, 51-241) He explained it when he wrote in "Statement on Untouchability-IX" in late November 1932 that 'the question whether *harijans* want to, or would enter into temples, if they were open to them, is irrelevant. The removal of untouchability is not a matter of bestowing patronage on *harijans*. It is one of penance and purification by the caste Hindus and one of the penances they have to do is to open the Hindu temples and invite the *harijans* to them'. (*CWMG*, 52-72) In "Statement on Viceroy's Decision" in January 1932 he said 'Economic and all other uplift will follow temple-entry as light follows dawn'. (*CWMG*,

53-131) Similarly in his "Letter to C.F. Andrews" he refers to 'the fundamental distinction I have drawn between the temple-entry and the economic and educational programme'. (*CWMG*, 53-163) Therefore, as in "*harijans* and Temple-Entry" in April 1933, 'The fact is temple-entry is not a substitute for any other uplift'. (*CWMG*, 54-336)

Gandhi, however, did not like to press the temples to open up. His method was to take the opinion of the regular goers to the temples still closed to Harijans. In the famous case of the Guruvayur Temple, near Trichur, in present Kerala, he advised in "Letter to K. Kelappan" of November 1932, that 'there should be a methodical taking of a referendum of temple-goers, say within a ten-mile radius. And in order to have the thing absolutely above the board, signatures should be taken at public meetings in the presence of witnesses…'. (*CWMG*, 52-43) The minute attention shown by Gandhi to the consciousness of the masses, and his eagerness to share it with the co-workers, were characteristic of him. In this case, as Gandhi wrote in "Statement on Untouchability-XIII", 'The Ponnani Taluk (where the temple is located) is the stronghold of orthodoxy and yet there was a decisive majority in favour of admission of the untouchables to that shrine now made famous throughout the length and breadth of the land'. (*CWMG*, 52-304)

On the impact of Temple-Entry on the *harijans*, Gandhi wrote in "Temple-Entry *vs*. Economic Uplift" in 1934, during the *Harijan* tour, that 'Only last week, between Dharwar and Belgaum, I opened three temples to *harijans* in the presence of crowds of *savarna* Hindus and *harijans*. If critics had been present at the opening and noticed the pleasure on the countenances of the *harijans* present as they bowed before the image and received the *prasad*, their criticism would have been silenced'(*CWMG*, 57-285) About this time Gandhi in "Speech at Public Meeting, Trivandrum" said that Malabar, together with Travancore and Cochin, the three components of Kerala, 'was the blackest spot in the untouchability map of India'. (*CWMG*, 57-22~23) On the untouchability in his own Gujarat also he said something harsh. He wrote in "Our Duty" that 'Perhaps the burden of untouchability falls on Harijans in one way nowhere so heavily as in Gujarat', (*CWMG*, 61-380) and in "Lathi's Example" that 'Indeed in some vital matters untouchability is worse in Gujarat than elsewhere and worst in Kathiawar' (*CWMG*, 65-254). He continued in "Water for *harijans* in Gujarat" that 'The ghastly form of untouchability which we find in Gujarat is not found anywhere else', (*CWMG*, 76-175) and finally in "Shocking If True" that he had been informed by the Gujarat Harijan Sevak Sangh that 'apart from Karadi nowhere are temples open to *harijans*, and nowhere may they use public wells'. (*CWMG*, 83-239)

There was organized opposition to the Temple Entry Movement. Gandhi told the audience in "Speech at Public Meeting, Tanjore" during his *Harijan* tour that 'I have been told not once but repeatedly that our *sanatanist* friends would associate with all other reforms with reference to untouchability, if only I would surrender the claim of Temple-Entry on behalf of the Harijans'. (*CWMG*, 57-160) If this was true, it would have proved Gandhi correct when he said that the Temple-Entry question was more significant than anything else. Many years later, in "Speech at Prayer Meeting" at Delhi at the end of 1947, Gandhi told the audience that the largest temple in Maharashtra at Pandharpur was now open, but 'Now they say that a large number of Brahmin priests are unhappy over this because the temple is visited by many Harijans every day. Some of the priests seem to have gone on a fast'. (*CWMG*, 90-327)

Partition and the Harijans

At the same time, as Gandhi was emphasizing in the same speech, the victimization of the *harijans* in the course of the Partition was going on and becoming extremely serious. He said that in Sind, which had become a part of Pakistan, 'Those Hindus who are called untouchables are particularly harassed there and they have no means of livelihood'. (*CWMG*, 90-32) He sent a couple of letters to Indian ship-owners in September 1947 and requested them to bring back *harijans* from there to Kathiawar by their ships free of charge. In one of them, "Letter to Shantikumar N. Morarjee", he wrote, 'There are many *harijans* in Sind. They are in great distress and are faced with starvation'. (*CWMG*, 89-235) The "Letter to Shoorji Vallabhdas" was of about the same content (*CWMG*, 89-236). In "Speech at Prayer Meeting" in December that year, he said that 'A doctor from Sind has written to say that the *harijans* left behind there are in a pitiable condition. If only *harijans* were left behind in Sind and caste Hindus went away, nothing but annihilation awaited them'. (*CWMG*, 90-168)

It was reported that '*harijans* in Sind and Baluchistan were being prevented from migrating to India under the Essential Services Ordinance' of the newly-created Pakistan. (*CWMG*, 90-168, fn. 1) Somewhat earlier, on 29 June, probably in the midst of carnage in the Punjab, he said in "Talk with Bhimsen Sacbhar", Leader of the Congress in the Punjab Assembly, that 'I shall be happy if you and your family do not leave Pakistan but all of you bravely sacrifice your lives there...I am sorry to say that the local leaders who have some influence are trying at any cost to transfer their property and family to safety. When this is happening, with what face can I advise the poor, the common people not to run away but to die wherever they are?' (*CWMG*, 88-236)

On East Bengal he said in "Speech at Prayer Meeting" in October of that year that 'Those people (from Noakhali) tell me that the Hindus in Dacca are fleeing...it is very wrong that influential people run away from there in order to save their lives while the poor, helpless people stay on there. There is a large population of *sudras* there. How can they be expected to show the requisite courage?... Wherever you go, you should always keep the poor with you'. (*CWMG*, 89-345) In Noakhali also, as he said in another "Speech at Prayer Meeting" later in the same month, 'I found in Noakhali that the rich had run away from there, leaving the poor behind. The villages in that area are full of people whom we...call untouchables'. (*CWMG*, 89-443) With stark candour he said in "Talk with Marwari Deputation" in the midst of the Calcutta riots, which prevented him from going to Noakhali to spend the independence day there, that 'The situation calls for sacrifice on the part of top-rankers. So far the unknown, nameless rank and file alone have been the victims of the holocaust with the one exception of the late Ganesh Shankar Vidyarthi. That is not enough'. (*CWMG*, 89-129)

Without saying so he was talking about manliness here. Vidyarthi's name had been mentioned several times before although quite a long time had passed since his death in 1931. It is as if the sharp hierarchical order in the Hindu society was reflected in the way people took flight to safety. More important was "Talk with

Laljibhai" of 21 October 1947. Though it overlaps with the previous talk it is worth quoting almost in full. Gandhi said, 'How can I ask anyone not to leave the land of his birth? The leaders were able to come so easily with their families and belongings but the poor, helpless villagers are in a sad plight. If even one of you had died there I would have danced for joy…Jinnah says he has provided protection for all and still people flee. But if a few of you had continued to wear *khadi* caps and Hindu dress as you used to and carried on your normal vocations and if then you had been killed, I could have asked Jinnah what had happened to his promise. But how can I say anything today? And so his lie carries the day. People are being coerced and it is being said that they are needlessly frightened…There has been some flaw somewhere in my *ahimsa*…How otherwise could they suddenly have lost the power of self-sacrifice?... If even people like you are coming away, how can I tell the refugees not to leave their homes but to die there, or that they must go back to their homes?' (*CWMG*, 89-378~379)

Here Gandhi was requesting the whole of the caste Hindus to restore their manliness, again without using the word, and their honour. He must have implied the repentance, and trusteeship, he thought the caste Hindus owed to the Harijans, who were actually in mortal danger. But in actual reality the caste Hindus have fled at the expense of the Harijans. In the end he became the victim himself, and almost the only one among the leaders. Would it not be possible to say that he became a martyr like Jesus Christ?

In Temple-Entry *versus* economic uplift, however, Gandhi did not simply support the movement for the former. He was also encouraging various village industrial skills to be imparted to the Harijans. As he said in "Speech At Harijan Industrial School, Delhi" in the middle of 1939, he attended the ceremony of the first batch of twenty-one students leaving the school to give them certificates. The training in the school, which was established in 1936, comprised carpentry, tailoring, leather work and paper-making. (*CWMG*, 70-32, fn.1) We wonder if the movements from among the Untouchables who were against Gandhi's emphasis on Temple-Entry had themselves put forward any counter-programme to match this school, for example, for the economic uplift of the Harijans.

Adivasis and Gandhi

Much of what has been said in the above on the untouchables may also be said on the tribals, or the Scheduled Tribes. But, although '*adivasis*' is listed in the Constructive Programme, Gandhi himself has given only a few sporadic observations about them. 'Thakkar Bapa and Khersaheb are working among the *adivasis*' (*CWMG*, 82-188), said Gandhi in "Letter to Mrs. S.R. Das", indicating his two main co-workers in this field. The term *adivasi* itself is said to have been coined by Bapa. Verrier Elwin may also be put in this category in view of his close association with Gandhi. Otherwise, he said in "Interview to N.G. Ranga" that 'Unfortunately very few Congressmen have taken to it'. (*CWMG*, 78-250) An ex-MLA from the Ho tribe at Chaibasa, Jharkhand, told the author who stayed there overnight in 2007 that in his opinion Gandhi had a philosophy for the *harijans*, but not for the tribals. In 1925, Gandhi travelled through Chaibasa. He left his impression in "*My Notes* (sub-title, The *Goshala at Chaibasa*)" thus, 'Chaibasa is a small town in Chhotanagpur', (*CWMG*, 28-245), and also in "*Bihar Notes* (sub-title, *With Aboriginals*)" that 'It was at Chaibasa that I made the acquaintance of the *Ho* tribe—a most interesting body of men and women, simple as children, with a faith that it is not easy to shake. Many of them have taken to the *charkha* and *khaddar*. Congress workers began the work of reformation among them in 1921. Many have given up eating carrion and some have even taken to vegetarianism'. (*CWMG*, 28-295)

It is clear that Gandhi had an idea to assimilate the tribals into Hinduism, just like the untouchables. Rodriguez, Editor of the *Essential Writings of Ambedkar*, writes in the "Introduction" on Ambedkar and the tribals that 'Ambedkar, however, did not explore the tribal cultures and did not attempt to build a political bridge-head with them, although in terms of deprivation, he felt, the 'Untouchables' and these communities formed a common constituency'.[91] The "Introduction" says, however, that 'Ambedkar took a great deal of interest in some of the major multi-purpose developmental projects such as the Damodar Valley Corporation and the Mahanadi River projects...this experience made him seek the portfolio of Planning'.[92] These large multi-purpose hydro-projects are known to have evicted much larger number of people than anything else from their places of residence and work, and great many of them are tribals. Was Ambedkar aware of it?

Are the tribals a distinct category of people? There seems to be a divergence of opinion among the scholars. It is natural given the fact that the concept basically owes to the British policy, which was accepted by the Government of India after independence, just like the Scheduled Castes. Anthropologist S.C. Dube, for example, wrote in 1977 that 'At no stage, however, did we have a set of clear indicators of tribalness'.[93] This means that the group of people who are called Scheduled Tribes, tribals, or *adivasis* are not a socially distinct one, let alone biologically.

At the other end, Ram Dayal Munda, an anthropologist mentioned above, wrote that the following points were characteristic of the belief system of the tribal people, namely, to look at the grand-parent and the grand-child as the most endearing, no need for the places of worship, to consider one's shadow as the departed souls, no perception of heaven-hell, no priesthood, and no *avatar* or a messiah or a prophet.[94] Which of these two views would Gandhi have agreed if he had known these differences?

In view of the victimization of many tribals in the process of constructing large-scale projects, the Maoists or Naxalites are often operating close to the *adivasi* areas. The Chenoys report that 'The Government claims that almost one-fourth of the 600 districts in twelve Indian States…are 'extremism-affected''.[95] We may wonder if Gandhi would have been urged to alter his indifference, if not quite opposition, to property redistribution.

Early in 2004, the author attended Fourth World Social Forum, under the slogan 'Another Society is Possible', in Mumbai, the first of its kind in Asia. There he came across with almost a shock of his life. One day we were at a large auditorium full of *dalits*, tribals, and women, with two large posters of Ambedkar. It was what seemed to be the anti-Gandhian atmosphere filling the hall, though unspoken, that was shocking.

Notes

1. *The Hindu*, Independent India at 60 Special Issue, 2007.

2. *Times of India*, 18 October 2013.
3. Hanumantha Rao, "Inclusive Growth", *Indian Economic Journal*, April-June 2010, 10.
4. *The Hindu*, 16 August 2010.
5. *The Indian Express*, 16 August 2010.
6. *The Hindu*, 15 November 2004.
7. *Business World*, 27 August 2007.
8. *Times of India*, 26 August 2007.
9. Ramachandra Guha, *India After Gandhi*, 697~8.
10. G. Balatchandirane, "India's BRICs Ambitions...", Rajaram Panda and Y. Fukazawa, eds. *India and Japan*, 198~9, 205~7.
11. Gurcharan Das, "The India Model", *Foreign Affairs*, July/August 2006, 7.
12. Dreze and Sen, "Putting Growth in its Place", *Outlook*, 14 November 2011, 52~3.
13. S. Hirashima, "Growth, Equity and Labour Absorption in Japanese Agriculture", 79-85.
14. Rothermund, *ibid.*, 117.
15. *The Hindu*, 7 February 2008.
16. Gopalkrishna Gandhi, *The Oxford India Gandhi*, 493~4.
17. E.M.S., "Minute of Dissent", *History, Society and Land Relations*, 150~73.
18. E.M.S. *History*... 230.
19. E.M.S. *Reminiscences of an Indian Communist*, 70.
20. Gilbert Etienne, "Mahatma Gandhi, Rural Development and Society", B.R. Nanda, ed., *Mahatma Gandhi 125 Years*, 337.
21. T.N. Jagadisan devotes Ch.18 of his autobiography to the "The First All India Leprosy Workers' Conference". *Fulfilment through Leprosy*, 119-130.
22. Yajnik, *ibid.*, 15.
23. Shriman Narayan Agarwal, *The Gandhian Plan*, 2.
24. Radha Kamal Mukerjee, *Planning the Countryside: First Report.*
25. P.C. Joshi, "Founders of the Lucknow School", *EPW*, 16 August 1986, 1455~69.
26. Bahuguna, Sunderlal, "Message from Our Experiences from the Chipko Movement and the Anti Tehri Dam Movement", *Asian Cultural Studies* 17, 2008, 97~106.
27. Ishizaka Shinya, "The Anti Tehri Dam Movement as a New Social Movement and Gandhism", *Journal of the Japanese Association for South Asian Studies*, 18, 2006, 76~95.
28. *Backward Classes Commission Report*, First Part, 60.
29. Kamaladevi, *Memoirs*, 123~4.
30. Shakuntala Narasimhan, *Kamaladevi Chattopadhyay*, 207.
31. Reena Nanda, *ibid.*, 29.
32. Jean Dreze and Amartya Sen, *India: Economic Development and Social Opportunity.*
33. JICA, *Nepal.*

34. Vinoba, *ibid.*, 426.
35. S.S. Gill, *ibid.*, 149.
36. Bose, Bose and Patwardhan, *ibid.*, 33.
37. *Ibid.*
38. Sukhamoy Chakrawarty, *Development Planning* (from Japanese translation).
39. *Writings of Bipan Chandra*, 37~8.
40. *Ibid.*, 37, fn. 55.
41. Sheela Reddy, "Gandhi, A Second Coming", *Outlook*, 11 September 2006, 32~8.
42. E.M.S., The Mahatma and the *Ism* (hereafter *Ism*), 153.
43. Rothermund, *ibid.*, 62~3.
44. B.R. Nanda, "Govind Ballabh Pant: A Biographical Sketch", *Selected Works of Govind Ballabh Pant*, Vol. 2, xvii.
45. B.R. Nanda, *Gandhi and His Critics*, 85.
46. B.R. Nanda, A Biographical Sketch", *ibid.*, xvii~xviii.
47. E.M.S. *Ism*, 127.
48. Sumit Sarkar, *Modern India*, 406.
49. *Ibid.*, 440.
50. EMS, A Short History of the Peasant Movement in Malabar, *History...*, *ibid.*, 174.
51. *Ibid.*, 178.
52. *Ibid.*, 194.
53. Weber, *Ibid.*, 23.
54. *Writings of Bipan Chandra*, 17.
55. *Ibid.*, 167.
56. Vinoba, *ibid.*, 384~5.
57. Yajnik, *ibid.*, 196.
58. *Ibid.*, 441.
59. Shriman Narayan, *Vinoba—His Life and Work*, 190~1.
60. *The Hindu*, 23 August 2007.
61. Shriman Narayan, *Vinoba*, *ibid.*, 210.
62. *Ibid.*, 213.
63. *Ibid.*, 210.
64. *Ibid.*, 262.
65. Shriman Narayan, *Vinoba*, *ibid.*, 241.
66. *Ibid.*, 245~6.
67. Vinoba, *ibid.*, 430.
68. Vinoba, *ibid.*, 431~2.
69. Bipan Chandra, *In the Name of Democracy*, 52.
70. *Ibid.*,141.
71. *Ibid.*, 288.
72. EMS, *Ism*, 168.
73. *Ibid.*, 169.
74. Tavleen Singh, *Lollipop Street*, 270.

75. P. Sainath, *Everybody Loves A Good Drought.*
76. *The Hindu*, 22 June 2004.
77. D.P. Mukerji, "Mahatma Gandhi's Views on Machines and Technology", *Diversities*, 205~27.
78. N.K. Bose, in Bose and Patwardhan, *ibid.*, 19.
79. M. Visveswaraya, *Planned Economy for India*, 294~5.
80. EMS, *Ism*, 104.
81. G.P. Pradhan, *Pursuit of Ideals*, 64.
82. *The Hindu*, 7 March 2008.
83. EMS, *Ism*, 169.
84. Shriman Narayan, *Vinoba*, *ibid.*, 256.
85. Ramachandra Guha, "A Nation Consumed by…", *Outlook*, 31 January 2011, 30~44.
86. Ramachandra Guha, *Gandhi Before India*, 546.
87. Vinoba, *ibid.*, 384.
88. *Essential Writings of Ambedkar*, 288.
89. M.N. Srinivas, *The Cohesive Role of Sanskritization and Other Essays*, Oxford University Press, 1989.
90. N. Jayaram, "Caste and Hinduism:Changing Protean Relationship", M.N. Srinivas, ed., *Caste—Its Twentieth Century Avatar*, Penguin, 1996, 77.
91. Rodriguez, Introduction, *Essential Writings of Ambedkar*, 29.
92. *Ibid.*, 14.
93. S.C. Dube, Introduction, *Tribal Heritage of India*, Vol. 1, 2.
94. R.D. Munda, *Adi-Dharam Religious Beliefs of the Adivasis of India*, 44~5.
95. A.M. Chenoy and K.A.M. Chenoy, *Maoist and Other Armed Conflicts*, 57.

FOUR
Gandhi against Communalism

'I am glad that you would rather be deceived by the whole world than deceive anyone'. "Speech at Wedding of Ramdas Gandhi", 27 January 1928, CWMG, Vol. 35, p. 499. 'To be killed but never to kill is the law that governs us, and women should surely excel in this field'. "Speech at Kasturba Gandhi National Memorial Trust Women Agents' Meeting".
—28 March 1946, *CWMG*, Vol. 83, p. 333.

1. Khilafat: The First Encounter

Pitfalls with the Khilafat Movement

Gandhi plunged into the Khilafat Movement almost blind-folded, in the sense that he had not studied the Arabs or Turks and their national aspiration by that time. He wrote a published "Letter to Viceroy" on 29 April 1918, during the First World War, at the end of which he called Viceroy Chelmsford's attention to 'definite assurances about Mahomedan States…the most scrupulous regard for the right of these States, and for the Muslim sentiment as to places of worship…'. (*CWMG*, 14-379) His "Speech on Khilafat, Bombay", on 9 May 1919, was made before a large Muslim audience. He said that there were three points in the question, namely 'the one regarding the Khilaphate and the possession of Turkey; second, regarding Holy Mecca and Medina; third, regarding Palestine'. (*CWMG*, 15-296) The latter half of the first and the second and the third are concerning the Arabs, on which it is doubtful if Gandhi knew enough. The former half of the first involved if the Turkish people would choose a secular state or not, and the Muslims of India or anybody else could not interfere with it. Therefore the whole *Khilafat* question was outside the interests of the Indian people, whether Hindu or Muslim, and should have been looked at as such. But he plunged into it as his duty of a Hindu to help his Muslim brethren, told so to his fellow Hindus, and succeeded in achieving a considerable measure of mass awakening.

About four months later, in September 1919, he again addressed what was said to be a predominantly Muslim meeting on the *Khilafat* question in Bombay. By this time the Peace Treaty had been signed with Germany, but the position of Turkey was still uncertain. The meeting passed "Resolution at Khilafat Meeting", which expressed 'the greatest anxiety over the threatened dismemberment of Turkey and removal of the Holy places of Islam from the Caliph's control…'. (*CWMG*, 16-153) Those were largely in consonance with Gandhi's three points mentioned above. On 19 January 1920 a delegation of six members, including Gandhi as the only Hindu, met the Viceroy. He gave his idea of NC for the first time on this issue at the Khilafat Conference on 26 January. Then he moved a resolution at a mass meeting at Bombay on 19 March, which suggested the possibility of 'complete withdrawal of co-operation from the Government'. (*CWMG*, 17-99)

The peace terms for Turkey were determined at San Remo on 26 April even while a Khilafat Deputation was in Britain. They became known in India on 14 May 1920. It did not abolish the Caliphate, but practically cut off almost all the non-Turkish territories, and possibly some parts of the predominantly Turkish areas also, from Turkey. Gandhi almost immediately wrote in his "Press Statement on Turkish Peace Terms" that 'There is no sacred character about the peace terms. They are capable of being revised'. (*CWMG*, 17-427) His remedy was to launch an NC. In an article "Khilafat: Mr. Candler's Open Letter" on 26 May, Gandhi repeatedly accused Lloyd George, the British Prime Minister, for going against his own pledge of January 1918 about the Turkish territories, and demanded that 'let these places (Armenia and Arab territories of Turkey) have full self-government with suzerainty to be retained with Turkey…'. (*CWMG*, 17-457) Interestingly Lloyd George said that after giving the pledge recruitment to the army from India very much increased, implying that the pledge was satisfactory to the Indian Muslims. Does it mean the Indian Muslims fought for the territorial integrity of an enemy country, which was what Turkey was at the time?

All-India Central Khilafat Committee approved Gandhi's plan for Non-Co-operation on 28 May 1920. Then the Committee of 3 June passed a resolution confirming the plan for NC, and appointed an eight-member sub-committee for that purpose, Gandhi being the only Hindu among the eight. Gandhi, however, wrote some time later in "The Non-Co-operation Committee" that 'The supreme committee can only be purely Mussulman…I am on the committee, therefore, as a specialist (of NC) and not because I am a Hindu'. (*CWMG*, 17-507) Of the seven Muslim members, as many as four were bearing the title of Maulana or Maulvi, suggesting the growing influence of the clergy men among the Muslims because of the Khilafat Movement (*CWMG*, 17-543). Then, there was the "Muslim Leaders' Representation to Viceroy" on 22 June, signed by ninety Sunni Muslims. It expressed Muslim displeasure with the Turkish peace terms, and said that if the situation would not improve, they would start from 1 August 1920, the third Khilafat Day, 'to withdraw co-operation from the Government and ask our co-religionists and Hindu brethren to do likewise'. (*CWMG*, 17-586~587) On 21 July it was published in "*Hartal* on First August" that the Central Khilafat Committee issued instructions that 1 August should be observed by *hartal*, prayer and fast. (*CWMG*, 18-78-79) 'As we have seen in Chapter Two, however the NC had come to a virtual halt almost three years ago'.

On 5 September, "The Non-Co-operation Resolution" by Gandhi proposing 'progressive non-violent non-co-operation' on 'the two aforementioned wrongs' of *Khilafat* and the Punjab was presented before the Special Session of the Congress at Calcutta. (*CWMG*, 18-230-231) It was passed. By this the *Khilafat* question for the first time became one for the whole Congress. Gandhi himself wrote that 'Never has the Congress been called upon to decide an issue so momentous as the one it was called upon to decide at its special session…' in "The Congress", and gave his own analysis of the votes there. (*CWMG*, 18-259-262) The Resolution, with a similar emphasis on 'the Khilafat and the Punjab wrongs' was confirmed at the Nagpur Session of the Congress at the end of 1920. (*CWMG*, 19-576~578)

After four years at the end of 1924, the Resolution ceased to exist as far as the Congress was concerned at its Session at Belgaum with Gandhi himself as the President. By this time the Congress had fought the NC struggle, Gandhi had been arrested, sentenced, and released much earlier than what the sentence said. In his "Presidential Address at Belgaum Congress" he said, 'non-violent non-co-operation as a means of attaining political freedom has come to stay...But we are face to face with a situation that compels us to cry halt...The *Khilafat* agitation in which Hindus made common cause with their Mussalman brethren and the non-co-operation that followed it caused an awakening among the hitherto slumbering masses...(but) I advise suspension of non-co-operation, for I see that the nation is not ready for it'. (*CWMG*, 25-471~89)

Gandhi's Mistake

Seen with hindsight of history, it was Gandhi's clear mistake that he pledged his support to the Muslims as a religious community as such, paying his respect to the community as a whole, and bringing into the movement a whole class of Ulemmas. All this helped to strengthen the solidarity of the Muslims as Muslims as distinct from other religious communities. After returning to India he wrote in his *Autobiography* that 'I had realized early enough in South Africa that there was no genuine friendship between the Hindus and the Mussalmans'. (*CWMG*, 39-350) This was a probable reason for his approaching the Muslim community for the *Khilafat* cause, and urging the Hindus to co-operate with them. In *Hind Swaraj* he had likewise assured that the Hindus had a good reason to support Muslims in the latter's petition to Morley, Secretary of State for India, in 1906, (*CWMG*, 10-32) which led to the leadership among the Muslims coming into the hands of their elite groups, introduction of the separate electorate, and the formation of the Muslim League.

Ulemmas' participation in the *Khilafat* may have been to him a compensation for the awakening of the Muslim masses. But it was a dangerous factor. From this time onward it became common for the leaders of the religious communities, away from even the awakened masses, to confer on important issues and reach agreements. This suited Gandhi with his S-T-S, but it often elevated the image of the negotiators on the opposite side, who may or may not have been religious leaders, especially Mohammad Ali Jinnah as the supreme leader of the Muslim community especially by the Gandhi-Jinnah Talks in 1944. Bipan Chandra looks at it still more critically. On the *Khilafat* he says, 'What is even more important, the very terms of the agreement prevented Gandhiji and other nationalist leaders from using this opportunity to impart to the Muslim masses a modern, secular, democratic outlook and anti-imperialist consciousness...When the Khilafat Movement was withdrawn, hardly any nationalist residue was left'.[1] Yajnik's criticism of the *Khilafat* is from a largely overlapping point. Because of the *Khilafat*, he said, 'India paid a heavy price. Large masses were addressed henceforth as Hindu and Mohammedan, instead of as Indians.[2] Yajnik's view is similar to Kamaladevi's of the Indian society getting fragmented, quoted before.

2. The Constitutional Question

Nehru Report, Jinnah, and the Congress

Attention has already been paid to the *Nehru Report* and the related constitutional questions in the late 1920s. On the most important electoral system, while the *Report* supported the joint electorate as against the separate electorates, the Muslims tended to defend the existing separate electorates. In his *Road to Pakistan: The Life and Times of Mohammed Ali Jinnah*, probably the only solid biography of Jinnah written so far by a non-Muslim author, B.R. Nanda quotes the *Report on the Indian Constitutional Reforms*, 1918 (Report of Montagu and Chelmsford) to show that the British themselves were aware of the adverse effect of introducing the separate electorates thus, 'Division by creeds and classes means the creation of political camps organized against each other, and teaches men to think as partisans and not as citizens; it is difficult to see how the change from this system to national representation is ever to occur.'[3]

It never occurred. The *Nehru Report* was the most important attempt to create this 'national representation' in India before independence. On the reaction to it, however, Dipak Malik has said that 'The genesis of partition can be traced right from the Motilal Nehru Committee Report which came out with a rather unilinear formula of parliamentary democracy with adult franchise. This created for the Muslim League and other leaders the spectre of being reduced to a minority forever.'[4]

Jinnah, however, in return for some concessions to the Muslims in terms of the seats in the central and provincial legislature, proposed to give up the separate electorate. It was a great gesture on his part which is well worth remembering. After some previous efforts came to nothing, Nanda writes that on 27 December 1928, Jinnah and his Muslim League delegation met the delegation of the National Convention (Nehru Committee's parent body) at Calcutta in the presence of Motilal Nehru. At this time 'Jinnah proposed six modifications (to the *Nehru Report*), of which three were important: reservation of seats for Muslims in the legislatures of the Punjab and Bengal, vesting of residuary powers in the provinces instead of at the centre, and the reservation of one-third seats in the central legislature for Muslims'. But 'The League was offered some minor concessions, but its three major demands were turned down'.[5] For Motilal Nehru the demands came perhaps too late.

Jinnah then on the next day 28 December moved the following resolution before the National Convention 'in a reasoned and eloquent speech'. It said in part, 'Majorities are apt to be oppressive and tyrannical and minorities always dread and fear that their interests and rights, unless clearly and definitely safeguarded by statutory provisions, would suffer and be prejudiced, and this apprehension is enhanced all the more when we have to deal with a communal majority…It is essential that you must get not only the Muslim League but the Musalmans of India, and here I am speaking not as a Musalman but as an Indian'.[6] It was a remarkable speech in that in about a decade he would no longer speak 'as an Indian'. What Jinnah said was very correct. After all he was a man who intended to be a 'Muslim Gokhale'.[7]

First Critical Moment Missed

Unfortunately, following the speech 'A number of speeches were delivered at the Convention, but none in support of Jinnah's proposals. No Congress leader spoke'.[8] This was one of the critical moments in the Hindu-Muslim relations in India, and it was missed. We have seen some political promises made in the Quit-India Resolution, especially the transfer of the residuary powers to the Provinces, but those came much too late, more than a dozen years later. It was a tragic mistake for the Congress, including Gandhi, not to respond positively to this 'reasoned and eloquent' speech then and there. Bimal Prasad writes about Gandhi at this time that 'Yet…he was the one Indian leader who understood the basic of the Hindu-Muslim problem in India and it was a pity that he did not evince much interest in the discussions on the preparation of the *Nehru Report* (1928), which considerably deepened Muslim distrust of the Congress'.[9] Very soon Jinnah put his demands in his Fourteen Points.

Syed Azmatullah wrote to Gandhi before his departure to the RTC, two years after Jinnah's Points, that 'If only you make it known to the Muslims that you would accept the other thirteen points of Mr. Jinnah, if separate electorates are given up, I assure you the Muslims would adopt a more accommodating attitude and agree to joint electorates…'. But Gandhi's reply in "Letter to Syed Azmatullah" of 14 May 1931 said, 'I thank you for your letter. I can only give you my assurance that I shall do my best to promote Hindu-Muslim unity. What I am striving for is a heart unity. The solution of the constitutional question rests in many other hands than mine'. (*CWMG*, 46-148, Azmatullah's letter included) This was disappointing, to say the least. Gandhi may not have been in possession of necessary know-how to solve the constitutional question. But he should have seriously addressed himself to what Jinnah and Azmatullah had entreated. Suppose the separate electorates had been done away with at this time, the ensuing political situation would have been vastly different. The 1937 Provincial Elections would have been fought under the joint electorate then, if not under the universal suffrage.

For one thing Gandhi might have looked at the issues lightly, and only as a scramble concerning the legislative seats and lower posts in the bureaucracy. For example, he said in "What it is Not" in 1930 that 'Does not the Hindu-Muslim question centre round a division of political power-spoils of office?'(*CWMG*, 43-55) Also in "Speech at Public Meeting, Delhi" in 1931, he said that 'What after all are the things you are quarrelling for?... It is for seats on legislatures and local bodies. What has the vast majority of you got to do with them? How many of you can go there?. (*CWMG*, 45-271) Or look at his "Speech at Birmingham Meeting" at the time of the RTC, where he said that 'What is offered is simply a share in the power of the bureaucracy to exploit India and this sets up an apple of discord in our midst'. (*CWMG*, 48-186) What he told his audiences on different occasions were all very correct. Some of them were piercingly sharp. Even then, the point remains that he had dealt with Jinnah politically unwisely. This was practically the first and the last chance for serious inter-communal dialogue.

The RTCs at London, including the second one Gandhi attended on behalf of the Congress, also did not produce the desired effect. Gandhi's "Speech at Minorities Committee Meeting" of the RTC on 13 November 1931 showed it well. He said, 'I would express my dissent from the view that you (Prime Minister of Britain) put before this Committee, that the inability to solve the communal question was hampering the progress of Constitution-making, and that it was an indispensable condition prior to the building of any such Constitution'. Then he went on, 'it was because of the emphasis that was laid last year and repeated this year upon this difficulty, that the different communities were encouraged to press with all the vehemence at their command their own respective views'. (*CWMG*, 48-293)

It shows that the failure to reach a constitutional agreement in the late 1920s cost India dearly. It also shows that the British saw it more and more important to encourage differences among different parties. It is worth remembering that Gandhi was rightly of the view that except him every other delegate at the RTC had been a Government nominee. But, after missing the opportunity in the late 20s, could not Gandhi have tried to have more Muslims among his seventy-eight fellow travellers in the Salt March, instead of just two or three? Did he ever think seriously over this matter of the scarcity of Muslims among his co-workers? The *CWMG* shows no sign of it. Ironically it fell upon Gandhi himself to declare in his "Speech at Congress Session, Lahore-II" on 31 December 1929 that 'As the British Government has failed to accept it within a year the *Nehru Report* ceases to exist for the Congress'. (*CWMG*, 42-346)

3. Change in Jinnah's Policy

Deepened Divide and Rule

Jinnah was a nationalist in 1928, but had transformed into a communalist by around 1937. We will briefly look at what had transpired between him and Gandhi by this time. When it became apparent that Gandhi's leadership was going to be established in the Congress in 1920, Jinnah and 19 others resigned from the All-India Home Rule League, affiliated to the Congress. Gandhi received a copy of their resignation letter, and wrote "Letter to M.A. Jinnah" of 25 October 1920. There Gandhi refused to accept the reasons Jinnah raised in their letter, such as the manner in which Gandhi presided over the alteration of the rules of the League as its newly elected President, the question of maintaining 'the British connection' in the future, and the interpretation of some technical terms.

Gandhi's argument seemed to be legally correct on all these points, which would suggest that Jinnah's reasons lay elsewhere. They could have been the *Khilafat* Movement as an anti-British one, the rise of the Muslim priests or of the Shaukat and Mohammed Ali brothers, the NC as a whole which might have, in case of a success, damaged Jinnah's prestige as a lawyer and a Member of the Legislature, Gandhi's Hindu style, or may be all of them. (*CWMG*, 18-370~372)

Gandhi wrote in "Note To Jagdish K. Munshi" many years later that 'Jinnah has hated me since the day I asked him in a meeting to give up English and speak in Gujarati'. (*CWMG*, 78-24) It was not what Gandhi said, but probably the fact that he said it in a meeting, that hurt Jinnah's pride. To that extent Gandhi may have been tactless, but whether it was something important is difficult to say.

Nanda quotes Srinivasa Sastri who said on the Muslim delegates there at the second RTC that 'They want India to have provincial autonomy and no responsibility at the Centre. The Mohammedans do not care for the latter at all'.[10] In other words they were not interested in the freedom of the country. If they would have to face the issue of independence, they would think of the ways and means of partitioning the country. We will see that Jinnah himself would reach this point in several years' time.

Meanwhile the long process of the constitution-making, started with the appointment of the Simon Commission in 1928, finally bore fruits, if it could be called that way, in the enactment of the new Government of India Act in 1935. One of its important stages was the hearings at the Joint Committee of both Houses of the British Parliament on the White Paper by the Government. M.J. Akbar writes in his *Nehru* that 'The committee was alive for eighteen months and examined 120 witnesses over 159 meetings, including twenty-eight Indians'. Only 28 out of 120! Moreover, they were 'strictly of the pro-British or at least non-Congress variety, like the Aga Khan, M.R. Jayakar, B.R. Ambedkar, Sir Akbar Hydari, Sir Mirza Ismail and Sir Tej Bahadur Sapru'.[11]

In other words, the new Act was not meant for the Congress, whose mass popularity had been testified by the Salt March almost beyond doubt, but for those pro-British or non-Congress elements. *The Viceroy at Bay*, a study of the viceroyalty of Linlithgow who was the Governor-General at the time of the first provincial elections under the new Act by his son, refers to the case of Hyde Gowan, the Governor of the Central Provinces, to show 'The surprise of the Governors' at the results. 'Here Congress had claimed that they would win 65 seats out of 112. On 17th December 1936, Gowan had called this 'an incredible boast'. On 4th February 1937, he forecast, on the basis of his District reports, that they would win 35 seats. By 10th February his estimate was up to 60:... On 7th March Gowan reported the final result. Congress had won 70 seats.' [12] The Congress victory appears all the greater in this light.

In the meantime the Congress Muslim leader M.A. Ansari died in 1936, and a discouraged Gandhi wrote in "Letter to Amtussalaam" on 17 May of that year saying 'We have no one to take his place'. (*CWMG*, 62-413) Nearly a year and a half later he wrote in "Letter to Syed Bashir Ahmed" that 'On questions relating to Mussalmans, the Congress is solely guided by Maulana Abul Kalam Azad'. (*CWMG*, 66-182) Narayanbhai, by the way, told the author in October 2012 that the Nationalist Muslim leaders were very poor in talking to the Muslim masses in their own easy language.

Second Critical Moment also Missed

When the League suffered a setback in the Provincial elections in 1937, Jinnah approached the Congress for making coalition governments in the two Provinces of UP and Bombay, as the League got more legislators elected in these two. When rejected, he turned to anti-Hindu communal policy. Rothermund writes that B.G. Kher, the Congress Premier-designate of Bombay, was thinking of having one minister from the League in his cabinet, but was not allowed a free hand in doing so.[13] Rothermund does not discuss the case of U.P.

What Akbar argues in *Nehru* is worth examining. He says that 'Three points are generally advertised as the landmarks on the road to Pakistan. The first is the collapse of the negotiations to settle the Hindu-Muslim question through the *Nehru Report* in 1928. The second is Jawaharlal Nehru's 'sabotage'...of the proposed congress-League coalition ministry in the United Provinces after the 1937 elections. And the third is Jawaharlal Nehru's rejection of the Cabinet Mission plan for a federal India in 1946'.[14] As Akbar says they are all 'pro-Pakistan argument', placing the responsibility for all the three failures on the shoulder of the Congress and stressing the inevitability of the separation of the Muslim India from the rest.[15]

It has been pointed out in the above, however, that much was left to be desired in the way the Congress dealt with Jinnah's demands around 1928. In 1937, the Congress had got an absolute majority in both of these Provinces, and was in that sense fully qualified to reject the League's demand for coalition.

Still, as we look back, was it not politically wise for the Congress to compromise? This was the first provincial elections under the new Act. If the League was turned down from sharing a seat or two in all the provincial Congress governments put together, such a minority status would continue for a long time to come, almost indefinitely, strengthening Jinnah's fear quoted above. This was the fear persistent since Syed Ahmad Khan. This was what Dipak Malik pointed out. As we have seen in connection with Pant's Premiership, the League was more pro-rich than the Congress, and it would not have been easy for the Congress to reach a set of common policies with them. Even then were Gandhi and other leaders of the Congress not sensitive enough to their sentiment?

It would be interesting to know in this connection that Ayesha Jalal, in her new book *The Pity of Partition*, which is an evaluation of Saadat Hasan Manto, an Urdu writer, sums up her earlier *The Sole Spokesman* in the following words. 'The British decision to split up India had usually been attributed to irreconcilable religious differences between Hindus and Muslims, and the intransigence of the Muslim League leader, Mohammad Ali Jinnah. I showed in *The Sole Spokesman* that the end result of partition must not be confused with the aims of Jinnah and the Muslim League to win an equitable share of power for the subcontinent's Muslims'.[16]

In the case of Nehru, he was looking at the Hindu-Muslim question mostly as an economic one, thinking that the economic upliftment would solve it. His attitude was the same on the caste question, and it was typical of the left-leaning intellectuals. Bipan Chandra writes that 'Above all, Nehru suffered from certain economistic, deterministic and reductionist biases in his treatment of the communal question which led him, in practice, to underplay the role of political-ideological struggle against communalism'.[17] In the absence of actual progress on the economic front, the communal unity was not forthcoming. Bimal Prasad writes that 'Even more disastrous was Gandhi's failure in 1937...' than at the time of the *Nehru Report*. And continues, 'Gandhi woke up after Jinnah declared war on the Congress...in October 1937, but by then it was too late.'[18]

Another thing which retarded the progress towards a united India at this time was the failure of the formation of the Federation stipulated in the Act of 1935 to materialize, and so the Act remained one only on the Provinces till the end. If a Federation had come into being, even flawed significantly, the different groups and communities would have been compelled to behave as a part of the system. In the absence of any such overall system they felt that much freer to act on their own. The Congress was hugely responsible for the non-starter of the Federal provisions, by declaring in its election manifesto, as we have seen, 'to prevent the introduction and functioning of the federal part of the scheme'. Could they not have compromised on this, so that an inclusive system of some kind came into being? It was the British who had put almost insurmountable hurdles in the way by introducing the element of Princely India into the question of the Federation. As soon as the Second World War broke out, moreover, the Viceroy closed the door even to this Federating by an announcement on 11 September (*CWMG*, 70-226, fn. 2), thus binding the Indian politics to the level of Provincial Autonomy and no more, not even a dyarchy in the central government. Hence all the more importance of the provincial coalition.

Nationalist Turned Communalist

Jinnah's transformation became known at the All-India Muslim

League's Session by "M.A. Jinnah's Speech at Lucknow" on 15 October 1937. It was all criticism of the Congress. (*CWMG*, 66-468~469) Gandhi wrote in his "Letter to M.A. Jinnah" on 19 October to say that 'I felt deeply hurt…the whole of your speech is a declaration of war'. (*CWMG*, 66-257) Jinnah retorted on 5 November that 'It is purely in self-defence'. (*CWMG*, 66-470) Gandhi said in another "Letter to M.A. Jinnah" on 3 February 1938 that 'In your speeches I miss the old nationalist' and asks 'Are you still the same Mr. Jinnah?'. (*CWMG*, 66-350) Jinnah had been known as a secularist, and was quoted to have said on 21 February 1936, at the age of 59, that 'I have never been to a mosque'.[19] It is true that Gandhi also may not be called a religious practitioner, but he was a devout Hindu whereas Jinnah was not a devout Muslim.

During the years when the League was in the opposition after the elections in most of the Provinces, Nanda writes, 'He (Jinnah) could not put forward any radical social and economic programme for British India because his party was dependent upon the powerful, feudal landowning politicians in the Punjab, Sind, the UP, the NWFP who dominated the Muslim League. So the only programme which seemed practicable to him was to slam the 'Congress tyranny', make allegations of establishing a '*Hindu raj*'…'.[20] Nanda also writes that 'Gandhi's stock was high in 1938 in official circles'.[21] He then quotes a letter of this time to Jawaharlal from Frances Gunthur, wife of John who was touring India, that 'Gandhi is practically considered the King-Emperor's personal representative in Congress…You, on the other hand, are considered so dangerous that if the British Empire ever falls, it will all be laid on you…Whenever we meet, interest-and fear-is centred on you, your thoughts, your plans, your projects and your influence'.[22] So the British did not presume that Nehru would speak Gandhi's language!

A nationalist should, almost by definition, be interested in achieving independence for his country more than anything else. Gandhi said in his interview with Louis Fischer, however, that when he and Jinnah along with Rajendra Prasad were summoned to the Viceroy 'Shortly after this war broke out', he proposed to Jinnah that they would together demand India's independence, but Jinnah replied that 'I do not want independence'. (*CWMG*, 76-434) This was not new for the League. We may recall what Srinivasa Shastri was writing in a similar tone at the time of the second RTC.

A.G. Noorani, in his *Jinnah and Tilak: Comrades in the Freedom Struggle*, quotes Jinnah's speech early in February 1938. This is a book which emphasizes the closeness of Jinnah to, and the distance of Gandhi from, Tilak. Jinnah said, '...there is an essential difference between the body-politic of the country and that of Britain. The majority and minority parties in Britain are alterable...But such is not the case with India. Here we have a permanent Hindu majority and the rest are minorities which cannot within any conceivable period of time hope to become majorities'.[23] Jinnah was giving vent to his complaint. When it demanded a greater outlet, he would openly want the Partition of the country.

But was there no way for Jinnah to form a majority party for him to lead? We wonder if it never occurred to him, an experienced lawyer and politician, to transform the Muslim League into a not-for-the Muslim-only-party, thus paving the way for taking the foremost political office in the country by a majority vote. The Partition might well have been averted then. As long as he continued to call the Congress a Hindu party, it would not have been possible. Exactly about two years later, Gandhi himself wrote "A Welcome Move", pointing out that Jinnah was joining forces with the Justice Party, Ambedkar, and was about to do so with the Hindu Mahasabha. Gandhi also wrote that 'He (Jinnah) is thus lifting the Muslim League out of the communal rut and giving it a national character...Nothing can be better than that we should have in the country mainly two parties—Congress and non-Congress or anti-Congress...'. (*CWMG*, 71-109) But the more Jinnah characterizes the Congress as a Hindu party, the less likelihood of secular Hindus joining such a non-Congress political group.

Later on in November 1940, already after the League's Lahore Session, Gandhi, in "Discussion with Kishorelal Mashruwala", said that 'The MacDonald Award and 'Pakistan' are nothing but projections of our mental attitude of treating the Harijans and Muslims as separate from us. Remember that the separation is not of their asking. It is what we have chosen to give them, what we forced them to ask for'. (*CWMG*, 73-175) This was a very honest observation, coming only from a man of his calibre. But the realization came too late.

Britain and the League Encircling the Congress

In the meantime, as Historian T.R. Sareen made clear in his *Jinnah, Linlithgow and the Making of Pakistan*, the League secured an assurance from the British on at least two occasions. The first was by Viceroy Linlithgow's letter to Jinnah on 23 December 1939, shortly after the resignation of all of the Provincial Congress governments in protest against drawing India into the War without consulting her. It was a reply to Jinnah's letter of 5 November, demanding that the future of India's constitutional question should be considered *de novo* under the changed circumstances, and no constitution should be made without the agreement of the two major communities. Jinnah's letter was as the President of the League, and was itself based on the resolution of the League Working Committee of 18 September. In his reply Linlithgow accepted Jinnah's demands. The League then passed the 'Pakistan Resolution' at Lahore on 23 March 1940 without a debate.

The second British assurance was by Secretary of State for India Zetland's speech at the House of Lords on 18 April 1940. It said that 'A substantial measure of agreement among the communities of India is essential if the vision of united India is to become a reality…But the fact of the matter is that the Congress Party has raised in the minds of many Muslims apprehensions which only they themselves can allay. Will the Congress refrain from closing the door upon unity in India? Upon their answer hangs the future fate of the country'. (*CWMG*, 72-21, fn. 1) The Secretary for India was clearly taking the side of the Muslim League. Sareen quotes a different portion of the same speech, which reads 'I cannot believe that any Government or Parliament in this country would attempt to impose by force upon, for example, the 80 million Moslem subjects of HM in India a form of Constitution under which they would not live peacefully and contentedly'. The Viceroy wrote to Jinnah the next day, quoting the latter part of the speech, and said that Jinnah must have noticed it.[24]

The Congress Session was also meeting at Ramgarh in March, shortly before the League Session. Its main resolution drafted by Gandhi said that 'Congressmen, and those under the Congress influence, cannot help in the prosecution of the war with men, money or material…The people of India alone can properly shape their own constitution…through a Constituent Assembly elected on the basis of adult suffrage…the Congress repudiates attempts to divide India…The Congress cannot admit the right of the Rulers of Indian States…to come in the way of Indian freedom'. ("A Resolution", *CWMG*, 71-440~441)

Zetland's speech was followed by L.S. Amery, the new Secretary of State for India in Churchill's cabinet, who said in the House of Commons on 23 May that 'as my predecessor made clear in his speech on April 18…We have no desire to delay any of the steps that may pave the way towards an agreed settlement that will take account of the legitimate claims of all communities and interests'. (*CWMG*, 72-95, fn. 2) He thus showed the basic continuity of the British policies. The League had these promises by Linlithgow, then Zetland, and also Amery, confirmed, so to speak, by "Statement made by the Viceroy on August 8, 1940", the so-called 'August Offer', by the same Linlithgow. It said, under Churchill's supervising eyes,[25] that 'It goes without saying that they (HMG) could not contemplate the transfer of their present responsibilities for the peace and welfare of India to any system of government whose authority is directly denied by large and powerful elements in India's national life…But His Majesty' Government authorize me to declare that they will most readily assent to the setting up after the conclusion of the war with the least possible delay of a body representative of the principal elements in India's national life in order to devise the framework of the new constitution…'. (*CWMG*, 72-473)

The August Offer was made several months after the Lahore Resolution. It is usually referred to as a critical British step towards Partition. It should, however, be truer to say, after Sareen's work, that it was the two British statements mentioned above, one preceding and the other following the Lahore Resolution, that can be termed that way. The League was assured by the 'Cripps Offer' of March 1942 one more time, which said that after the war a new constitution would be framed to give India a Dominion status, the Indian States would participate in the process, it would be possible for 'non-acceding Provinces' of British India to make a separate constitution, and during the war-time the Defence of India would be Britain's responsibility. This time also, Churchill was careful to see that Cripps would not concede to the Indian leaders on the war-time distribution of the power on defence, and for this 'the Linlithgow-Churchill Axis' came into being 'behind Cripps's back', although Cripps was Lord Privy Seal in the War Cabinet.[26]

When Gandhi saw it he immediately told Cripps, 'If this is your entire proposal to India, I would advise you to take the next plane home'. ("Interview with Louis Fischer", *CWMG*, 76-427) Interestingly, Sheikh Abdullah from Kashmir writes in his autobiography on the Cripps proposals that 'Had the Congress party accepted them as well (like the League), the partition of the country might have been avoided'.[27] He must have known the above response by Gandhi, who was the man he called 'The only Hindu Congress leader against Partition'.[28]

Lahore Resolution

The Muslim League's Lahore Resolution demanded first that 'Muslim India will not be satisfied unless the whole constitutional plan is reconsidered *de novo* and that no revised plan would be acceptable to the Muslims unless it is framed with their approval and consent'. Thus it spoke on behalf of the whole Muslims of India. Then it goes on to put their own demand that 'geographically contiguous units are demarcated into regions which should be so constituted with such territorial adjustments as may be necessary that the areas in which the Muslims are numerically in a majority, as in the north-western and eastern zones of India, should be grouped to constitute "independent states" in which the constituent units shall be autonomous and sovereign'.

Various, at least five, territorial concepts like unit, region, area, zone, and "independent state" are mixed up without clear explanation. Nowhere in Pakistan so far has a constituent unit been autonomous and sovereign. Here it is taken for granted that the Muslims have their own specific interests, but the idea was exploded once and for all by the independence of Bangladesh in 1971. Perhaps with Gandhi's criticism of the vivisection of India in mind, to be discussed later, the Resolution further says that 'adequate, effective and mandatory safeguards should be specifically provided in the constitution for minorities in the units and in the regions', for the Hindus and other non-Muslims in the future Pakistan, and 'in other parts of India where the Mussalmans are in a minority' the same sort of safeguards should be provided for them and other minorities. Finally the Resolution provides that the respective regions will assume 'all powers such as defence, external affairs, communications, customs and such other matters as may be necessary'. ("Resolution Passed by All-India Muslim League", *CWMG*, 71-444~445) This last phrase practically precluded the Rajaji Formula in advance. It is not clear where the residuary power would reside.

The next day, 24 March, Jinnah in his Presidential speech said, 'They (Hindus and Muslims) neither intermarry, nor interline (*sic*) together and, indeed they belong to two different civilizations which are based mainly on conflicting ideas and conceptions. Their aspects on life and of life are different. It is quite clear that Hindus and Mussalmans derive their inspiration from different episodes. Very often, the hero of one is a foe of the other and, likewise their victories and defeats overlap'.[29] Jinnah spoke as if to fill a gap in the Resolution as to the specific interests of the Muslims, although what he said here would, and did, lead to a mono-cultural Muslim country made that much poorer deprived of its mixed and composite elements.

It is as if Linlithgow's letter to Jinnah had anticipated, even approved Lahore beforehand, and the Lords speech rubber stamped it. We may even say with hindsight that the Lords speech was the decisive climax in the whole process of the Partition.

Stakes in August 1942

As for Gandhi, whose criticism of the vivisection was answered by the Resolution, at least by words, by its reference to the safeguards for the minorities in both of the future states, the next step was to take up instances where such promises were broken. First, it was the case of some riots. In "Communal Riots" of 4 May 1941, a little more than a year from the Resolution, Gandhi wrote, with the riot in Ahmedabad of 18 April and others in mind, that 'the Congress produced little or no influence over either the Muslims or the Hindus in the affected areas…it seems that Muslim fanatics in Dacca and Ahmedabad did their worst in inflicting damage on Hindu property by looting and burning with a deliberation that showed premeditation'(*CWMG*, 74-26). When another riot had broken out in

Ahmedabad on 1 July 1946 he said in "Speech at Prayer Meeting" at Poona that 'In Ahmedabad…Hindus and Muslims had always lived together in peace'. (*CWMG*, 84-400) He also wrote about this time in "Letter To Vallabhbhai Patel" that 'Personally I believe it is a civil war that has started' (*CWMG*, 74-99), in "Letter to Agatha Harrison" that 'The riots this time have no resemblance to the former ones. This time it is a rehearsal for a civil war' (*CWMG*, 74-132), and in "Letter to Manu Subedar" that 'I am convinced that the riots in Sind, Dacca and Ahmedabad were intended to intimidate the Congress. But I am ready to ignore this'. (*CWMG*, 74-319) The 'intimidation' here must have meant to pressurize the Congress to recognize the League as the only representative of the Muslims, and in doing so to agree to the partition of India.

It was in these circumstances of riots and violence that Gandhi called upon the Congress and the people to start the 'Quit-India' Movement in 1942. His objectives were to find ways and means of resisting the possible Japanese invasion with non-violence and with the villages as the base, and of giving more help to China which was in a life-and-death struggle with Japan. One would wonder if he had also in mind curbing the communal violence. It was like the case of the Salt March which was also meant to curb the terrorist, communal and even official violence. In the case of 'Quit-India', however, the situation was much more difficult, as the War was going on which had fortified the Government's hand, and the Muslims were more organized under the League's banner and with more British backing.

B.R. Nanda had at least some reason to say that it was Gandhi's 'a serious, almost inexcusable, miscalculation'.[30] The Quit-India Movement, and its early collapse, paved the way for the expansion of the League's influence and there is no doubt about it. So the stakes were extremely high in 1942, but from Gandhi's point of view there was no alternative. Narayanbhai told this writer, by the way, that the 8 August 1942 Resolution with its 'Do or die' *mantra* got a tremendous welcome at the AICC meeting where he was present with his father.

Gandhi-CWC Relations

To understand those heavy stakes it may be worth looking at the political process of the above period from the point of Gandhi and the CWC relations. The Congress had been expecting the 'August Offer' to make some concessions or overtures to them. In the "Discussion at Congress Working Committee Meeting" of 3~7 July 1940, Gandhi said that 'I have been oppressed all the time by the fact that I now represent a totally different mentality from that of the Working Committee'. (*CWMG*, 72-235) The difference was on non-violence.

Gandhi had desired to be absolved from the Congress responsibility at the previous CWC meeting in June (*CWMG*, 72-235, fn. 1). According to "Both Happy and Unhappy", the CWC passed a resolution on 21 June, which said that 'they (CWC) are unable to go the full length with Gandhiji…and, therefore, absolve him from responsibility for the programme and activity which the Congress has to pursue…' (*CWMG*, 72-194, fn. 2). Rajaji opposed Gandhi's thinking in the July meeting saying that 'Ours is a political organization not working for non-violence but for the political ideal', and Nehru supported him (*CWMG*, 72-237). In the end, the CWC endorsed "Resolution Passed at Congress Working Committee Meeting at Delhi" on 7 July. Drafted by Rajaji, and with what N.K. Bose called 'rare independence of judgment'[31], it demanded the complete independence of India and a provisional National Government, and said that 'if these measures are adopted, it will enable the Congress to throw in its full weight in the efforts for the effective organization of the defence of the country'. (*CWMG*, 72-467)

The CWC thus went out of the way to show its interest in the defence of the country, and to catch the heart and mind of the British even at the expense of Gandhi's leadership. If the British had conceded some of their demands even half-way, there would have been no Quit-India Movement. Gandhi, who was not present on this day, issued "The Delhi Resolution" the next day, and called it a 'fateful resolution', 'an undoubted departure from its (Ramgarh Resolution's) spirit'. (*CWMG*, 72-255) He said that in the voting on the Resolution five members remained neutral. (*CWMG*, 72-256) He also said in the above "Discussion" that 'I am not satisfied with *swaraj* for the few. It is for millions. They must feel it. By violent means they cannot feel it'. (*CWMG*, 72-239) Writing in "Of Civil Disobedience" on the AICC meeting held at Poona at the end of July to ratify the CWC's Delhi Resolution, Gandhi said 'The opposition on the part of so many members of the A.I.C.C. to the ratification of the Delhi resolution is...a sign of their resentment at the feeling that the High Command was letting the British Government to get the better of the Congress'. (*CWMG*, 72-340)

But the 'August Offer' that the CWC had thus been looking to was not simply a negative answer to the Congress, or did not simply refuse to talk about Dominion. It was also a positive encouragement to the League. Gandhi wrote in "Letter To Lord Linlithgow" the next day that 'I have very carefully read your pronouncement and slept over it. It has made me sad. Its implications frighten me. I cannot help feeling that a profound mistake has been made'. (*CWMG*, 72-370) Did he mean by 'implications' a possible division of the country? Two months later, after a meeting with the Viceroy, he issued a "Statement to the Press". One sentence of it said that 'I felt that the putting up by the Viceroy, and then the Secretary of State, of want of agreement by the Congress with the Princes, the Muslim League and even the Scheduled Classes as a barrier to the British recognition of India's right to freedom was more than unjust to the Congress and the Indian people'. (*CWMG*, 73-78)

The CWC after the 'Offer' debated a "Draft Resolution for Congress Working Committee", probably Gandhi's own as it is in the *CWMG*, which says that 'It is well known that the offer (by the Congress in the Delhi Resolution) was made against Gandhiji's advice...The W.C., therefore, wish it to be known that the effect of the resolution must be regarded as exhausted...The W.C. must revert to Gandhiji's position and so far as the Congress is concerned it must strive to build up a non-violent society and believe with Gandhiji in the possibility of building up a State able to defend its liberty against the whole world by its own sheer goodwill towards the whole of mankind working under a democratic system which will eschew all violence and which by its simple code will afford no temptation to an invader...' (*CWMG*, 72-409~410) This was approved by "All-India Congress Committee Resolution" in September (*CWMG*, 73-1~3), repairing the gap between Gandhi and the Congress, at least on the surface and for the time being.

Accordingly Gandhi started his Civil Disobedience Movement, as he wrote in "Civil Disobedience" in October, as the so-called individual *satyagraha*. Did not both Gandhi and the CWC lose precious time in going separate ways and then coming together again? Incidentally, if we compare the CWC resolution quoted above, namely 'defend its liberty…by its own sheer goodwill towards the whole of mankind' with Gandhi's own words, quoted in Chapter Two, written in February the same year, namely 'unarmed peaceful India would rely upon the goodwill of the whole world', we find closeness in expression, although the direction of 'goodwill' is the other way round.

The individual *satyagraha* came to an unfortunate end as after about one year Gandhi decided to call it off. N.K. Bose looks into the reason this way, 'On October 30th, 1941, Gandhi reviewed the whole situation and issued a very important statement…In that statement Gandhi said that he had come to realize that Congressmen who had joined in the (individual) *satyagraha* were mostly not opposed to war because of their faith in non-violence, but because they wanted to force the British Government to yield favourable terms so that they might join in the war against the Axis Powers…The *satyagraha* was accordingly withdrawn…'.[32] In other words they returned to the position of the Delhi Resolution without saying so, and practically absolved Gandhi.

Perhaps encouraged by these events, the Foreign Committee of the League (the Haroon Committee) sent its Report on Pakistan Scheme at the end of 1940. Ultimately it did not find its place in the Partition Plan. But besides recommending setting up one State each in the North-West and the North-East of India, it had several surprises. Delhi and a part of UP up to Aligarh were to be incorporated into the Punjab, and thus into the North-West. Then, the whole of Bengal minus Bankura and Midnapur Districts, but plus Purnea District of Bihar, as well as the whole of Assam, were to constitute the North-East. Finally, all the Princely States under Muslim rulers were to become sovereign, and Hyderabad in particular was to form the Muslim triangle together with the North-West and the North-East. The ratio of the Muslim population included in all those areas was estimated to be 72.5 per cent, much higher than the ratio which was actually to constitute Pakistan.[33] This may have been a reason why the League did not pay attention to what Gandhi repeatedly said about the fate of the minority surrounded by the majority population in case of a Partition.

These schemes were closely guarded. In "Interview To Bombay

Suburban and Gujarat Congressmen" in mid-May 1942, after a year and a half since the above Report was made, Gandhi said that 'Rajaji concedes Pakistan. But has Jinnah even moved an inch to discuss matters with him?... He (Rajaji) believes that he will achieve Hindu-Muslim unity. But what, after all, is Pakistan? What does it mean?... What really is Pakistan? Jinnah has never really explained…Indeed, when I am asked to solve the deadlock, I admit I can't do anything about it'. (*CWMG*, 76-108) Even in the middle of July 1944, two months before the Gandhi-Jinnah Talks, Gandhi had to say in "Answers to Questions" that 'Neither Qaid-e-Azam Jinnah nor the Muslim League have pronounced their opinion on Rajaji's Formula', which would have made clear their Pakistan plan. (*CWMG*, 77-387) Jinnah at last 'spoke at length criticizing Rajagopalachari's formula and Gandhiji's association with it' at a Muslim League meeting on 30 July. (*CWMG*, 78-16, fn. 4)

When Cripps visited India in March 1942, there was not much of divergence of views between Gandhi and the CWC, as the Cripps Proposal was such that neither, especially Gandhi, had much expectation from it. Gandhi summed up his position in "That Ill-Fated Proposal" which he wrote in the middle of April at Sevagram, where he had returned without being involved in the negotiations. He wrote that 'It contemplated Pakistan, and yet not the Pakistan of the Muslim League's conception. And last of all it gave no real control over defence to responsible (Indian) ministers'. (*CWMG*, 76-28) The Quit-India was in reality Gandhi's counter-proposal to Cripps.

But another near-split came about not long afterwards when Gandhi sent Mirabehn carrying his "Draft Resolution for A.I.C.C." at the end of April, which said that 'the British should withdraw from India'. He had already written in "Foreign Soldiers in India" dated 19 April that 'her (India's) real safety and Britain's too lie in orderly and timely British withdrawal from India. All talk of treaties with the Princes and obligations towards minorities are a British creation designed for the preservation of British rule and British interests'. (*CWMG*, 76-50) This was the birth of the 'Quit-India' Movement. It was another product of Gandhi's genius, but he wanted to have it approved by the Congress and make it a Congress movement.

The draft resolution also said that 'India will attain her freedom through her non-violent strength and will retain it likewise…', reflecting his idea of non-armament. But it continues to say that 'if Japan attacks India…the Committee would expect all those who look to Congress for guidance to offer complete non-violent non-co-operation to the Japanese forces and not render any assistance to them'. (*CWMG*, 76-63~64) The AICC debated it from 27 April to 1 May, in Gandhi's absence, and finally adopted a revised draft, proposed by Nehru (*CWMG*, 76-63, fn. 1), which said that 'The All-India Congress Committee is convinced that India will attain her freedom through her own strength and will retain it likewise'.

It does not make sense. Continuing it says, 'In case an invasion takes place it must be resisted. Such resistance can only take the form of non-violent non-co-operation as the British Government has prevented the organization of national defence by the people in any other way'. (*CWMG*, 76-425) This is a return to Gandhi's Eleven Points of 1930, a return to the pre-Lausanne days. It was not non-violence, at least not of Gandhian conception. What would they have done if they had captured weapons from the invading Japanese? It was due to this spirit that the historic Quit-India Resolution as was finally adopted by the AICC at Bombay on 8 August retained such words to the end as 'to defend India and resist aggression with all the armed as well as the non-violent forces'. (*CWMG*, 76-459) Thus the split remained between them. But Gandhi wrote around this time in "A Challenge" that 'What little energy I have, I am storing up for what promises to be the last fight of my life' (*CWMG*, 76-231), in "Letter to Amrit Kaur" that 'I am satisfied with things as they are shaping themselves' (*CWMG*, 76-233), and in "Letter to G.D. Birla" that 'As far as I am concerned, I am fully prepared'. (*CWMG*, 76-246) They were all written in the latter half of June. Having found an answer to the question of how to resist the Japanese, though unable to convince others, he was high-spirited as almost never before, except the few years preceding the Salt March.

4. The Two-Nation Theory

A Two-Nation Theory

Jinnah's argument for Pakistan was based on the 'two-nation theory'. It is a theory of demarcating the Muslims and Hindus without seeing any commonalities between them. It is a theory of intolerance, preaching that a religion constitutes a nation, and a nation should have a state of its own. It was similar in logic to the Hindu communalism by, say, Vinayak Damodar Savarkar. When the Congress was about to accept the Partition of India, Gandhi in "Letter to J.B. Kripalani" called it accepting 'the two-nation theory'. (*CWMG*, 88-32) He had already been used to this way of thinking, as the Reader in *Hind Swaraj* was saying that 'Hindus and Mahomedans are old enemies. Our very proverbs prove it. Mahomedans turn to the West for worship, whilst Hindus turn to the East. The former look down on the Hindus as idolaters'. (*CWMG*, 10-28)

A proto-type of the latter-day two-nation theory was already in vogue then, which Gandhi had to argue and win over. Some of the words here are reminiscent of Jinnah's Lahore speech mentioned above. Therefore Gandhi writes in *Hind Swaraj*, 'In no part of the world are one nationality and one religion synonymous terms; nor has it ever been so in India'. (*CWMG*, 10-29). He continues, 'Religions are different roads converging to the same point'. (*Ibid.*) Years later, when he arrived in Bihar from Noakhali and gave his first "Speech at Prayer Meeting" at Patna on 5 March 1947, he concluded it with those words, 'Ishwar, Allah both are your names, Oh God, grant wisdom to us all'. (*CWMG*, 87-46) He wrote in *Hind Swaraj* also, 'Those who do not wish to misunderstand things may read up the *Koran*, and they will find therein hundreds of passages acceptable to the Hindus; and the *Bhagavad Gita* contains passages to which not a Mahomedan can take exception'. (*CWMG*, 10-31)

When Smuts wanted to squeeze out the Indians from South Africa with his "Black Act" and other measures, on the basis of allegedly different civilizations between the East and the West, Gandhi fought it with his feet on what he thought to be the Eastern civilization. He said 'I am and I have been a determined opponent of modern civilization' at a "Speech at Y.M.C.A., Madras' shortly after his return from Africa. (*CWMG*, 13-65) He also characterized his *Hind Swaraj* as 'a severe condemnation of 'modern civilization" in a short essay ""Hind Swaraj" or the "Indian Home Rule"" early in 1921.

Gandhi, however, did not clarify what constituted the specific features of what he called the Indian civilization. When he said, for example, in his "Letter to Mrs. Maddock", in March 1924, that 'My own motive is to put forth all my energy in an attempt to save Indian, that is, ancient culture, from impending destruction by modern, that is, Western culture being imposed upon India' (*CWMG*, 23-243), is it clear what he intended to defend, or to 'save' out of the then existing Indian milieu? Did he intend to defend the duty-oriented, as against the right-oriented, characteristic of the Indian society, as he once said half sarcastically? But that would nullify a great deal of his effort to reform the society. Much later, he told at the "Speech at Inter-Asian Relations Conference", organized by Nehru in April 1947, that 'I want you to go away with the thought that Asia has to conquer the West through love and truth'. (*CWMG*, 87-193) This is equally vague. But it was all right because it was given at a conference as a greeting on behalf of a nation. But many of his speeches and writings similarly lacked concreteness as to the nature of the Indian or Eastern civilization he said he wanted to defend. The above letter would even give the impression that, by equating 'Indian' with 'ancient', he had mostly the Hindu culture in mind. That would be dangerous.

Then what did he try to defend in South Africa? It was mostly those values and rights with more or less universal nature, such as the right to reside, to move, to vote, to marry according to one's custom, and so on. There may have occurred some conflict between Hindus and Muslims, as many Hindu labourers came into the struggle much later while the big Muslim merchants, originally responsible for inviting Gandhi to South Africa, had got tired of it. And the inter-religious relations were not always at their best as he himself looked back. Still, the objectives of the struggle were of universal value and as such got supported by growing circles of Indians both inside and outside South Africa, and by non-Indians.

Jinnah, to reinforce his patched-up two-nation theory, relied on *ulemmas*, violence, and, for socio-economic programme, the CPI (Communist Party of India) which was against the Quit-India because of their pro-USSR stand and was supporting the Partition. In a recent work entitled *The Sickle and the Crescent*, the authors write that 'In the path of becoming the sole spokesman of the Muslims, there were two road-blocks, viz., the Unionist coalition in Punjab and the Krishak Praja Party in Bengal, both having the support of the majority of the Muslims in those two provinces.'[34] Out of these, in the Punjab 'In the opposition to the Unionists, the League needed all the support and readily got it from the Communists'. In Bengal also the two came to an understanding.[35] In order to attract the masses, a prominent Muslim League speaker in his address at Bombay on 16 August 1946, the first day of the Direct Action, went so far as to say that 'Islam stands for Socialism. In Pakistan, all the industries will be nationalized and capitalism abolished'.[36]

Gandhi, on the other hand, continued to stress that the Congress was representing India as a whole. In his extremely rich "Speech at Chatham House Meeting" during the RTC, he said that 'Those who fought and went to gaols were not all Hindus. They had several thousand Mussalmans amongst them, and Sikhs and Christians too'. As has been seen there were only two Muslims among his seventy-eight fellow travellers in the Salt March. But the five-member 'War Council' Sarojini Naidu constituted at the time of the Dharasana Raid included four Hindus and one Muslim.[37] According to Gandhi's "Special Task Before Women" the two ladies selected as leaders at the women's conference at Dandi on 13 April 1930 were both non-Hindus, a Muslim (President) and a Parsi (Secretary). (*CWMG*, 43-271) Judith Brown writes that 'in all only just over 1,000 Muslims were in gaol in mid-November (1930), out of a total of 29,000 prisoners'.[38] But Narayanbhai writes that 'It was not a small achievement that about twelve thousand Muslims had courted prison during the Civil Disobedience Movement…in Bombay, one lakh Muslims took out a procession during the Movement'.[39]

As to the difference in language and script, an important criterion of nationhood, Gandhi said in "Hindustani, Hindi and Urdu" in late 1938 that 'There are thousands of Hindus whose mother tongue is Urdu and there are hundreds who can be aptly described as Urdu scholars', (*CWMG*, 68-24) and mentioned Motilal Nehru and Tej Bahadur Sapru as examples. In Bihar while he was combating communal fire, he said in "Speech at Prayer Meeting" in March 1947 that 'Brijkishore Babu and Rajendra Babu who accompanied me during those early days in Champaran normally used to write in Urdu only'. (*CWMG*, 87-124) Perhaps he should have gone deeper and enquired why Urdu was lost to Hindi in later years. He resigned from the Hindi Sahitya Sammelan in 1945 as 'the Sammelan could not commit itself to Gandhiji's policy that the national language should neither be Persianized nor Sanskritized but should be harmonized under the name Hindustani and should be written in both Devanagari and Persian scripts'. (*CWMG*, 82-9, fn. 2) This was his consistent attitude since *Hind Swaraj*. In "Speech at Prayer Meeting" about two months before independence, he said that 'If we adopt the attitude that since Urdu will be the language of Pakistan we should have Hindi (and not Hindustani) as our language then the charge of separatism against us also will be proved'. (*CWMG*, 88-140)

Nationalist Muslims

One of Jinnah's tactics that was ingenious in pulling the Muslims to him and the League was to cry loudly that they were the only representative of the Muslims in the sub-continent. Its starting point was probably the "Letter from M.A. Jinnah" to Gandhi on 3 March 1938, after the defeat in the elections and two years before the Lahore Resolution. Jinnah said, in response to Gandhi's earlier one, that he was ready to meet him, but 'We have reached a stage when no doubt should be left that you recognize the All-India Muslim League as the one authoritative and representative organization of the Mussalmans of India and on the other hand you represent the Congress and other Hindus throughout the country. It is only on that basis that we can proceed further and devise machinery of approach'. (*CWMG*, 66-481)

Gandhi was not in a position to oblige Jinnah, as it would mean to disown the Nationalist Muslims, and to completely identify politics with religion. In spite of his refusal, however, Jinnah did not mind calling the Nationalist Muslims and, in fact, all those Muslims who did not support the League, traitors, and this, probably more than anything else, generated tremendous ill-will towards the years of the Partition. It is obvious that the separate electorate had made it easier for Jinnah to adopt this policy. Gandhi quotes a letter from a Muslim in "I Wonder" in September 1940 which mentions 'the fifth-columnist Mussalmans like Khan Abdul Ghaffar Khan and Abul Kalam Azad'. (*CWMG*, 73-50)

Unfortunately for Gandhi, he was not able to concentrate on taking on Jinnah's claim at the time. For one thing, he had to see to it that Subhash Chandra Bose would not continue to be the Congress President for two consecutive terms. This was, so to speak, a difficulty of his own creation. The fact that as many as twelve members of the

CWC, almost all the 'Gandhites', signed their resignation against Bose's re-election showed that their and Gandhi's leadership was being endangered, or that may have been how Gandhi felt about it. The increasing bitterness between the Congress and the Kisan Sabha in Bihar and elsewhere which has been discussed before should also be brought into this picture. Still it was quite possible to accommodate Bose. There was no personal animosity, at least not much, between Gandhi and Bose. In "Letter To Subhash Chandra Bose" of 29 December 1940, almost two years since Bose's resignation, Gandhi wrote '...so can you too (come to Sevagram). You know, you will be well looked after here'. (*CWMG*, 73-264) But he went on to say that the political co-operation between the two was 'with the fundamental differences between you and me, it is not possible', thus refusing Bose's offer. (*CWMG*, 73-457~458)

It was on 17 January 1941, barely three weeks afterwards, that Bose disappeared from his Calcutta residence (*CWMG*, 73-304, fn. 1). Gandhi's "Telegram to Sarat Chandra Bose", Subhash' elder brother, of 28 January read 'Startling news about Subhas. Please wire truth. Anxious. Hope all well'. (*CWMG*, 73-304) But all was not well. It was too late for Gandhi to hope so. If Gandhi had agreed to Bose's offer of cooperation, the latter would not have taken this drastic action, and there would have been no INA episode later. For Gandhi the Bose affair started with his famous "Statement to the Press" of 31 January 1939, in which he said that 'the defeat (of Pattabhi Sitaramayya, Bose's rival in the Congress Presidential election) is more mine than his' (*CWMG*, 68-359), and continued till Bose's resignation on 29 April, taking three months of his precious time.

For another, there was the conflict of popular movement with the Prince in the Indian State of Rajkot, which overlapped the Bose affair and equally called his attention, took more of his time and even more of his energy. In "Statement to the Press" of 24 April, he said 'Rajkot seems to have robbed me of my youth...I never knew what it was to lose hope'. (*CWMG*, 69-168) His first visit to Rajkot in this connection was on 27 February 1939, and his last departure from there was on 1 June, covering three months.[40] So Gandhi was not able to concentrate his attention on what Jinnah had said in the above. He met Jinnah late in April 1938, and they jointly issued a "Statement to the Press" to say that 'We had three hours' friendly conversation over the Hindu-Muslim question…' (*CWMG*, 67-50). But when they met again fairly soon, Gandhi wrote in "Letter to C. Rajagopalachari" of 21 May that 'I had two hours and a half with friend Jinnah yesterday. The talk was cordial but not hopeful…' (*CWMG*, 67-90). Several months later he wrote in "Letter to Vallabhbhai Patel" that 'The door is closed now so far as Jinnah is concerned. His letter also is in the same strain'. (*CWMG*, 67-433) The letter suggests that both Gandhi and Jinnah chose to go the way of non-communication with each other. Hiren Mukerjee is also right when he said that 'he (Gandhi) found himself too busy confounding the Left' to seriously face the Hindu-Muslim relations.[41]

Gandhi's Counter Measures

In October 1939, Gandhi made two inter-connected points to counter the two-nation theory in "Am I a Messenger of God?". One is more theoretical. He said, 'How are the Muslims of the Punjab different from the Hindus and the Sikhs? Are they not all Punjabis, drinking the same water, breathing the same air and deriving sustenance from the same soil?' Here he talks in terms of what is usually understood to be a nationality like the Punjabis. Each of those nationalities may include different religious groups, but those groups need not necessarily be hostile to each other. He cited the instance of Sind in "Economic Ruin in Sind" in 1940 to say that 'The Hindus of Sind are enterprising. They supply the felt wants of the Muslim agriculturists. The two are closely intertwined'. (*CWMG*, 72-461) It would not be easy, however, to persuade the believer in the two-nation theory in this way. The latter may retort that even so one is the exploiter and the other is the exploited, or their cultures are different.

The second is more pragmatic, and in a way threatening. He said, 'Is India to be vivisected into two parts…? And what is to happen to the handful of Muslims living in the numerous villages where the population is predominantly Hindu, and conversely to the Hindus where…they are a handful?'(*CWMG*, 70-283) This was the first time he talked about the 'vivisection' of India. And this was the first time, too, that he talked about the possible tragedy that would visit the minorities, whether Hindu or Muslim, in such a case. Gandhi and the Congress should have talked more, much more, at this time about such danger, together with the theoretical drawback of the two-nation theory. This was a crucial period, as in a matter of five months the League passed the Pakistan Resolution. Gandhi was not idle. He met Jinnah in Delhi on 1 and 2 November. (*CWMG*, 70-354, fn-5) He talked more on the danger arising from the vivisection. In "My Position" in April 1940 he said that 'I would employ every non-violent means to prevent it (vivisection). For it means the undoing of centuries of work done by numberless Hindus and Muslims to live together as one nation'. (*CWMG*, 71-412) In "Speech At A.I.C.C. Meeting, Bombay-III" in the middle of September that year, he said, 'It is worse than anarchy to partition a poor country like India whose every corner is populated by Hindus and Muslims living side by side. It is like cutting up a living body into pieces'. (*CWMG*, 73-25)

He spoke as a real nationalist. But not only the League, but also some others, some Congressmen included, did not listen to him. Even Jawaharlal was reported to have said at this time that 'The communal problem, he said, was not a major issue and was capable of solution if India's right to be treated as a free country was conceded'. (*CWMG*, 71-12, fn. 3) We may be reminded of his reductionist approach we have seen. We may also listen to what Historian S. Gopal writes of Nehru from a similar angle. He talks of 'Jawaharlal's general indifference to communal issues and his belief that they would be submerged once the emphasis was shifted to economic matters affecting the common people...'.[42] Such an attitude is characteristic of the leftist intellectuals, but it is not Marx's fault but theirs.

Quit-India: Gandhi's Miscalculation?

B.R. Nanda wrote on Gandhi's 'miscalculation' in offering the whole political field to the League by the Quit-India Movement.[43] August 1942 was the time of the war when India was a very important base for supplying China. Kunming, the capital city of Yunnan Province in South China, was the gateway to China for such Allied activities from India then, and it was full of American soldiers.[44] A little later, the US heavy bombers were deployed into the Chinese airfields from India to conduct long-range bombing against Japan. The first American air-raid on the Yahata Steel Works in northern Kyushu was made on 15 June 1944, which coincided with the US landing on the

Japanese Mandated Territory of the Marianas in the Central Pacific. The bombers were later shifted to the Marianas after they fell into the US hands as they were better located for attacks on Japan. The planes that dropped atomic bombs on Hiroshima and Nagasaki in 1945 came from a small Mariana island of Tinian[45]. But there were two full years from the Quit-India and the fall of the Marianas, and India's strategic place in this period was extremely important. This was behind the prompt action by the British against the Congress.

Gandhi on the other hand had said in "Interview to Foreign Correspondents" in the middle of July that 'I am not ready with a planned programme as yet…Assuming that the A.I.C.C. confirms the resolution there will be some time but not very long-taken. As far as I can see just now it may be a week or two'. (*CWMG*, 76-299) Also he said in "Telegram to Rathindranath Tagore", "Letter to Amrit Kaur" and "Instructions to the Ashram Inmates" a little later that he would be back from Bombay to Sevagram 'about 10th' (*CWMG*, 76-326), 'I hope to be back in Sevagram before 14th and not before 10th' (*CWMG*, 76-349) and 'I hope to be back by August 11, and in any case not later than August 13' (*ibid.*), respectively. The S-T-S formula thus held till the end.

Even at Bombay on 8 August itself, his last free day, he said in his two speeches, 'I will now wait upon the Viceroy and plead with him for the acceptance of the Congress demand. The process is likely to take two or three weeks' (*CWMG*, 76-391), and 'Let me tell you at the outset that the real struggle does not commence today. I have yet to go through much ceremonial as I always do' (*CWMG*, 76-396). We must conclude from them that he had not grasped the urgency of the situation as seen from the British point of view, although it is difficult to imagine what he would have done if he had done so. This does not imply that he was not in a hurry. He was, in view of the possible Japanese invasion and the need to help China. He even said in the first speech on 8th that 'Freedom cannot now wait for the realization of communal unity'. (*CWMG*, 76-389) In fact, while the Muslim League did not oppose the Salt March in 1930, this time Jinnah condemned the CWC resolution, which convened the AICC on 7 August, as blackmailing the British to establish a Hindu *raj*. (*CWMG*, 76-368, fn. 2)

Nanda, on the other hand, remains silent on the resignation of the Congress provincial ministries. To the author, however, it seems the resignation was equally important in making it easy for the League to act as it liked. It took place almost three years before the 'Quit-India', meaning that the League had already three years of freedom to move about. The Congress Governments may have been dismissed by the British sooner or later anyway, but during whatever interval that may have existed, they could have resisted the *Raj* trying to oppress the mass movement, or freedom of 'expression', as was said in the Individual *Satyagraha*. They did not consult the people of those Provinces where they were ruling. But the "Congress Working Committee Resolution" of 22 October 1939 said that 'As a first step in this direction the Committee call upon the Congress Ministries to tender their resignations'. (*CWMG*, 70-420)

N.K. Bose writes that 'But some, like Mr. M.N. Roy, questioned the wisdom of the step, holding that it was necessary for the Ministers to continue in office for 'the very useful purpose of defending the maximum possible civil liberties against the operation of the Defence of India Act".[46] Had the Congress been trapped into resignations? But Gandhi himself supported the resignations and said in "Politics *vs*. Morals", refuting M.N. Roy who said that they were not necessary (*CWMG*, 70-344, fn. 2), 'I feel sure that they (resignations) have added to the prestige of the Congress...To remain in office after the discovery of their impotence would have been to court ignominy'. (*CWMG*, 70-344) In October 1941, he wrote in "Letter to Agatha Harrison" that 'The Congress cannot be party to the war efforts and, therefore, cannot take office'. (*CWMG*, 75-38)

Journalist Frank Moraes, however, writes on 'The disastrous withdrawal of the Congress provincial ministries in November 1939, leaving Jinnah a free field...', and that the mistake was repeated by the rejection of the Cripps offer and the launching of the Quit-India Movement.[47]

5. Gandhi-Jinnah Talks and After

Rajaji Formula

Gandhi had prolonged talks with Jinnah by visiting him at his house in Bombay in September 1944. Azad said that the Bombay meeting of the two raised Jinnah's prestige. Many would have agreed with this view. True, Gandhi should never have met Jinnah at this time. He was a nationalist, but the other was not by now, and they were not on the same footing. Especially so after a series of the Muslim riots in several cities in March to April 1941 which Gandhi called a rehearsal (of a Civil War). The moment they could have met with profit was long gone by now. Nevertheless Gandhi told the press that he was meeting Jinnah as there was a great deal of popular expectation. People wanted communal peace, and he, known for his touch on the pulse of the people, was aware of it.

The main topic in 1944 was nothing other than the partition of India. The major material that was provided was the 'Rajaji Formula'. According to Bipan Chandra, there has been no study of it so far. When Bimal Prasad said 'seldom any effort made' on Gandhi and partition, he may have had this Formula also in mind. It is a six-point programme for partitioning India, drafted by Rajaji at Gandhi's bedside in prison in 1942. Since Gandhi made use of it in his talks with Jinnah, it is difficult to say, as is often said, that Gandhi is innocent of partition. He was not.

Briefly, "C. Rajagopalachari's Formula" states that, the Muslim League will co-operate with the Congress to form 'a provisional interim government' (Item 1). After the end of the war, 'contiguous districts' with the Muslim majority will be demarcated, there will be 'a plebiscite of all the inhabitants held on the basis of adult suffrage' there, and if the majority is in favour, those will be separated from India (Item 2). In that case mutual agreements between the two new nations will be made for safeguarding defence, commerce, and communications (Item 4). These will be effective only after the transfer of power by Britain (Item 6). (*CWMG*, 76-456) It may be presumed that the Items 1 and 6 were necessary as Jinnah might not be interested in achieving the independence of India as one united body, or before the British withdrawal. The stipulation in the Quit-India Resolution for a federal structure with autonomy for the units and the residuary powers vesting in the units is not here.

Rajmohan Gandhi, a grand-son of both Gandhi and Rajaji, says in his *Rajaji Story* that Jinnah rejected the Formula because (1) the Pakistan there was 'too small', (2) 'Jinnah feared that the bonds (to be arranged between the two new countries) would abridge Pakistan's sovereignty', (3) concerning whether independence should come first or the partition, Jinnah 'did not trust a Congress-ruled India to implement a Pakistan promise', and (4) why the non-Muslims should take part in the plebiscite.[48] Rajmohan also says that when Rajaji showed the Formula to Jinnah prior to the Gandhi-Jinnah Talks, 'As Jinnah studied the piece of paper, C.R. (Rajaji) waited for a positive reaction on Jinnah's face. It never came.'[49] Was Rajaji not shrewd enough to anticipate this? Rajmohan's *Eight Lives* is a book on the life and work of eight prominent Muslims under the *Raj*. In its chapter on Jinnah also he says that 'He did not find it (the Pakistan in the Formula) large enough—it excluded the Hindu-majority districts of Bengal and Punjab…'.[50] Rajmohan quotes there an interesting remark by Choudhry Khaliquzzaman of the Muslim League that 'The right of self-determination of an area with the vote of one community alone (as demanded by Jinnah) formed a demand without parallel in world history'.[51]

Jinnah Rejects the Formula

Pakistan, as was actually born, was demarcated by the Muslim majority Districts. In that sense, its birth followed this Formula. But the latter provided for a plebiscite of all the adults, and as such was much more democratic than what had actually taken place. That was perhaps one of the reasons Jinnah rejected it. The Congress had taken the universal suffrage for granted for years, and put it into practice the moment India had its first General Elections in 1951-52. But it was in 1971 that Pakistan had its first General Elections by universal suffrage, and their results gave a call to the negation of the two-nation theory and the breaking up of the country itself. Jinnah also rejected the proposal for mutual agreements. As to the timing of the Partition, too, the Formula wanted to see to it that there would be no room for the British maneuver, while Jinnah wanted to depend on the British till the last.

Even early in 1947 Gandhi was firm in "Talk with Muslim Youths" in Noakhali that 'Only after independence has been won can there be a question of granting Pakistan…Once freedom is secured for the country as a whole then we can decide about Pakistan or Hindustan'. (86-354) This was the same attitude he took at the time of the Cabinet Mission Plan as to the sovereign status of the

Constituent Assembly, which, according to some, led to the failure of the Plan.

The Formula, together with Rajaji-Jinnah correspondence, was released to the Press on 9 July 1944, after Gandhi's release from his imprisonment since August 1942 and before the Talks. Pyarelal wrote to Amrit Kaur the next day that 'Bapu had shown his preparedness for exploring some such formula even as far back as August 4 1942, when he wrote to C.R. about it...'. (*CWMG*, 77-363, fn. 2) What Pyarelal wrote would fit in well with the easiness with which Gandhi had taken to the Formula. Gandhi, for instance, wrote in "Telegram to S. Sadanand" that 'Regard Formula Consistent with National Integrity...' (*CWMG*, 77-367). He also wrote in "Letter to Agatha Harrison" that 'Ere this reaches you, you will have known from the Press about the attempt I made to solve the communal tangle in collaboration with Rajaji...' (*CWMG*, 77-373), and in "Interview to the Press" that 'Rajaji's offer has seen the light of day only now, but I had personally subscribed to it when I was fasting in prison camp. It is now sixteen months old'. (*CWMG*, 77-405) These three were written in the middle of July 1944. What Pyarelal said also fits in well with what Gandhi and Rajaji were corresponding immediately before the AICC Resolution of August 1942. This would suggest that Gandhi was not all for 'Quit-India'.

He was basically against the partition. He said in "Unity is Vital in India" in April 1942 that 'I myself could never subscribe to the partitioning of the country. I would fight it with every means at my disposal...'. (*CWMG*, 76-24) In "For Muslim Friends" in July of the same year he wrote, after quoting Jinnah who said that 'Pakistan is an article of faith with Muslim India...' that 'If Pakistan as defined above is an article of faith with him, indivisible India is equally an article of faith with me'. (*CWMG*, 76-315) Then why did he agree to the Formula?

It may be that he was impressed by the prospect of democratic decision-making through universal suffrage, the lasting peace between the two newly born countries, and the impossibility of the British interference, which were all implied in the Formula. Above all the last point, namely, the idea that the Indians alone would be the arbiter of things, and that he would negotiate it on behalf of the Congress, something he could not succeed at the RTC, must have made him happy, and encouraged him to make so many visits to his rival, almost on bended knees, in the hot and humid September of Bombay.

There is a second factor which may have impressed him equally. Gandhi wrote, shortly before the Talks, in "Interview to United Press of India" that 'I know my present attitude has puzzled and pained many people…I was also a party to the self-determination resolution of the A.I.C.C. I hold that the Rajaji Formula gives effect to that resolution'. (*CWMG*, 78-16) He was talking here of the resolution about which he wrote in "Note to Jagdish K. Munshi" that 'The Delhi Resolution of April 2 (of 1942) was concerned with self-determination' (*CWMG*, 78-23), and not the 'Quit-India' Resolution.

The former, "A Resolution" of the CWC, declared at the end that they are 'unable to accept the proposals' of the Cripps Mission on the ground that the proposals 'relate principally to the future', and for the present 'It has been made clear that the Defence of India will in any event remain under British control'. But significantly it also says that 'the Committee cannot think in terms of compelling the people in any territorial unit to remain in an Indian Union against their declared and established will. While recognizing this principle, the Committee feel that every effort should be made to create conditions which would help the different units in developing a common and co-operative national life…Each territorial unit should have the fullest possible autonomy within the Union, consistently with a strong national State'. (*CWMG*, 78-397~399) It was apparently this resolution that Gandhi talked about in the above "Note". It certainly does not close the door to the vivisection of India, but it clearly encourages the opposite direction.

Therefore what Gandhi said is not quite understandable. Almost one year afterwards from the failure of the Talks, he said in "Interview to *The Hindu*" on the Rajaji Formula that 'It was my settled conviction though originally derived from Rajaji…I shall stick to it so long as I retain my sanity'. But he continued to say that 'I hold it to be substantial and also directly derivable from the Congress Resolutions and immediately from the Resolution of August 8 1942. Only I have given it concrete shape' (*CWMG*, 81-74). It is doubtful whether he was right, especially in his interpretation of the August resolution. He further said in the "Note" that 'According to him (Azad, Congress President)…I still retain the authority to discuss the matter with Jinnah because the Resolution of April 2 still stands'. (*CWMG*, 78-23) About the same time "Interview to Shyama Prasad Mookerjee" was published by Mookerjee, who wrote that 'He also said that the Rajaji Formula was a way of reducing to a concrete form the Congress resolution on self-determination…'. (*CWMG*, 78-12)

Gandhi the Loser at the Talks

The Formula, with Gandhi's backing, was more than enough to show Jinnah that the Congress would not reject the Partition out of hand. Jinnah was the winner in this sense. Against this Gandhi had to fight a losing battle. The failure of the Talks also greatly strengthened the position of the British. Gandhi was writing in the above "Note to Jagdish" about a month before the Talks that 'I wish to conquer even Jinnah with trust and love…Jinnah too has complete faith in me'. (*CWMG*, 78-24) They met and talked almost every day from 9 to 26 September 1944. In this period Gandhi wrote eleven letters to Jinnah and was reciprocated by Jinnah's ten, to supplement the talks. But his hope was not to be materialized. From the beginning he tried hard to call Jinnah's attention to the Formula, and even said 'you can call it Pakistan if you like'. (*CWMG*, 78-88) But when Jinnah said that 'We will have independence for Pakistan and Hindustan', presumably while the British were here, Gandhi had to reply that 'I said I could never be a party to that. I could never ask the Britishers to impose partition on India'. (*CWMG*, 78-88~89)

Jinnah also said 'Why should you ask non-Muslims (to vote)?' (*CWMG*, 78-89), to which Gandhi answered that 'there must be clear proof that the people affected desire partition'. (*CWMG*, 78-122) Jinnah must have been afraid that the Hindus in the Punjab and in Bengal would vote against the Partition *en masse* but not all the Muslims for it. Gandhi said, 'The Lahore Resolution is indefinite. Rajaji has taken from it the substance and given it a shape'. (*CWMG*, 78-92) But he was opposed to Jinnah's two-nation theory and asked, 'Will the two nations become one if the whole of India accepted Islam? Will Bengalis, Oriyas…cease to have their special characteristics if all of them become converts to Islam?'. (*CWMG*, 78-101) He also said that 'I am unable to accept the proposition that the Muslims of India are a nation, distinct from the rest of the inhabitants of India. Mere assertion is no proof'. (*CWMG*, 78-122)

Thus Gandhi did not really concede any of the points which were dear to him. The April resolution was really meant not to divide the country but to consolidate its unity. It was wrong to put it, and the Formula, together with the Lahore Resolution. Gandhi had to do so in order to make the Talks a success. Jinnah said in his statement at the end that 'I have placed before him (Gandhi) everything and every aspect of the Muslim point of view'. (*CWMG*, 78-418) But he did not define Pakistan, or tell anything over and above the Lahore Resolution. Whenever he found himself in difficulty he talked about himself representing the Muslims but Gandhi not representing anybody. The Talks failed.

Wavell's Letter to Amery

The Indian Nationalist Movement, 1885-1947—Select Documents, edited by B.N. Pandey, includes a letter from "Lord Wavell to L.S. Amery on the failure of the Gandhi-Jinnah talks, 3 October 1944", taken from *Transfer of Power*, Vol. V. The letter contains some points worth considering.[52]

It says that 'Gandhi propounded the Rajagopalachari formula, but made it clear that he did not really believe in it'. It may be true that Gandhi did not really believe that Jinnah would accept it for the reasons discussed already. But it is doubtful if he was not serious about convincing Jinnah. About three years afterwards, Gandhi, who was on fast in Calcutta in the midst of the communal trouble, told in "Discussion with Sarat Chandra Bose" on 2 September 1947 that 'If only Jinnah had accepted my offer embodied in the Rajaji Formula, all this could have been avoided ...I was prepared to go even further.' (89-139) Would he have said so if he had not believed in it, though it is not clear what he meant by 'going even further'?

Wavell also wrote that 'Jinnah was arguing for something which he has not worked out fully, and Gandhi was putting forward counter proposals in which he did not really believe at all'. As we have just seen, the second part is incorrect. And it is also difficult to believe that the first part is correct. It was already four and a half years after the Lahore Resolution. Had not Jinnah worked out his plan for Pakistan in the meantime? He simply did not care to tell it to Gandhi, for Wavell also wrote that 'He (Jinnah) told Gandhi that he was dealing only with British India and was not considering the Indian States', but we have seen that the Haroon Report was with Jinnah for some time which covers both the British India and the Indian States.

Criticism of the Rajaji Formula

Back to the Rajaji Formula, we see that it faced criticism from different quarters. In "Letter from K.M. Munshi" the author (Jagdish's father) wrote that 'Today, none but the Muslims are honestly welcoming the Rajaji Formula'. (*CWMG*, 78-401) Gandhi in his reply "Letter To K.M. Munshi" wrote that 'A believer in non-violence, I can maintain the unity of India only if I accept the freedom of every part'. (*CWMG*, 78-25)

Immediately after the Talks, M.R. Jayakar wrote to Gandhi that 'I am not surprised. There could be no meeting-ground between you two…It is frankly my opinion that the Muslim League leader has gained more from you than he has lost to you…Your formula is in Mr. Jinnah's hands and…he will use this formula as a bargaining counter with the British Government and also as the starting point in future negotiations with Indian leaders'. (*CWMG*, 78-145, fn. 1) When the Simla Conference, convened by Wavell in June to July 1945, ended in failure, Jayakar wrote to Gandhi that 'it does not suit Mr. Jinnah, to accept any arrangement, however shortlived, which brings Hindus and Muslims together…he called the Wavell arrangement a snare…if he accepted the interim arrangement Pakistan would be shelved…'. (*CWMG*, 81-14, fn. 1)

V.S. Srinivasa Sastri was also outspoken. In a letter of 4 August 1945 he cautioned Gandhi that 'The price is too big, the purchase will be a bogus article'. (*CWMG*, 81-90, fn. 1) Gandhi was still not convinced. In another of 18 February 1946, written in his death-bed and delivered to Gandhi personally by T.N. Jagadisan, Sastri said, 'Rajaji is not sound on this matter. Do not let him lead you again. The Punjab and Bengal would be ruined and blast your memory, if you gave them up. Do not let any part of India go out and become independent. It is bound to be a lasting enemy and a blistering sore to India'. (*CWMG*, 83-159, fn. 2) Sastri died two months afterwards. What he said was like a prophecy, but it came too late. Gandhi replied in "Letter to V.S. Srinivasa Sastri" that 'Do not worry. My support cannot be had for dividing Hindustan into two parts. I do not think Rajaji's opinion is different. If it is, it will not be acceptable to me'. (*CWMG*, 83-159) Gandhi, in October 1947, in "Talk With Muslims" said that 'Hindus are very much annoyed with me. You should be knowing, if you do not, how furious Hindus are with me. I shall not be surprised if one day I fall a prey to this fury'. (*CWMG*, 89-384) Sushila Nayar wrote on this point that Gandhi was at the time of partition against 'occupying vacant Muslim evacuee houses, mosques and the like' and 'those without shelter were outraged'.[53]

Was this fury, by the way, simply due to his alleged pro-Muslim policies? Was it not motivated also by his alleged pro-Harijan policies? If so, there were two varieties of fury against him and, geographically, they may have probably been overlapping in Western Maharashtra stretching to Konkan.

Some time after the Lahore Resolution, Gandhi got a request from a Muslim living in Lucknow, probably a well-wisher. It said that in view of the communal riots happening mostly in North India, he should move his ashram from Sevagram to some Muslim-majority village in U.P. (*CWMG*, 72-90, fn. 1) This seems to be, with hindsight, a sound idea. Gandhi himself mentioned this in "Letter To Jawaharlal Nehru" and said that 'I have told the writer that his suggestion attracts me and if I see my way clear I shall act up to it in part or wholly'. (*CWMG*, 72-90) During the last fifteen months of his life, Gandhi kept himself busy alongside the Grand Trunk Road, from Noakhali in the East to Delhi in the West, and was almost on the verge of going to the Punjab. To move his Headquarters to the North would have meant that he was permanently in Noakhali-like situation. In "Speech at Prayer Meeting" in Delhi about a month before independence, he talked about the Muslims and said that 'the Muslims of U.P. are walking in fear. They do not know whether they can continue to live there or not. But why can't they live there, I ask?'. (*CWMG*, 88-329~330) Three months since then, in another "Speech at Prayer Meeting" in Delhi he said that 'One-fourth of the entire Muslim population is concentrated in the U.P. They speak Urdu. If we want them to stay there the Devanagari script should not be forced on them…After all, Muslims have left their stamp all over the U.P….'. (*CWMG*, 89-339~340) His transfer to the U.P., therefore, would have made a difference.

Talking of UP, economist P.C. Verma told the author an episode in one of our many conversations. When the country was partitioned, his would-be father-in-law, teaching in Dhaka, came to India as a refugee. He got an appointment in Lucknow. It so happened that he arrived there on the day Gandhi was murdered. Without knowing anything about it, he hired a tonga in an unfamiliar city. Then, there appeared a Hindu mob who took the driver, a Muslim, away. But the people soon got to know that the assassin was not a Muslim, and the driver returned to his tonga safely.

Prelude to the Cabinet Mission

Gandhi's Noakhali mission was preceded by the failure of the Cabinet Mission Plan earlier in 1946 which intensified the political deadlock in India. It was, in its turn, preceded by the failure of the Simla Conference in June and July of the previous year 1945, shortly before the War came to the end in Asia and the Pacific. The Conference was convened by Wavell, the Viceroy. He made a "Speech Broadcast by the Viceroy" on 14 June (*CWMG*, 80-440~443), and on the same day there was a "Statement Made in Parliament by Secretary of State for India" (*CWMG*, 80-446~449). Both spoke on the aim of the Conference. Both referred to the proposed reconstitution of the Viceroy's Executive Council where all the Members except the Viceroy and the Commander-in-Chief would be appointed from among the Indians.

That itself was a step forward. But both told their audiences that those Indian Members would be from the caste Hindus and the Muslims in equal numbers. The divide and rule had come this far. There was nothing on the Constituent Assembly. The Secretary of State went so far as to say that 'The offer of March 1942 (by Cripps) stands in its entirety without change or qualification', and even referred to 'the future permanent constitution or constitutions for India' along that line. The Conference was thus half doomed even before it met.

In about six months' time, and shortly before the arrival of the Cabinet Mission, there was the Royal Indian Navy's Mutiny in February 1946. On hearing the news at Poona, Gandhi sent "Statement to the Press" on 23 February, stressing that 'This mutiny in the navy and what is following is not, in any sense of the term, non-violent action', having damaged churches, tram-cars and so on, and 'A combination between Hindus and Muslims and others for the purpose of violent action is unholy…'. (*CWMG*, 83-170~171) We will look at this Statement. Unlike the INA soldiers, the sailors were not fighting a war. They could have been easily persuaded to abandon the arms. The sailors would have welcomed Gandhi's blessings as much as the INAs, apart from the fact that, as Samar Guha writes in *The Mahatma and the Netaji*, the majority among the senior officers of the INA were Muslims who chose to belong to Pakistan in the end.[54]

Gandhi's abhorrence of violence is understandable, especially as the violence on property was involved, and *kisans* and labourers joined hands with the sailors. But could not Gandhi have seen it as a new form of Hindu-Muslim unity when, as a matter of fact, he was not able to see any way out on the communal front? Did not the Thebhaga *kisans* ask him if such a unity would not be forged out of a concrete political programme? After alienating the sailors and their supporters, were there any hope of Hindu-Muslim unity left with him? He left it to Vallabhbhai Patel to deal with the Mutiny. He wrote in another "Statement to the Press" three days later, which was a critique of Aruna Asaf Ali, not exactly for her support of the mutiny but more for her underground activity, and said, 'It is a matter of great relief that the ratings have listened to Sardar Patel's advice to surrender'. (*CWMG*, 83-184) Did it not occur to him that whatever communal unity achieved on this occasion could be looked at in a more sympathetic way, in the sense that the violence here was after all not much and would be much less compared to the violence likely to be generated in the serious communal clashes, let alone a 'civil war'?

About the same time elections to the Provincial Assemblies were held under the same 1935 Government of India Act as in 1937 with its limited franchise. The Congress got 81 per cent of the total votes cast in the General constituencies. From this point of view it was a victory for the Congress, and India moved forward towards independence. At the same time the Muslim League obtained 75 per cent of the total votes polled in the Muhammadan constituencies. In this sense it was a victory for the League, and India also moved forward towards partition.[55] India was going to be sandwiched between these two moves.

Cabinet Mission's Failure

On 16 May 1946 "Statement of Cabinet Delegation and Viceroy", one of the most important documents in Indo-British history, was issued (*CWMG*, 84-467~476). Although it said that 'The (Muslim) League...insisted that the principle of Pakistan should first be acknowledged', it made a historic announcement that 'We have, therefore, been forced to the conclusion that neither a larger nor a smaller sovereign State of Pakistan would provide an acceptable solution for the communal problem'. Did the Statement then support only the idea of a united India and contain no germ from which the two states of India and Pakistan ultimately came to be born? Unfortunately that was not so.

The Statement said that its purpose was two-fold, to present an idea for the 'machinery' for the future constitution-making, namely the Constituent Assembly, and to pave the way for setting up the Interim Government in the centre.

Out of the twenty-four paragraphs of the Statement, only one was devoted to the latter task. But a large part of the rest was not exactly on the constitution-making machinery as such, but on grouping within the 'Union of India' of Muslim-majority Provinces in the north-western area as Section B, and in the north-eastern area as Section C. The other, Hindu-majority Provinces would form Section A. The paper says that the Provinces are free to form groups in 15(5), but it also talks as if the members of the Constituent Assembly should immediately divide up into A, B, and C in 19(iv). The B and C would easily be led into forming groups. Note here from the 'Table of Representation' that the Punjab and Bengal were each undivided Punjab and Bengal. It was said in the paper as an argument against the creation of Pakistan that 'Bengal and the Punjab each has its own common language and a long history and tradition'. But now it was used as an argument for creating two expanded *de facto* Pakistans. The residuary powers, by the way, 'should vest in the Provinces' by 15(3).

Gandhi was paying close attention to the activities of the Delegation from the beginning. He wrote in "Draft Letter to Lord Pethick-Lawrence", the Secretary of State for India and Leader of the Delegation, ten days before the Plan was announced, that 'we are entirely opposed to any executive or legislative machinery for a group of provinces or units of the Federation... If that is to come, it should come through the Constituent Assembly free of any influence of the present Paramount Power'. (*CWMG*, 84-108)

Significantly Gandhi also wrote in this letter that 'In our discussions yesterday (5 May) repeated references were made to 'groups' of provinces functioning together...This method of grouping has not so far been discussed by us but still our talks seemed to presume all this'.

This would suggest that the idea of grouping came into the thinking of the Delegation only about this time. The fact that it was retained in spite of Gandhi's opposition would suggest that it was necessary to do so to appease the League. Whether the Delegation and the Viceroy had anticipated the birth of Pakistan at this time or not, seen in the above light, the Statement was clearly in conformity with the series of the British appeasement of the League from Linlithgow's letter to Jinnah in 1939 onwards. When the Statement came out, Gandhi spent 'four days of searching examination' of it and wrote "An Analysis". He was rather non-committal and optimistic, saying that 'It has no compulsion in it'. (*CWMG*, 84-170) The "Congress Working Committee's Resolution" of 24 May, which Gandhi called 'a good resolution' in "Letter to Lord Pethick-Lawrence" (*CWMG*, 84-198), was also non-committal and took a wait-and-see attitude, although it said that India wanted 'a strong, though limited, central authority, full autonomy for the provinces...' but 'it would appear that a measure of compulsion is introduced which clearly infringes the basic principle of provincial autonomy'. (*CWMG*, 84-482~483)

Two days later Gandhi wrote "Vital Defects", which was not as alarming as it may have sounded. One of the points he raised was important if only to know his view of the international scene at this time. He said that 'Troops (British troops) ...are to remain during the interim period...their presence will act as a damper on the Constituent Assembly and is more likely than not to be wanted even after the establishment of independence so called. A nation that desires alien troops for its safety, internal or external, or has them imposed upon it, can never be described as independent in any sense of the term'. (*CWMG*, 84-210) This view may well have been a reflection of his caution of the then Super Powers including Britain.

In the meantime, a "Resolution of Muslim League Council" passed on 6 June said that 'the attainment of the goal of a complete sovereign Pakistan still remains the unalterable objective of the Muslims in India, for the achievement of which they will, if necessary, employ every means in their power…'. However, as 'the basis and the foundation of Pakistan are inherent in the Mission's plan by virtue of the compulsory grouping of the six Muslim provinces, in Sections B and C…', the Muslim League is accepting the scheme. (*CWMG*, 84-487~489)

Gandhi on the other hand said in "Speech at Prayer Meeting" on 23 June that, 'He had commended the State document because of its voluntary character. But…A telegram from Assam had drawn attention to the fact that under Rules of Procedure for the election of members to the Constituent Assembly that had been issued from the Viceroy's office to the Speakers of the various Provincial Assemblies, no one could stand as a candidate unless he signed a declaration that he would abide by clause 19 of the State Paper of May 16. As they all knew, clause 19 referred, among other things, to grouping'. (*CWMG*, 84-360) Another question with Gandhi at this time, as is clear from "Speech at Congress Working Committee Meeting" of 19 June, was that of 'the non-inclusion of a nationalist Muslim' in the Interim Government proposed by Viceroy Wavell on 16 June. (*CWMG*, 84-347) The CWC passed a resolution on 26 June saying that the Congress would join the Constituent Assembly and demanding the formation of a representative and responsible Provisional National Government. (*CWMG*, 84-418, fn. 1) The AICC ratified it on 7 July by 204 to 51. (*CWMG*, 84-423, fn. 1)

Noorani argues that it was a trick by Cripps, a member of the Delegation, and Gandhi, who together tried to make it possible for the Congress to join the Interim Government even though it did not really accept the Statement as regards the grouping, while Jinnah had conceded much in abandoning the demand for a separate Pakistan.[56] To pass a judgment on Jinnah, however, the meaning of the above League Council's resolution should be examined. It seems to speak for itself. It would not have been possible to expect that Hindu-Muslim reconciliation could have been achieved under the circumstances even if the Cabinet Mission Plan had been accepted. Another thing is the League's Direct Action, which came within three months after the said Council resolution talked of 'employ(ing) every means'.

Narayanbhai writes on the communal background of the Calcutta police at that time and said that 'On 16 August, the Direct Action Day, 22 out of 24 police stations in Calcutta had Muslim officers in command, the remaining two were under the charge of Anglo-Indian officers'.[57] What was it that the Muslim League planned to do in Calcutta with this deployment? Noorani writes that Jinnah himself said that 'he must at all costs have Calcutta' for Pakistan, the Muslims were 'quite as capable of causing bloodshed', and 'he himself would welcome two years' rest in the Aga Khan's palace'.[58] Did all this amount to the acceptance of the Statement? The Direct Action in Calcutta spread to Noakhali, and Bihar, caused great losses among the Muslims especially in the latter. Indeed Moraes notes that 'It is curious that the British at that time should have taken no action against Jinnah for openly inciting the Calcutta killings: one of Jinnah's sympathetic biographers reveals that he expected to be arrested at any moment (Hector Bolitho in *Jinnah*), and in similar circumstances Nehru or Patel would have received short shrift'.[59]

Back to the AICC's ratification, Nehru, the new Congress President and as the head of the majority party the natural Prime Minister-designate in the Interim Government, said in his Press Statement within a few days that the Congress would enter the Constituent Assembly 'completely unfettered by agreements'. (*CWMG*, 85-5, fn. 2) Gandhi wrote in "Letter to Jawaharlal Nehru" that 'Your statement as published in the papers does not sound good. If it is correctly reported, some explanation is needed. It must be admitted that we have to work within the limits of the State Paper'. (*CWMG*, 85-5~6) Here Gandhi was in tune with the above CWC and the AICC resolutions. But Nehru's Statement was consistent with what Gandhi wrote in the above-mentioned Gandhi's Draft Letter to Pethick-Lawrence before the publication of the Statement.

We will again quote two scholars. Bimal Prasad said, concluding his paper on "Gandhi and India's Partition", that 'although strongly opposed to partition, Gandhi did not in fact seriously oppose it.'[60] He also writes, 'When (Rajendra) Prasad called on Gandhi on May 31, 1947', which was shortly before the fatal decision on the partition of India, 'the latter told him that it was a mistake on the part of the

Congress leaders to assume that their acceptance of partition would lead to the restoration of peace in the land'.[61]

In Bipan Chandra's words, 'Gandhiji's major political failure lay on the communal front'.[62] He, however, concludes by saying that 'Gandhiji was the only one to wage, however inadequately, a personal, life-long campaign for Hindu-Muslim unity'.[63]

Was Gandhi reaping as he had sown? Yes, though there were moments, at least in 1928 and 1937, that he could have turned the tide in the direction of forging Hindu-Muslim unity. How about 1946? It was too late, as the mutual suspicion had gone too deep by that time.

We may here look at how Wavell saw the relationships among the Indian politicians. His judgment may not have always been correct, but he was an honest man to himself. In a long note titled "A Retrospect: Summary of Cabinet Mission's Work" dated 1 July 1946, he wrote that 'no Hindu admitted that a Muslim could possibly have a grievance or any reason for mistrusting the 'democratic' predominance of the Congress, no Muslim would admit any possibility of justice or fairness from Hindu hands. The only people who put their case in some spirit of moderation and realism were the Princes, one or two of their Diwans, and (Percival) Griffiths on behalf of the Europeans.'[64] In the same note Wavell called Gandhi 'the real wrecker' of the Cabinet Plan, in more or less the same way as Noorani in the above.[65]

Incidentally Wavell wrote several lines when he heard the news of Gandhi's murder. He said, 'Whether he did more harm or good for India it would be hard to say, but Indians will have no doubt, and he certainly hastened the departure of the British, which was his life's aim. But he wrecked the plan of the Cabinet Mission which might possibly have secured a united India and saved all the massacres. I do not believe that he really worked for an understanding with the Muslims, when his influence might have secured it'.[66] The editor of Wavell's book, Penderel Moon, himself a British ICS, sort of intervened and said some words as if to defend Gandhi. He said that 'In judging, or perhaps one should say misjudging, Gandhi, Wavell was strongly influenced by his recollection that in 1942, when he as Commander-in-Chief was trying to secure India against Japanese invasion, Gandhi had let loose the 'Quit India' rebellion which for some weeks paralysed communications with the Eastern Front…Wavell was never able to rid his mind of the memory of it and it coloured his judgment'.[67]

Would it be useful to quote some words of what a British ex-Governor of Bengal, R.G. Casey, already quoted in Chapter Three, said of Gandhi? He wrote, 'Gandhi was the most interesting individual I met in India…His personality was lively and he had great charm. He was innately courteous, tactful, and a good listener. He had a good sense of fun, and I think probably also a good sense of humour…He seldom, if ever, spoke ill of any man'.[68]

When the CWC's decision to partition India was put before the AICC on 14 June 1947, Gandhi spoke on it. It was a remarkable speech in that he was honest to himself and to the AICC, and confessed his and the Congress' defeat although he did not use the term. It also showed him a democrat. In "Speech at A.I.C.C. Meeting" he said, 'The Working Committee has on your (A.I.C.C.'s) behalf accepted partition…But our (the Congress') constitution permits it and your duty demands it that if you feel that the Working Committee is in the wrong you should remove it, you should revolt and assume all power. You have a perfect right to do so, if you feel that you have the strength. But I do not find that strength in us today. If you had it I would also be with you and if I felt strong enough myself I would, alone, take up the flag of revolt. But today I do not see the conditions for doing so'. (*CWMG*, 88-153~7) He thus gave up once for all an idea of launching what promised to be his very last NC he may have surely been entertaining in one small corner of his mind, although people like N.K. Bose and Pyarelal have had a different idea on Gandhi's mind at this time, as we have seen elsewhere.

Kamaladevi, who was strongly opposed to the partition, was pressing Gandhi to rise against it. Gandhi's reply was 'It is too late. If it had been ten years earlier…'. This was about himself. Then he said on the Congress leadership that 'You see my colleagues came to me when they were still in their prime of life, giving up their bright careers, plunging into an unknown destiny'. Gandhi was saying that they too were old. But why is it that the "Old Guard" had stayed on so long until they were too old to take a new initiative? And who was responsible for that? Kamaladevi continued that 'I presumed he was conveying that they too had had a stake'.

The AICC approved the partition plan the next day. Kamaladevi cast an opposing vote and parted with politics then and there.[69]

Gandhi's Last Fifteen Months

Toward the end of 1946, in "Fragment of Letter to Jagneswar Ghosh", N.K. Bose wrote on Gandhi's behalf that 'What Gandhiji objects to is the redistribution of population on the basis of religion. That would mean an admission that people of different faiths cannot live on friendly terms within the same state. The Muslim League has suggested a similar remedy for the present Hindu-Muslim tension, when the minority who remain over in each Province will be held as hostages for the good behaviour of the majority in the neighbouring Province. This would amount to an armed truce and not peace on terms of equality, friendship and mutual trust. To cut up India into specifically religious zones, and then redistribute population to fit in with such an artificial scheme would, in Gandhiji's opinion, be monstrous. For it will cut across many of the linguistic, cultural and fundamental bonds of co-operation which have held together our people in the past'. (*CWMG*, 86-220)

Gandhi himself had said in "Talk to Relief Workers" almost on arrival in Noakhali a little earlier that 'No police or military in the world can protect people who are cowards...Your trouble is not numerical inferiority but the feeling of helplessness that has seized you and the habit of depending on others. The remedy lies with you. That is why I am opposed to the idea of your evacuating East Bengal *en masse*'. (*CWMG*, 86-89) Note the word 'coward'.

It was for the first time that he expressed his opinion on the population exchange. While in Noakhali, he also said in "Interview to the Press" in December that 'The question of the exchange of population is unthinkable and impracticable'. (*CWMG*, 86-182) When, as Bose explained, the Hindu Mahasabha people came to discuss a 'project of segregating the Hindu population in Noakhali for purposes of safety' (*CWMG*, 86-199, fn. 2), Gandhi in "Discussion with Hindu Mahasabha Leaders" responded that 'If they (the Hindus) lived in clusters, it would really mean accepting the Muslim League's mischievous two-nation theory'. (*CWMG*, 86-199)

On hearing the news from the Punjab, in "Speech at Prayer

Meeting" at Calcutta a week after independence, he said that 'He felt sorrow and shame to learn that the Hindus were leaving Lahore and the Muslims were leaving Amritsar'. (*CWMG*, 89-79) His intention to go to the Punjab to stop such exodus and help in the resettlement of the refugees must have been fortified by these news. He made his intention of going to the Punjab clear for the first time when he said that 'I shall proceed to the Punjab as soon as there is a call from God' in "Talk with Goswami Ganesh Dutt" on 7 April of that year, one month after the fatal Punjab Resolution (*CWMG*, 87-228). He was actually in Lahore for a day in August and said in "Talk with Congress Workers" that 'The rest of my life is going to be spent in Pakistan, may be in East Bengal or West Punjab, or perhaps, the North-West Frontier Province...My present place is in Noakhali and I would go there even if I have to die. But as soon as I am free from Noakhali I will come to the Punjab. I hope I am free from Noakhali very soon'. (*CWMG*, 89-10~11) He was on board a train the next day intending to go to Noakhali to spend the day of independence there. But he was not to see Noakhali again, nor the Punjab. He said in "Speech at Prayer Meeting" in the middle of September that 'For me, transfer of millions of the Hindus and the Sikhs and the Muslims is unthinkable. It is wrong. The wrong of Pakistan will be undone by the right of a resolute non-transfer of population'. (*CWMG*, 89-189)

In "Speech at A.I.C.C. Meeting" in the middle of November he said that 'Let all Muslims who have left their homes and fled to Pakistan come back here'. (*CWMG*, 90-42) But that would be a tremendous task. Twice, on 10 November and 2 December, Gandhi went to see the refugee camps at Panipat. In between, on 12 November, the Diwali Day of that year, he made "Broadcast to Refugees at Kurukshetra Camp" from Delhi, to thousands of people who had escaped Pakistan, when he introduced himself as 'To suffer with the afflicted and try to relieve their suffering has been my life's work'. (*CWMG*, 90-15) On 28 November he said in "Speech at Guru Nanak Birthday Function' that 'I found to my shame that as our motor-car was passing through Chandni Chowk, which used to be filled with Hindus, Sikhs and Muslims, I did not notice a single Muslim passer-by'. (*CWMG*, 90-123) In "Speech at Prayer Meeting" on 19 January 1948, one of his last, he said that 'Hindu and Sikh women should go to the Muslim sisters and establish friendship with them'.

He also said that 'Delhi is poorer for the disappearance of the exquisite workmanship of the Muslims'. (*CWMG*, 90-462)

These statements were made by Gandhi a nationalist who believed in the essential inviolability of the unity of India. He was a believer in the composite Indian culture. He should have put these points more strongly and tenaciously before Jinnah and the nation. In early May 1947, when the communal conflict was on the increase, Gandhi said in "Speech at Prayer Meeting" at Delhi that 'Jinnah Saheb has stated that the Hindu and the Sikh minorities would be absolutely safe in Pakistan...But why are such conditions not obtaining today? I can have a glimpse of Pakistan in only what is happening in the Punjab and Bengal, isn't it?'(*CWMG*, 87-400) Also he said in "Discussion with Muslim League Leaders" that 'Today the Hindus asked him (Gandhi) if Noakhali was an indication of what they were to expect in Pakistan'. (*CWMG*, 86-94)

At the same time he had to face antagonism by the Hindus. In "Speech at Prayer Meeting" on 2 January 1948, he showed a long letter by a Hindu, which said that if there were any Muslim loyal to India he should keep them and send the rest away, otherwise what would happen in the case of a war between India and Pakistan. (*CWMG*, 90-346) In "Speech at Prayer Meeting" on 12 January 1948, he all of a sudden announced that he would begin an indefinite fast from the next day (*CWMG*, 90-408~409). In "Speech at Prayer Meeting" on 15, he clarified that 'My fast...is undoubtedly on behalf of the Muslim minority in the Union and, therefore, it is necessarily against the Hindus and Sikhs of the Union and the Muslims of Pakistan. It is also on behalf of the minorities in Pakistan as in the case of the Muslim minority in the Union'. (*CWMG*, 90~428~429) It became clear that Gandhi wanted seven conditions, all concerned with the rights and liberty of the Muslims in India, fulfilled before he broke his fast (*CWMG*, 90-440, fn. 1). A seven-point declaration was signed and submitted to him on 18 January. They satisfied him. A little earlier, apart from these conditions, the Government of India in its "Government Communique" announced that in view of the fast it changed its policy concerning the cash balances between India and Pakistan and decided to pay to Pakistan the amount due. (*CWMG*, 90-556) In "Speech at Prayer Meeting" on 16 January Gandhi hailed this decision and said that 'They deserve the warmest thanks from the whole country'. He added that 'This is no policy of appeasement of the Muslims'. (*CWMG*, 90-435) He must have thought that these conditions and a decision would also help pave his way to Pakistan.

When Nelson Mandela died in December 2013, in the midst of this writing, David Cameron, the Prime Minister of Britain, said that 'Tonight one of the brightest lights of our world has gone out'. Many in India may have been reminded that, when Gandhi was assassinated, Jawaharlal Nehru said in his broadcast, 'the light has gone out of our lives and there is darkness everywhere'.

Communal Relations after Independence

Rajmohan Gandhi writes in his *Gaffar Khan* that he visited India for the first time after the Partition in 1969, Gandhi's centenary. But 'Whether by accident or by design, the Gandhi centenary saw communal riots in different parts of India, including in Gandhi's Ahmedabad'.[70]

The author spent ten days at Ahmedabad in August to September 2002 when the large scale riots had taken place in Gujarat, and had a look at some of the refugee camps and the burnt-down houses. Here we will see what Vibhuti Narain Rai, IPS officer, has written in his study *Combating Communal Conflicts—Perception of Police Neutrality during Hindu-Muslim Riots in India.*

In the riots in Ahmedabad in 1969, the number of dead was 24 Hindus, 430 Muslims and 512 in total (including others). By this time mixed localities were emerging together with the growth of the Muslim middle classes. But with every riot since then the differentiation between the communities proceeded, and with the riots in 1985 it became complete. In this the role of the land mafia at Ahmedabad was 'amazing'. They created riots and sold colonies.[71] It was also ascertained that in 1969 half a dozen Muslim religious facilities were destroyed which were located near the police, but none of such Hindu facilities.[72]

Rai continues on the psychology of the police that 'Like an average Hindu, an average Hindu policeman also believes that Muslims, generally, are cruel and violent by nature...I spoke to a large number of policemen working in various ranks. I was amazed to find that most of them seriously believed, that apart from being cruel and violent, Muslims were untrustworthy, anti-national and easily influenced by fanatical leadership and could indulge in rioting at the slightest provocation'.[73] Therefore, in the riots, 'arrest' was usually that of the Muslim, 'search' was that of the Muslim house, 'firing' was against the Muslim. The Hindu mobs, even when warned of firing, did not take it seriously.[74] Rai's foremost recommendation was to recruit Muslim policemen up to the population ratio. In the case of the PAC (UP), its one battalion consists of 72 sections each with 7~9 policemen. It is the minimum unit to be deployed in the case of a riot. But 60~65 of the 72 has no Muslim at all. More than 85 per cent of Hindus prefer PAC and the Civil Police deployed at the time of the riots, but the equally high ratio of the Muslims prefer CRPF or the Army to be deployed.[75]

The book came out in pre-2002 days. After the riots, Rai wrote a "Letter" under the title 'Gujarat holocaust: a lesson to learn for IPS cadre'.[76] He said that what was taking place everywhere from Ahmedabad to the rural areas was 'the same old story...(but) on an unprecedented scale'.

A newspaper article describes 'the same old story' in a somewhat more sociological way. Raka Roy writes under "Where women bore the brunt" that 'The populations were identified at Partition and then stored in the collective memory to be whipped to frenzy when necessary. The violence was kept alive by stories, jokes, implicit rules, and writings that swirled underground in the darkness of both Hindu and Muslim subconscious...'.[77]

We will wind up this Chapter by showing some excerpts from the *Sachar Committee Report,* 2006 (Prime Minister's High Level Committee on Social, Economic and Educational Status of the Muslim Community of India, Chaired by Justice Rajindar Sachar), a document showing the contemporary position of the Muslims in India.

According to the *Report*, while the total population of India increased by 134 per cent during the four decades of 1961~2001, the Muslim population increased by 194 per cent in the same period, thus enhancing their ratio to the total from 10.7 per cent to 13.4 per cent. In real terms the Muslims increased from 47 million to 138 million. This change, however, is not because the Muslims were in better living conditions.

In the educational sphere, the *Report* says that 'The data clearly indicates that while the overall levels of education in India, measured through various indicators, is still below universally acceptable standards, the educational status of the Muslim community in particular is a matter of great concern.'[78] It also says that it is being seen that 'traditionally under-privileged SCs/STs catching up and overtaking the Muslims in several contexts'.[79] But 'Muslim parents are not averse to modern or mainstream education and to sending their children to the affordable Government schools. They do not necessarily prefer to send children to *madarsas*'.[80]

On the employment situation, the *Report* says that many of the Muslims are engaged in 'self-employed manufacturing and trade activities' in the informal sector'.[81] On infrastructure, the Report says that 'Muslims are concentrated in locations with poor infrastructural facilities. This affects their access to basic services like education, health facilities, transport, etc.'[82] At the time of Partition the flight of the educated and wealthy Muslims to Pakistan left the living conditions all the more difficult for those who remained.

How much of the above condition is still to be called the legacy of the Partition?

Notes

1. *Writings of Bipan Chandra*, 191.
2. Yajnik, *ibid.*, 117.
3. B.R. Nanda, *Road to Pakistan*, 32.
4. Dipak Malik, "Political Economy of Communalism", John P. Neelsen and Dipak Malik, eds., *Crisis of State and Nation*, 388.
5. B. R. Nanda, *Road to Pakistan*, 118.
6. *Ibid.*, 118~9.
7. *Ibid.*, 47.
8. *Ibid.*, 119.
9. Bimal Prasad, Amit Kumar Gupta, ed., *Myth and Reality*, 103.
10. *Ibid.*, 154.
11. Akbar, *Nehru*, 255.
12. John Glendevon, *The Viceroy at Bay*, 49.
13. Rothermund, *ibid.*, 87~8.
14. Akbar, *ibid.*, 275.
15. *Ibid.*, 276.
16. Ayesha Jalal, *The Pity of Partition*, 4-5.
17. *Writings of Bipan Chandra*, 134~5.
18. Bimal Prasad, *ibid.*

19. B.R. Nanda, *Road to Pakistan*, 182.
20. *Ibid.*, 225.
21. *Ibid.*, 243.
22. *Ibid.*, 243~4.
23. A.G. Noorani, *Jinnah and Tilak*, 132.
24. T.R. Sareen, *Jinnah, Linlithgow and the Making of Pakistan*, 75~9, 203~4, 244.
25. Churchill himself remodelled Linlithgow's draft. R.J. Moore, *Churchill, Cripps, and India*, 35.
26. *Ibid.*, 96~104.
27. Sheikh Abdullah, *Flames of the Chinar*, 56.
28. *Ibid.*, 73.
29. Sareen, *ibid.*, 234.
30. B.R. Nanda, *Road to Pakistan*, 303.
31. Bose, *Studies*, *ibid.*, 281.
32. Bose, *Studies*, *ibid.*, 287.
33. Sareen, *ibid.*, 251~67.
34. Sunanda Sanyal, Soumya Basu, *The Sickle and the Crescent*, 67~8.
35. *Ibid.*, 68, 70~1.
36. *Ibid.*, 134.
37. Narayanbhai, *ibid.*, II, 654.
38. Judith Brown, *Gandhi*, 243.
39. Narayanbhai, *ibid.*, III, 11.
40. Suhrud, 145, 155.
41. Hiren Mukerjee, *ibid.*, 126.
42. S. Gopal, *Essential Writings of Nehru*, 1-209.
43. Nanda did not call it that way in his first biography of Gandhi, *Mahatma Gandhi.*
44. Sydney Rittenberg and Ananda Benett, *The Man Who Stayed Behind* (from Japanese translation).
45. H. Yamaguchi, *Japan*, 45-6.
46. Bose, *Studies*, *ibid.*, 281.
47. Moraes, Witness to an Era, 105.
48. Rajmohan Gandhi, *The Rajaji Story*, 102~5.
49. *Ibid*, 100.
50. Rajmohan Gandhi, *Eight Lives*, 160-1.
51. *Ibid.*, 163.
52. B.N. Pandey, ed., *The Indian Nationalist Movement*, 156-7.
53. Sushila Nayar, "This I Saw", *ibid.*, 279.
54. Samar Guha, *ibid.*, 108.
55. Kuwajima Sho, Table V, 243-5.
56. Noorani, Jinnah and Tilak, 177~231.
57. Narayanbhai, *ibid.*, IV, 231.
58. A.G. Noorani, *ibid.*, 171.
59. Moraes, 145.

60. Bimal Prasad, *ibid.*, 113.
61. *Ibid.*, 110.
62. *Writings of Bipan Chandra*, 166.
63. *Ibid.*, 197.
64. Wavell, *The Viceroy's Journal*, 311.
65. *Ibid.*, 314.
66. *Ibid.*, 439.
67. *Ibid.*, 461-2.
68. Gopalkrishna Gandhi, 493~4.
69. Kamaladevi, *Memoirs*, 304~5.
70. Rajmohan Gandhi, *Ghaffar Khan*, 247.
71. V.N. Rai, *Combating Communal Conflicts*, 87.
72. *Ibid.*, 101.
73. *Ibid.*, 105.
74. *Ibid.*, 106~7.
75. *Ibid.*, 91~2.
76. *Azad Academy Journal*, May 1-31, 2002, *The Milli Gazette*, 1-15, June 2002.
77. *The Hindu*, 11 May, 2002.
78. *Sachar Committee Report*, 84.
79. *Ibid.*, 85.
80. *Ibid.*
81. *Ibid.*, 106.
82. *Ibid.*, 150.

Five
Gandhi an Internationalist

'If there is anything to be learnt from India, it is non-violence'. "Speech at Prayer Meeting".
—4 December 1947, *CWMG*, Vol. 90, p. 177

1. The Meaning of India's Independence

India's Contribution to Peace

India's independence prompted the independence of other colonial nations, particularly those in Asia, Middle East and Africa. There was naturally a certain time lag between the independence of India and of other countries, like, for example, the ten years' interval between India's and Ghana's independence. Ghana was the first British colony in Black Africa to achieve freedom after the Second World War, first as a Dominion and later turning to a Republic, just like India. In the course of time those newly independent nations made up the majority in the United Nations, with 1960, "The Year of Africa", as the watershed when as many as seventeen African countries became independent and joined the UN. The independence of so many nations itself made it difficult, almost impossible, for the imperialist powers to start a new war of conquest and redistribution of colonies among them, as in the case of the two World Wars, in search of new market for export or investment, or new sources of raw materials and energy. India thus made a great contribution to the cause of world peace by achieving her own independence.

Needless to say it is impossible not to associate the name of Gandhi with this process. He himself was broadly aware of the role of India, and wrote a number of times on the significance of India's becoming independent, although his emphasis was probably more on getting it with non-violence. It would be appropriate to cite a few examples of how he looked at India's achieving independence in a wider context. In his "Speech at Meeting in Lausanne" toward the end of 1931, Gandhi said in answering a question on the future of Egypt that 'If India becomes independent, Egypt becomes independent automatically. India becoming independent is such a huge and far-reaching event that every country will pulsate with a new life'. (*CWMG*, 48-412) In "Interview with Louis Fischer", Gandhi asked 'What about the Negroes?' (*CWMG*, 76-440) In July 1944, after he came out of prison, he said in "Interview to Stuart Gelder" that 'Freedom for India will bring hope to Asiatics and other exploited nations. Today there is no hope for the Negroes, but Indian freedom will fill them with hope'. (*CWMG*, 77-351) Also as to Black Africa, he had a "Discussion with Negro Soldiers" in Madras after the end of the war. They were from West Africa and reportedly came to see him 'with a long list of questions indicative of the deep stirring in their consciousness'. (*CWMG*, 83-11, fn. 1~3) His last message on this subject was in "Speech at Prayer Meeting" at Delhi in early May 1947, about a month after the Inter-Asian Relations Conference. In the Speech he said that 'it is universally hoped that with India becoming independent, the whole of Asia and then Africa too would become free. This would mean a new birth for the whole world'. (*CWMG*, 87-404) We thus see that Gandhi's sense of history had not been clouded by the uninterrupted stream of domestic troubles he had encountered one after another. We may even be allowed to think if his long African experience had sustained him till the end in keeping his perception of the world broad and extensive. We have seen that he had already had a vague idea of how India would achieve independence when he left Africa. He may have been building upon it ever since.

Mention must also be made here that Gandhi represented one of the sources of the thinking on the United Nations. It expressed itself in the Quit-India Resolution. It says 'the Committee is of opinion that the future peace, security and ordered progress of the world demand a world federation of free nations...On the establishment of such a world federation, disarmament would be practicable in all countries, national armies, navies and air forces would no longer be necessary, and a world federal defence force would keep the world peace and prevent aggression'. (*CWMG*, 76-460) This part is not in the CWC Resolution of 14 July which became the basis of the AICC Resolution. (*CWMG*, 76-451-3) One might be allowed to think if it was added by Gandhi himself at the last moment.

Gandhi on Palestinian Question

Gandhi's active interest in the Middle East, for the first time after the collapse of the Khilafat Movement, was aroused by the way the Jewish people were brought into Palestine in spite of the opposition of the local Arabs in the absence of their explicit or implicit consent. He wrote four short articles, or gave interviews, on the subject from 1931, while he was in Britain, to 1947, on the eve of the Partition of both India and Palestine. If we recall the three points he was raising as the core of the Khilafat question shortly after the First World War, and the lack of understanding of the Arab and Turkish nationalism implied there, we are struck by the advance in his knowledge and judgment of the Arabs in a matter of a little more than ten years.

The first was an "Interview to "*The Jewish Chronicle*" of 2 October 1931. He begins with 'I have a world of friends among the Jews. In South Africa I was surrounded by Jews...'. But he soon came to the point and said, 'I can understand the longing of a Jew to return to Palestine, and he can do so if he can without the help of bayonets, whether his own or those of Britain. In that event he would go to Palestine peacefully and in perfect friendliness with the Arabs'. Britain was the country which promised a 'Jewish National Home' in Palestine by the Balfour Declaration of 1917, and also had Palestine under its League of Nations Mandate during the inter-war years. (*CWMG*, 48-105~6)

His second one, titled "The Jews" published in his *Harijan* of 26 November 1938, was the most important of those four. Here also Gandhi had the history of the persecution of the Jews in mind and wrote, 'My sympathies are all with the Jews...They have been the untouchables of Christianity. The parallel between their treatment by Christians and the treatment of untouchables by Hindus is very close'. Still, 'The cry for the national home for the Jews does not make much appeal to me'. And 'Palestine belongs to the Arabs in the same sense that England belongs to the English or France to the French. It is wrong and inhuman to impose the Jews on the Arabs'. Then Gandhi puts a fundamental question to the Jews. 'The Palestine of the Biblical conception is not a geographical tract. It is in their hearts. But if they look to the Palestine of geography as their national home, it is wrong to enter it under the shadow of the British gun. A religious act cannot be performed with the aid of the bayonet or a bomb. They can settle in Palestine only by the goodwill of the Arabs'. (*CWMG*, 68-137~41)

There was no change in his attitude after the Second World War. In "Jews and Palestine", *Harijan* on 21 July 1946, his third one, he wrote, 'they (the Jews) have erred grievously in seeking to impose themselves on Palestine with the aid of America and Britain and now with the aid of naked terrorism. Their citizenship of the world should have and would have made them honoured guests of any country'. This was the first time Gandhi criticized the US on the Palestinian question. It came almost on the heels of the publication of his criticism of dropping the atomic bombs on Japan, which appeared in *Harijan* of 7 July, eleven months after the dropping, entitled "Atom Bomb and *Ahimsa*". (*CWMG*, 84-440~1)

In his fourth and final piece, Gandhi said to the "Interview to Reuter" on 5 May 1947 that if I were a Jew, I would tell them: 'Don't be so silly as to resort to terrorism, because you simply damage your own case which otherwise would be a proper case...They should meet the Arabs, make friends with them, and not depend on British aid or American aid or any aid...". Perhaps here, the worth of what he said, and repeatedly, is shining even more at present. (*CWMG*, 87-417)

It may be interesting to note here that A.G. Noorani, in his book *Savarkar and Hindutva: The Godse Connection*, writes that V.D. Savarkar, a believer in the two-nation theory on the Hindu side, who was very close to N.R. Godse, Gandhi's assassin but himself got acquitted, 'lauded the establishment of Israel...for Savarkar Arab meant simply Muslim'.[1]

It may also be interesting to look at the book *Gandhi and the Middle East: Jews, Arabs and Imperial Interests* by Simone Panter-Brick. It has focused on the role played by Hermann Kallenbach, a very close friend of Gandhi in his South African days, himself a Zionist who approached Gandhi after his return to India.

The book asks 'did Gandhi…ever do something positive to resolve the conflict between the Arabs and the Jews?' and answers 'yes'.[2] The book then follows Kallenbach who came to see Gandhi in 1937 at Sevagram, and made him promise that he would read Zionist literature without prejudice. Gandhi kept it.[3] But, while Gandhi wanted to do something with the help of Kallenbach, several factors stood in the way, such as the Rebellion in the Palestine, hiatus in British policy, delay in Kallenbach's second visit, Gandhi's illness, and Jinnah's retaliation against the Congress.[4] When Kallenback finally came in January 1939, for a second time, it was too late, and he went back at the end of March. Thus, '…the Mahatma failed in the Middle East because of strictures at home'.[5] The work is remarkable in that it not only focused on Kallenbach's hitherto unknown secret contact with Gandhi, but it did it on the basis of the letters its author found in the newly available Volume 96 of the *CWMG*.

Gandhi and Tagore on Korea

There was, however, one area in international affairs where Gandhi's knowledge was almost zero and that of Rabindranath Tagore much superior. It was on Korea under the Japanese rule since 1910. Tagore, unlike Gandhi who never visited Japan, was in Japan five times in all, made detailed observation of the country, and, very importantly, paid attention to the position of the Koreans as well. Since Japan did not introduce any higher education in Korea, many Koreans had to come to Japan for study, and Tagore was contacted by some of them. Tagore wrote a poem "The Song of the Defeated" for the Koreans in 1916, during his first visit to Japan. Then he handed a short poem for a Korean daily during his last in 1929, which was published in that daily on 2 April of that year. The original was as follows.

- In the golden age of Asia
- Korea was one of its lamp bearers,
- And that lamp is waiting to be lighted once again
- For the illumination in the East.

The above is from a presentation by a Korean scholar at the Symposium on "India and East Asia: Learning from Each Other", organized by the University of Delhi to commemorate the reorganization of its Department of Chinese and Japanese Studies into one of East Asian Studies, held in March 2003. The presentation also says that many of Tagore's writings have been translated into Korean. Surprisingly it says that 'Mahatma Gandhi also sent a letter to the same paper in January 1927, in which he hoped that "*Chosun* will be on its own in non-violent ways"'. It is not possible to find it in the *CWMG*.[6]

Tagore's poem was in 1929. The next year 1930 was that of the Salt March. According to *The Mahatma and the Poet*, compiled and edited by Sabyasachi Bhattacharya, Mahadev Desai wrote on Tagore's visit to Sabarmati Ashram in the middle of January. It said, 'The Poet talked in his usual manner on all varieties of subjects, all of us listening with rapt attention. He had vivid in his memory the picture of a Korean who had visited him. The man was dreaming dreams of a new Korea. "How will you fight exploiting Japan?" the Poet had asked him, and he had said: "The world may be divided into two classes—exploiters and the exploited, and it is only by means of the combination of the exploited that we can fight Japan. "That combination is coming, and one day we will find all the exploited people together, and we will find even the Japanese exploited fighting by the side of us". "Won't it be true, Mahatmaji? Prosperous people can never combine, it is only the oppressed and the downtrodden who can combine. That was his idea".

Mahadevbhai also wrote that 'He (Tagore) talked with intimate knowledge of the affairs in China and elsewhere...'. He also adds that 'The Poet was keen on knowing what exactly Gandhiji wanted to place before the country during the present year. "I am furiously thinking night and day", said Gandhiji, "and I do not see any light coming out of the surrounding darkness"'. The conversation is not in the *CWMG*. Even after this, there is nothing to show that Gandhi's interest was aroused in Korea. His interest in China, however, became more and more intensive as the Second World War progressed, ultimately leading to the 'Quit-India' Movement.[7]

NAM—A Different Aspect of India's Role

We have seen that India's independence together with its wider effect has made another world-scale war almost impossible. India has made a contribution to the cause of peace still in another way and in a much more conscious manner. It was by becoming one of the main architects of the Non-Aligned Movement (NAM). The NAM was an outcome of the then developing global Cold War, and a response to it, and India's role in, for instance, bringing ceasefire to the Korean War (1950-53) is not to be forgotten.V.K.R.V. Rao must have been aware of all this when he wrote on the role of Gandhi and Nehru in the NAM in his *The Nehru Legacy* that '...the one thing Gandhi succeeded in stamping upon Nehru was the method of attaining peace, that peace has to be fought for and won, and that there are peaceful methods for winning peace'. Rao said that the main means of attaining this was non-alignment. He quoted Nehru who said that 'I do not believe in blocs. My country will not join any of these military blocs. My country will remain a non-aligned country'. Rao goes as far as to say, but with a good reason, that it was Nehru who prevented tensions from exploding into a hot war, and it is a pity that Western historians do not appreciate it.[8]

The spirit and the theoretical thinking of the NAM, however, were already seen developing even before the Cold War. Its remarkable instance in India was a long letter Kamaladevi wrote to Gandhi on the eve of the Second World War. There she said that 'the world is mainly torn between these two (camps)' who were about to start fighting in a war for 'the usual scramble for colonies', but 'there is a third view...the voice of the people who are mere pawns in the game.' 'You (Gandhi) are eminently fitted to give voice to it. India has, I think, a peculiar place today in the colonies of the world. It has both a moral prestige and organizational strength enjoyed by few colonies'. (*CWMG*, 70-235~237) None of the three biographies of Kamaladevi, by Jamila Brijbhushan, Sakuntala Narasimhan, and Reena Nanda, respectively, that the author had an opportunity of reading, and not even her own *Inner Recesses Outer Spaces: Memoirs*, has quoted this letter.

But Kamaladevi wrote her thought in some more detail in her *Memoirs*. She writes, 'In the anti-imperialist vortex, India had attained a notable position'. She said that the CD and Nehru's anti-colonial, anti-Nazi and pro-China activities in Europe 'had served to build India up as a powerful manifestation of subject peoples' champion'. And then 'Gandhiji's avowal of the close identity of the Indian freedom struggle with the world colonial struggle had added a universal dimension to our objectives and actions. Gandhiji had touched the global nerve centre when he proclaimed that India's freedom would mean the liberation of British colonies and by chain reaction, of other subject people. That the Indian struggle was crucial in a larger context, he never tired of reminding us and the world'.[9]

That was how Kamaladevi, and for that matter Gandhi himself, understood the meaning of India's attaining independence. As such her thought may be seen as one of the original streams of the NAM. We do not have to think of NAM solely as a Cold-War phenomenon. Its origin preceded the Cold War and it has not yet exhausted its usefulness for the peace of the world as long as there still exist military alliances which are clearly the legacy of the Cold War. Nor do we have to think of NAM only as an official, namely an inter-governmental organization.

Mary King's Study on Gandhi and the African-Americans

Gandhi's connection with the African-Americans' movements has so far been relatively little known. But Chapter 3 of Mary King's hefty *Mahatma Gandhi and Martin Luther King Jr* is devoted to this topic, and makes a very interesting reading. She begins by saying that 'The overwhelming white news corps in the United States tended habitually to report on (Martin Luther) King's Gandhian approaches in the Montgomery bus boycott as if they were a new phenomenon.' But 'The more informative story is how, for decades, a detailed transmission of Gandhian philosophies and procedures had been underway to the US black community…'. More concretely, 'as early as the 1920s, years before the Salt March, an undeniable association had been established in the collective African-American mind between Gandhi's freedom struggle and the aspirations of black citizens for equality.' It would be quite natural that 'Gandhi's campaigns against untouchability drew instant recognition by African-Americans'. Also, a number of representatives of African-Americans visited Gandhi in India while he was active. Martin Luther King Jr came to be inspired by Gandhi through some of these streams.[10] Homer Jack's article "Mohandas Karamchand Gandhi and Martin Luther King Jr." is helpful in understanding King's background in connection with India.[11]

How much of this Gandhi and African-American connection are we able to know from the *CWMG*? It is not clear. They include at least three meetings of Gandhi with the African-Americans, all in 1936-7. They are (1) "Interview to American Negro Delegation", headed by Howard Thurman (*CWMG*, 62-198~202), (2) "Interview to Prof. Mays" (*ibid.*, 64-221~5), and (3) "Interview to Dr. Tobias" (*ibid.*, 64-229~30). On all the occasions the conversation centred upon the question of non-violence.

Mary King's book, incidentally, devotes its final Chapter 5 to "Seven struggles" which discusses the non-violent movements in Burma, Poland, the then East Germany, the former Czechoslovakia, Thailand, Palestine, and Guatemala.

2. The Place of Gandhi in Modern Asian History

Three Epochs of Asian History and Gandhi

We will conclude this small work on Gandhi with a few words on his place in the modern Asian history. We may broadly identify three more or less distinct epochs in this era of Asian history. First came the period of independence or decolonization. It was roughly from around the First World War to the mid-1950s, when we saw the arrival of peace in Asia and the Pacific in the ceasefire in Korea, the end of the first Vietnam War, and the Bandung (Afro-Asian) Conference. This was the time when Gandhi was very active for India's, and for other countries' independence.

The second was the period of Cold War in Asia. Gandhi was no longer there on the scene, but his thought on fighting for and winning peace exerted influence, largely through Jawaharlal Nehru's foreign policy in the case of India, at least till India had her own serious domestic and border problems. Journalist Kuldip Nayar once wrote that while India was economically and militarily not yet up to the standard, the big powers tried to get her support and opinion, but now her Prime Minister was making a round of Moscow, New York and London so that she would not slip off their radar.[12] Akbar writes in his *Nehru* how Norman Cousins described Nehru at the Bandung Conference in 1955. Cousins says, 'At Bandung, Chou En-lai was surrounded by bodyguards, Nehru by men who wanted to talk to him—men from new nations who suddenly were obliged to make history and needed the kind of confidence that a Nehru could impart to them'.[13]

The third is the present post Cold War age when peace and poverty alleviation are the two major tasks before us. They are inter-related. Peace in this case means not simply no war but drastic disarmament, scrapping of the deterrence theory, and democratization of the political system. Poverty alleviation here does not simply address the per capita income and the poverty line. It also means man's safety, dignity, health, education, quality of life.

It was largely in the context of the world today that we have examined the thinking and practice of Gandhi, as we believe that he is still one of the important sources from which the mankind will be able to extract wisdom and ideals for solving those two-fold problems before us. In other words we need Gandhi, particularly his insight into non-violence and into the underprivileged. In our view Gandhi is valid for 50 per cent of the problems India and the mankind are facing. Thus Gandhi has basically withstood the test of time all through the above three periods of modern Asian history. Has there been any other Asian leader comparable to Gandhi in this respect? Perhaps 'Uncle Ho'—Ho Chi-Minh—was one such person.

Notes

1. A.G. Noorani, *Savarkar and Hindutva*, 93.
2. Simone Panter-Brick, *Gandhi and the Middle East*, 10.
3. *Ibid.*, 33~7.
4. *Ibid.*, 94~5.
5. *Ibid.*, 162.
6. Jeong Ho Lee, "Literary Contacts and Influences between India and Korea", in: Sushila Narasimhan and G. Balatchandirane, eds., *India and East Asia*, 425~40.
7. Sabyasachi Bhattacharya, *The Mahatma and the Poet*, 190~3.
8. V.K.R.V. Rao, *The Nehru Legacy*, 31~6.
9. Kamaladevi, *Memoirs*, 218.
10. Mary King, *Mahatma Gandhi and Martin Luther King Jr*, 175-200.
11. Homer A. Jack, "Mohandas Karamchand Gandhi and Martin Luther King Jr.", Radhakrishnan, S. ed., *Mahatma Gandhi 100 Years*, 129~144.
12. Kuldip Nayar, *The Indian Express*, 6 November 2001.
13. Akbar, *Nehru*, 567.

Summing Up

We will briefly summarize what we have been discussing.

Gandhi's conception of manliness *vs.* cowardice was an important yardstick by which he measured his and other people's behaviour. He looks at an oath as something individualistic, calls upon others even to face the world with its help. This may have led him to regard others as having their own will, as composing a civil society. He, however, did not look at men and women as equal.

Among the *Ekadasi*, namely the eleven-fold vows, Non-stealing would lead to earning one's relief in the event of difficulties, and Non-possession to simplicity of life and to respecting physical labour.

His Hinduism means, in part, assimilating the 'untouchables', and tends to neglect their own way of life. He stressed penance on the part of the Hindus, particularly by opening the temples to the Harijans, rather than to welcome the emergence of their own consciousness from within the Harijans. His approach was the opposite of the reductionist one. He was against the inter-marriage, inter-caste, inter-provincial, and inter-faith, at first, but gradually came to embrace it.

His *satyagraha*, including non-co-operation (NC) and civil disobedience (CD), encouraged people and moved them from fear and subservience to fearlessness and peaceful rebellion. The idea behind was that the power, even the dictatorship, depends on the will of the common people. He seems to have learned this lesson from several historical precedents. CD needs training compared to NC. His *Hind Swaraj* discusses mainly the former, but the NC can be more fatal to a regime.

He was an adherent of Non-violence. But on occasions he permitted relatively less violence. From 1931 he became convinced that not only India would gain her freedom by Non-violence but the independent India would need no armed forces to defend herself. This conviction made him search for the way to resist the possible foreign invasion non-violently during the Second World War. The result was the Quit-India movement, which was a stroke of genius, although it is susceptible to the criticism that it offered the political arena to the Pakistan Movement.

Gandhi was a democrat. Already in the 1930s he called India the largest democracy, even with its limited franchise. He made various attempts to make the masses familiar with politics, to have Congress Sessions in the villages, for example. His "Talk with Workers" in 1947, quoted in Chapter Two, is superb in urging the provincial ministers to be together with the masses. There has been no mass organization in Indian politics after him. Therefore, the Governments tended to depend more and more on the bureaucracy since then.

He, however, used to say that in the new India there should be a place for the capitalists, landlords, and the Princes. He said he wanted to change their heart. This was often put forward with the concept of trusteeship. But it leads to the question of whether after all he was on the side of the rich, or the masses?

This question becomes serious since there was relatively little land redistribution in the sixty-odd years since independence, the enforced idleness of the peasants he often talked about has continued, the size of the average operational holding keeps shrinking, and the migration to the cities is increasing.

Gandhi tried to tackle the question of poverty by founding five voluntary organizations, each for *khadi*, village industries, *nayee talim*, service to the Harijans, and cow protection. His wider concept of uplifting the villages was called the Constructive Programme. But he had a great difficulty in recruiting workers for these village works. He believed in reconstructing 'village republics'. It was combined with the idea of political decentralization.

For uplifting the villages, an integrated programme including education, drinking water, prevention of diseases, forest and soil conservation, organic fertilizer, and irrigation, in addition to land distribution and employment creation, is called for. He did work in some of these fields, for example on *nayee talim* in education, which shows his remarkable interest in training the common people. He showed attention to minute details and constantly urged his co-workers and others to drink only boiled water, avoid mosquitoes and so on.

Sometimes he did say that the peasants should have access to the title of the land and to a greater share of the produce. But he did not believe in non-violent redistribution of the land/property. Vinoba went ahead of Gandhi, though even his Bhoodan Movement could not bring about transformation of the land system.

Gandhi's dealing with the Muslims, especially M.A. Jinnah, was full of miscalculation. His first contact with the Muslims, the Khilafat Movement, helped to strengthen the solidarity among the Muslims simply because they were Muslims, and in that sense was a failure. Gandhi could have done more, may be much more, to bridge the gap between the Motilal Nehru Committee and Jinnah in incorporating the Muslim representation, even though for the tiny elite among them.

In 1937, his responsibility was much heavier as he was the supreme leader of the Congress which was going to rule in the majority of the Provinces. But he failed to incorporate the League into the same political set-up as the Congress.

His support to the Rajaji Formula and his three-week long talks with Jinnah were his great mistakes. But his fight against the two-nation theory should be remembered. Way back in South Africa, when he fought the "Black Act" and other discriminatory policies, he claimed that he fought to save the Eastern Civilization. Actually he fought for the universal values. His fight against the two-nation theory had a similar characteristic. Even after it exploded in Pakistan by the secession of Bangladesh, it has reappeared here and there in many different forms, mixing religion or ethnicity with a nation. The second Maliki Government in Iraq from 2010~4 is one of its latest.

When there was a Mutiny of the Royal Indian Navy, he condemned the 'unholy' alliance of the Hindus and Muslims. But should he not have explored if it would not provide a hitherto unknown way of the communal unity? It might have involved violence, but compared to the possibility of an all-out communal warfare it would be negligible. The same would apply to the Thebhaga Movement.

India's independence, though not completely by non-violence as Gandhi wished, has triggered the waves of independence in the colonies. They have made it extremely difficult for the Third World War to take place, and we must thank India for that. India has also contributed to the growth of the Non-aligned Movement, which has yet to work hard to achieve the non-aligned and that much more peaceful world order. All this owes much to Gandhi. His call for the non-armed world federation with only the world federal defence force is still something of an ideal for mankind.

Whether Gandhi was a charming man or not depends on the individual viewpoint. But he is worth remembering as a man from whom we may still extract answers, or hints of the answers, to our problems today.

Within India, he led the freedom movement, characterized as S-T-S, organized the masses, gave them hope, and endeared him to them. The hope should be realized, no matter how late it is. India being a hierarchical society in many ways, land/property should have been redistributed, preferably by non-violence but not necessarily with compensation, the caste system should have been abolished, and the widow remarriages should not have remained a taboo. These are some of the measures by which he could have become really pro-poor. He has sown at least some of the seeds in that direction.

Internationally, his name will be remembered as a man who has encouraged and shared his views with among others the Africans, with whom he lived for two decades, Arabs and Palestinians, the Chinese, and African-Americans. His name is known much more widely as a messenger of peace. His life, work and thinking have basically withstood the three different phases of modern Asian history.

For those reasons he is still alive and relevant.

Appendix

List of Gandhi's Co-Workers

Sources are *CWMG* unless otherwise indicated

Thirteen names whom, Narayanbhai says, Gandhi found as his associates between 1916 and 21, 'who dedicated all their abilities to the service of the country'. They were, 'Vinoba, Kishorlal Mashruwala, Kakasaheb, Mahadevbhai, Narharibhai, Swami Anand, Rajendra Prasad, Kripalani, Thakkarbapa, Pyarelal, Valijbhai, Ravishankar Maharaj, Jamnalal Bajai—how many names shall we mention?' Sardar Patel's name was soon added. (Narayanbhai, II-19)

When the Satyagraha Pledge was taken at the Sabarmati Ashram on 23 February 1919, 'Some twenty people...Vallabhbhai, Sarojini Naidu, Horniman...Umar Sobani, Shankarlal Banker and Anasuyaben Sarabhai attended the meeting.'(Narayanbhai, II-133) Indulal Yajnik says there were twenty-four. (Yajnik, 70) This was taken from Gandhi's *Autobiography* which also mentions those six names. (39-363) B.R. Nanda writes that Bombay politicians led by Horniman and including Banker, Sobhani, Sarojini, Jamnadas Dwarkadas, called 'the Jinnah clique', came to see Gandhi and were joined by Patel, Yajnik and others who fought together with Gandhi at Kheda. (Nanda, *Road to Pakistan*, 58-9)

Narayanbhai lists seven names as the teachers who left the government schools and colleges to join the newly created national schools. Those were 'Acharya Kripalani. Acharya Gidwani, Zakir Hussain, Narendra Dev, Dada Dharmadhikari, Jaykrishna Bhansali and Ramnarayan Pathak'. (II-209)

The *Young India* of 6 October 1921 published "A Manifesto", dated two days back, demanding the freedom of expression, and calling upon the soldiers and civilians in the service of the Government to resign. It was signed by Gandhi and 46 others including Lajpat

Rai, Motilal and Jawaharlal Nehru, and Rajagopalachari. Eleven of them seem to be Muslims like Abul Kalam Azad, Ajmal Khan and M.A. Ansari. (21-235~6) Before this, Gandhi had sent a "Circular Letter" to 23 persons requesting them to come to Bombay for a meeting, adding that 'You will please bring any other friend whose presence may be helpful'. (21-138~9)

Maganlal K. Gandhi, Gandhi's uncle's grandson, died on 23 April 1928. Gandhi writes in "My Best Comrade Gone" that 'He whom I had singled out as heir to my all is no more'. (36-261)

Gandhi's "Satyagraha Ashram" lists the members of the Management Committee of the Ashram as of the middle of 1928. There were eleven persons, with Mahadev Desai as Chairman, Imam Abdul Kadar Bawazir as Vice-Chairman, and Chhaganlal Joshi as Secretary. (36-407~8)

Early in 1928, Gandhi wrote in "Gujarat Vidyapith" that under the leadership of Vallabhbhai Patel it played a great role in the relief work at the time of 'the late disastrous floods' of 1927. He also lists 18 names here out of whom the members of the newly created Board of Trustees would be appointed. (36-4~6) In his "Letter to Motilal Nehru" in August 1928, he wrote that the struggle at Bardoli was possible because there was the Ashram which prepared the workers, and 'If I could but make of the Ashram what I want, I should be ready to give battle on an extensive scale'. (37-194)

In February 1929 Gandhi wrote "Letter to Jairamdas Doulatram" requesting him to be a whole-time secretary to Gandhi who has taken charge of the Committee for Boycott of Foreign Cloth, as there is 'nobody so suitable like you'. (40-20~1)

At the time of the Salt March also he greatly depended on the Ashram. The March itself started from the Ashram. Already in October 1929 he wrote in "Letter to Chhaganlal Joshi" that 'something can certainly be done through them'(the Ashram inmates). (41-519) His "Speech at Prayer Meeting, Sabarmati Ashram" on 15 February 1930 shows that already some inmates have given their names. (42-477~8) This is because the Congress Working Committee 'authorizes him (Gandhi) and those working with him…to start civil disobedience…', (42-480) thereby placing Gandhi's Ashram-based movement outside the sphere of the Congress and characterizing it as Gandhi's. Gandhi wrote to Jaysukhlal Gandhi on 6 March that 'I will start on the march on the 12th, accompanied by most of the men in the Ashram'. (43-21) The list of "Persons who accompanied Gandhiji on the Dandi March" gives 78 names except Gandhi, region-wise. Gujarat tops the list with 31, but there is a separate Cutch list of six. (43-454~5) Gandhi said in "Speech at Bhatgam", in Surat District, that 'more than in any other part of Gujarat, in this district are concentrated workers who have come in closest touch with me'. (43-146)

When a raid was made on the Dharasana Salt Depot after Gandhi's arrest, Sarojini Naidu constituted the 'War Council' consisting of herself, Imam Saheb, Manilal Gandhi, Narhari Parikh and Pyarelal. (Narayanbhai, II-654)

From the prison Gandhi wrote "Letter to R.V. Martin" in which he mentioned about 150 names 'who are intimately connected with me and are not known to political fame' and who, he hoped, would be allowed to visit him. The list includes Chhaganlal Joshi, Vinoba or Sarojini Naidu. The relatives are not there. (44-10~13) Gandhi wrote a similar, but much shorter list during his next prison term after coming back from the RTC, giving description of 19 'non-political associates' beginning with Indira Nehru. (49-335~7) Soon he wrote "Letter to Devdas Gandhi", and wrote about nearly twenty co-workers who were in jails at different places. Some of them were with him together, but not his wife. (49-421~4)

At the time he was about to begin the 'Fast unto Death' in protest against the Communal Award, he wrote or sent a large number of letters and telegrams to bid farewell to people including Elwin, Romain Rolland, Sarojini, Chhaganlal, Vinoba, Tagore, Srinivasa Sastri, Mirabehn, Kalelkar, Bajaj, Mashruwala. (51-58~140) After his release, Gandhi made a Harijan tour from 1933 to 34. There was a core of about six persons in his entourage. They were, in his words in "Letter to Narayan M. Khare", 'Chandrashankar, Mirabehn, Nayar (Pyarelal) and Jamnalalji's Om…Ramnath 'Suman'…And of course Thakkar Bapa.'(56-189) The "Letter to Kasturba Gandhi" he wrote on 29 March 1934 was a remarkable one in that in a short space he gave information on 44 persons including two of their sons and their wives, and his programme for the moment. (57-324~5)

Several years later, when Subhas Chandra Bose was re-elected Congress President, twelve members of the Working Committee jointly wrote "Resignation Letter of Congress Working Committee

Members" on 22 February 1939. It was signed by Abul Kalam Azad, Sarojini Naidu, Vallabhbhai Patel, Rajendra Prasad, Bhulabhai Desai, Pattabhi Sitaramayya, Shankarrao Deo, Harekrushna Mahtab, Kripalani, Abdul Ghaffar Khan, Jamnalal Bajaj and Jairam Doulatram. (68-486~7)

This is similar to what happened at the Working Committee meeting of 29 June 1936 when seven members submitted their resignation opposing Jawaharlal Nehru the then President. Six names are in the above also, who were Patel, Prasad, Deo, Kripalani, Bajaj and Doulatram, and the seventh was Rajaji. (63-127, fn. 1)

In the field of education, especially of *Nayee Talim* or Basic Education, Narayanbhai lists 18 names, including Zakir Husain, Asha Devi, E.V. Aryanayakum, Vinoba, Kakasaheb, Kishorelal Mashruwala, and writes that they and 'many committed educationalists' worked on it. (Narayanbhai, III-221) He also lists nine names as Gandhi's associates in constructive programme. (*Ibid.*, III-390~1)

When disturbances started in Noakhali, Gandhi wrote instructions to many as a part of his preparation to go there. In "Statement to the Press" of 20 November he clarified that he left the work of editing 'the *Harijan* and the allied weeklies' in the hands of Kishorelal, Kakasaheb, Vinoba and Narahari Parikh. (86-139) A little earlier on 4 November, in 'Letter to Kishorelal G. Mashruwala", who was the oldest person in the Ashram, he wrote many things small and large on 14~15 co-workers and asked the addressee to 'Read this to all'. He was not bidding farewell to anyone this time, unlike in 1932 which was the only such occasion. There were not many who accompanied him to Noakhali. They were Sushila Nayar (Pyarelal's sister), Amtussalaam, Satis Chandra Das Gupta, Thakkar Bapa, Sucheta Kripalani (Acharya Kripalani's wife), N.K. Bose, Renuka Ray, Sushila Pai, Manu Gandhi, Pyarelal, Kanu and Abha Gandhi (husband and wife), Prabhudas Gandhi and Parasuram (stenographer). Nehru, together with Acharya Kripalani, Shankarrao Deo, and Mridula Sarabhai visited Gandhi at Srirampur village on 28 December 1946. ("Speech at Prayer Meeting", 86-283)

Bibliography

Apart from the *Collected Works of Mahatma Gandhi* (*CWMG*).

Abdullah, Sheikh, *Flames of the Chinar* (translated by Khushwant Singh), Viking/Penguin, 1993 (originally in Urdu in 1986).

Akbar, M.J., *Nehru*, Roli Books, 2002.

Ambedkar, B.R., *The Essential Writings of B.R. Ambedkar* (edited by Valerian Rodriguez), Oxford University Press, 2002.

Azad, Maulana Abul Kalam, *India Wins Freedom*, Orient Longmans, 1959.

Backward Classes Commission (Chair; B.P. Mandal), Government of India, *Report*, 2 parts., 1980.

Bahuguna, Sunderlal, "Message from Our Experiences from the Chipko Movement and the Anti Tehri Dam Movement", *Asian Cultural Studies* 17, International Christian University Publications 3-A, 2008.

Bakshi, Rajni, *Bapu Kuti*, Penguin, 1998.

Balatchandirane, G., "India's BRICs Ambitions, Human Capital and Japanese Lessons", Rajaram Panda and Yoo Fukazawa, eds., *India and Japan in Search of Global Roles*, Promilla & Co., 2007.

Banerjea, Surendranath, *A Nation in Making*, Humphrey Milford and Oxford University Press, 1925.

Bhattacharya, Sabyasachi, ed., *The Mahatma and the Poet*, National Book Trust, India, 1997.

Bhave, Vinoba, "Gandhi: Jaisa Dekha-Samjya", Gautam Bajaj, ed., *Vinoba Sahitya*, Vol. 17, Parandham Prakashan/Laximinarayan Devasthan, 1997.

Bipan Chandra, Mridula Mukherjee, Aditya Mukherjee, K.N. Panikkar, Sucheta Mahajan, *India's Struggle for Independence*, Penguin, 1989.

Bipan Chandra, *In the Name of Democracy*, Penguin, 2003.

Bipan Chandra, *The Writings of Bipan Chandra* (edited by Aditya Mukherjee), Orient Black Swan, 2012.

Bondurant, Joan V., *Conquest of Violence*, revised ed., University of California Press, 1971.

Bose, Nirmal Kumar, *Studies in Gandhism*, 2nd edition, Indian Associated Publishing, 1947.

Bose, Nirmal Kumar, *Selections from Gandhi* (2nd and enlarged edition), Navajivan, 1957.

Bose, Nirmal Kumar, *My Days with Gandhi,* Orient Longman, 1974.

Bose, Nirmal Kumar and P.H. Patwardhan, *Gandhi in Indian Politics*, Lalvani, 1967

Bose, Sarat Chandra, *I Warned My Countrymen*, Netaji Research Bureau, 1968.

Brown, Judith M., *Gandhi*, Yale University Press, 1989.

Brown, Judith M., *Nehru*, Oxford University Press, 2003.

Campbell-Johnson, Alan, *Mission with Mountbatten*, Robert Hale, 1951.

Chakravarty, Sukhamoy, *Development Planning—The Indian Experience*, Oxford University Press, 1987.

Committee appointed by the (All Parties) Conference to determine the principles of the Constitution for India, *Report* (*Nehru Report*), AICC, 1928.

Committee (Prime Minister's High Level, Chair; Rajindar Sachar) for Social, Economic and Educational Status of the Muslim Community of India, *Report*, 2006.

Das, Durga, ed., *Sardar Patel's Correspondence*, 10 Vols. Navajivan, 1971-4.

Das, Gurcharan, "The India Model", *Foreign Affairs*, July/August 2006.

Desai, Bhulabhai, "Address for Defence", Bimal Prasad, ed., *Towards Freedom*, Oxford University Press, 2008.

Desai, Meghnad, "Communalism, secularism and the dilemma of Indian nationhood", Michael Leifer, ed., *Asian Nationalism*, Routledge, 2000.

Desai, Narayan, *My Life is My Message* (translated by Tridip Suhrud), 4 Vols., Orient Black Swan, 2009.

Dreze, Jean, and Amartya Sen, *India: Economic Development and Social Opportunity*, Oxford University Press, 1995.

Dreze, Jean, and Amartya Sen, "Putting Growth in its Place", *Outlook*, 14 November 2011.

Dube, S.C., "Introduction", S.C. Dube, ed., *Tribal Heritage of India*, Vol. 1, Vikas, 1977.

Etienne, Gilbert, "Mahatma Gandhi, Rural Development and Society", B.R. Nanda, ed., *Mahatma Gandhi 125 Years*, Indian Council for Cultural Relations, 1995.

Gandhi, Gopalkrishna, ed., *The Oxford India Gandhi; Essential Writings*, Oxford University Press, 2008.

Gandhi, Rajmohan, *The Rajaji Story:1937-1972*, Bharatiya Vidya Bhavan, 1984.

Gandhi, Rajmohan, *Eight Lives*, Roli, 1986.

Gandhi, Rajmohan, *The Good Boatman*, Viking/Penguin, 1995.

Gandhi, Rajmohan, *Ghaffar Khan*, Penguin/Viking, 2004.

Gandhi, Rajmohan, *Mohandas*, Viking/Penguin, 2006.

Gandhi, Rajmohan, "What If Gandhi Had Lived On?" *Outlook*, 23 August 2004.

Gill, S.S., *Gandhi: A Sublime Failure*, Rupa, 2001.

Glendevon, John, *The Viceroy at Bay*, Collins, 1971.

Gopal, S., ed., *Selected Works of Jawaharlal Nehru*, Vol. 3, Orient Longman, 1972.

Gopal, S. and Uma Iyengar, eds., *The Essential Writings of Jawaharlal Nehru*, 2 Vols., Oxford University Press, 2003.

Guha, Ramachandra, *India After Gandhi*, Picador, 2008.

Guha, Ramachandra, *Gandhi Before India*, Penguin, 2013.

Guha, Ramachandra, "A Nation Consumed by the State", *Outlook*, 31 January 2011.

Guha, Samar, *The Mahatma and the Netaji*, Sterling, 1986.

Hampton, Henry, and Steve Fayer, *Voices of Freedom*, Bantam Books, 1990.

Herman, Arthur, *Gandhi and Churchill*, Arrow, 2009.

Hirashima, Shigemochi, "Growth, Equity and Labour Absorption in Japanese Agriculture", Ishikawa Shigeru, Yamada Saburo and Hirashima Shigemochi, *Labour Absorption and Growth in Agriculture: China and Japan*, ILO (ARTEP), 1982.

Imhasly, Bernard, *Goodbye to Gandhi* (translated by Ritu Khanna), Penguin/ Viking, 2007.

Ishizaka, Shinya, "The Anti Tehri Dam Movement as a New Social Movement and Gandhism", *Journal of the Japanese Association for South Asian Studies*, 18, 2006.

Iyer, Raghavan, ed., *The Moral and Political Writings of Mahatma Gandhi*, 3 Vols., Clarendon Press, 1986~7.

Jagadisan, T.N., *Fulfilment Through Leprosy*, Kasturba Kushta Nivaran Nilayam, 1988

Jalal, Ayesha, *The Pity of Partition*, Princeton University Press, 2013.

Jayaram, N., "Caste and Hinduism: Changing Protean Relationship", M.N. Srinivas, ed., *Caste—Its Twentieth Century Avatar*, Penguin, 1996.

JICA, *Nepal* (Chair; Yamaguchi Hiroichi), 1993.

Joshi, P.C., *Bharatiya Gram*, Rajkamal Prakashan, 1966.

Joshi, P.C., *Mahatma Gandhi: The New Economic Agenda*, Har-Anand, 1996.

Joshi, P.C., "Founders of the Lucknow School and their Legacy", *Economic and Political Weekly*, 16 August 1986.

King, Mary, *Mahatma Gandhi and Martin Luther King Jr*, UNESCO, 1999.

Kumarappa, J.C., *Economy of Permanence*, Sarva Seva Sangh Prakashan, 1997.

Kuwajima, Sho, *Post-War Upsurge of Freedom Movement and 1946 Provincial Elections in India*, Osaka University of Foreign Studies, 1992.

Lee, Jeong Ho, "Literary Contacts and Influences between India and Korea: A Comparison between the Poetry of Rabindranath Tagore and Han Yong Woon (Man Hae)", in Sushila Narsimhan and G. Balatchandirane, eds., *India and East Asia*, Manak, 2004.

Mahajan, Sucheta, "British Policy, Nationalist Strategy and Popular National Upsurge, 1945-46", Amit Kumar Gupta, ed., *Myth and Reality*, Manohar, 1987.

Malhotra, Inder, *Indira Gandhi*, National Book Trust, India, 2006

Malik, Dipak, "Political Economy of Communalism: A Response from the Left", John P. Neelsen and Dipak Malik, eds., *Crisis of State and Nation*, Manohar, 2007.

Mishra, Anil Dutta, *Revisiting Hind Swaraj*, Concept, 2010.

Mishra, Anil Dutta, *Mahatma Gandhi on Untouchability*, Concept, 2015.

Moon, Penderel, *Gandhi and Modern India*, The English Universities Press, 1968.

Moon, Penderel, ed., *Wavell: The Viceroy's Journal*, Oxford University Press, 1973

Moore, R.J., *Churchill, Cripps and India*, Clarendon Press, 1979.

Moraes, Frank, *Witness to an Era*, Vikas, 1973.

Mukerjee, Hiren, *Gandhiji: A Study*, 2nd edition, People's Publishing House, 1960

Mukerjee, Radha Kamal, *Planning the Countryside: First Report*, Hind Kitabs, 1946.

Mukerji, D.P., "Mahatma Gandhi's Views on Machines and Technology", D.P. Mukerji, *Diversities*, People's Publishing House, 1958.

Mukherjee, Aditya, Introduction, *The Writings of Bipan Chandra*, Orient Black Swan, 2012.

Munda, Ram Dayal, *Adi-Dharam: Religious Beliefs of the Adivasis of India*, Sarini Occasional Papers, No. 3, n.d.

Naito, Masao, "Japanese Approach towards Gandhi during the Sino-Japanese War", Radhika Seshan, ed., *Convergence*, Primus Books, 2014.

Namboodiripad, E.M.S., *The Mahatma and the Ism*, second edition, Left Word, 2010.

Namboodiripad, E.M.S., *Reminiscences of an Indian Communist*, National Book Centre, 1987.

Namboodiripad, E.M.S., *History, Society and Land Relations*, Left Word, 2010.

Nanda, B.R., *Mahatma Gandhi*, George Allen & Unwin, 1958.

Nanda, B.R., *Gandhi and His Critics*, Oxford University Press, 1985.

Nanda, B.R., "Govind Ballabh Pant:A Biographical Sketch", Nanda, B.R. ed., *Selected Works of Govind Ballabh Pant*, Vol. 2, Oxford University Press, 1994.

Nanda, B.R., *Road to Pakistan*, Routledge, 2010.
Nanda, Reena, *Kamaladevi Chattopadhyaya*, Oxford University Press, 2002.
Narasimhan, Shakuntala, *Kamaladevi Chattopadhyay: The Romantic Rebel*, Sterling, 1999.
Narayan (Agarwal), Shriman, *The Gandhian Plan of Economic Development for India*, Padma Publications, 1944.
Narayan (Agarwal), Shriman, *Gandhian Constitution for Free India*, Kitabistan, 1946.
Narayan, Shriman, *Vinoba—His Life and Work*, Popular, 1970.
National Commission (Chair; Arjun Sengupta) on Enterprizes in the Unorganized Sector, *Report*, 2007.
Nehru, Jawaharlal, *A Bunch of Old Letters*, Asia, 1958.
Noorani, A.G., *Savarkar and Hindutva*, LeftWord, 2002.
Noorani, A.G., *Jinnah and Tilak*, Oxford University Press, 2010.
Pandey, B.N. ed., *The Indian Nationalist Movement*, Macmillan, 1979.
Panter-Brick, Simone, *Gandhi and the Middle East*, J.B. Tauris, 2008.
Parulekar, Godawari, *Adivasis Revolt*, National Book Agency, 1975 (originally in Marathi in 1970).
Pinto, Vivek, *Gandhi's Vision and Values*, Sage, 1998.
Pradhan, G.P., *Lokamanya Tilak*, National Book Trust, India, 1994.
Pradhan, G.P., *Pursuit of Ideals*, Ameya, 2005.
Prasad, Bimal, "Gandhi and India's Partition", Amit Kumar Gupta, ed., *Myth and Reality,* Manohar, 1987.
Pyarelal, *Mahatma Gandhi: The Last Phase*, 2 Vols., Navajivan, 1956~58.
Pyarelal, Sushila Nayar, *In Gandhiji's Mirror*, Oxford University Press, 1991.
Radhakrishnan, S., ed., *Mahatma Gandhi 100 Years*, Gandhi Peace Foundation,.2009 (originally 1968).
Rai, Vibhuti Narain, *Combating Communal Conflicts*, Anamika Prakashan, 1998.
Rai, Vibhuti Narain, "Gujarat holocaust: A lesson to learn for IPS cadre", *Azad Academy Journal*, May 1-31, 2002.
Rao, C.H. Hanumantha, *Agricultural Growth, Rural Poverty and Environmental Degradation in India*, Oxford University Press, 1994.
Rao, C.H. Hanumantha, "Inclusive Growth", *The Indian Economic Journal*, April-June, 2010.
Rao, M. Chalapathi, *Gandhi and Nehru*, Allied, 1967.
Rao, V.K.R.V., *The Nehru Legacy*, Popular, 1971.
Reddy, Sheela, "Gandhi, A Second Coming", *Outlook*, 11 September 2006.
Rittenberg, Sydney and Amanda Benett, *The Man Who Stayed Behind*, Simon and Schuster, 1993.
Rodriguez, Valerian, Introduction, *The Essential Writings of B.R. Ambedkar*, Oxford University Press, 2002.

Rothermund, Dietmar, *Mahatma Gandhi*, Manohar, 1991.
Sainath, P., *Everybody Loves A Good Drought*, Penguin, 1996.
Sanyal, Sunanda, and Soumya Basu, *The Sickle and the Crescent*, frontpage, 2011.
Sareen, T.N., *Jinnah, Linlithgow and the Making of Pakistan*, Uppal, 2010.
Sareen, T.N., *India and the Allied Occupation of Japan*, Life Span, 2013.
Sarkar, Sumit, *Modern India*, Macmillan, 1983.
Sharp, Gene, *Gandhi as a Political Strategist*, Porter Sargent Publishers, 1979.
Sharp, Gene, *From Dictatorship to Democracy*, 4th US edition, The Albert Einstein Institution, 2010.
Singh, Khushwant, *Train to Pakistan*, Roli, 2006 (originally in 1988).
Singh, Tavleen, *Lollipop Street*, Viking, 1999.
Srinivas, M.N., *Social Change in Modern India*, University of California Press, 1966.
Srinivas, M.N., *The Cohesive Role of Sanskritization and Other Essays*, Oxford University Press, 1989.
Srinivas, M.N., ed., *Caste: Its Twentieth Century Avatar*, Penguin, 1996.
Suhrud, Tridip, *Reading Gandhi in Two Tongues and Other Essays*, Indian Institute of Advanced Study, 2012.
Tendulkar, D.G., *Mahatma: Life of Mohandas Karamchand Gandhi*, 8 Vols., Vithalbhai K. Jhaveri and D.G. Tendulkar, 1951-54.
Terchek, Ronald J., *Gandhi*, Vistaar, 1998.
Thapar, Raj, *All These Years*, Penguin, 1991.
Visveswaraya, M., *Planned Economy for India*, Bangalore Press, 1934.
Weber, Thomas, *Gandhi, Gandhism and the Gandhians*, Roli Books, 2006.
Weber, Thomas, *Gandhi as Disciple and Mentor*, Cambridge University Press, 2007.
Yajnik, Indulal, K., *Gandhi as I Know Him*, Revised and Enlarged, Danish Mahal, 1943.
Yamaguchi, Hiroichi, *Japan*, National Book Trust, India, 2006.
Yamaguchi, Hiroichi, "Some Issues Latent in *Hind Swaraj*", *Journal of Gandhian Studies*, January 2012.

Index